Crystal Programming

A project-based introduction to building efficient, safe, and readable web and CLI applications

George Dietrich

Guilherme Bernal

BIRMINGHAM—MUMBAI

Part 3: Learn by Doing – Web Application

This part will continue the *Learn By Doing* paradigm with another common type of application: a web framework. This part will build upon the information from the first two parts. Most commonly, a web application is created with the help of a framework. Thankfully, Crystal's ecosystem has various frameworks to choose from. While the best framework to use varies from use case to use case, we are going to focus on Athena Framework.

This part contains the following chapters:

- *Chapter 8, Using External Libraries*
- *Chapter 9, Creating a Web Application with Athena*

Part 5: Supporting Tools

Crystal comes bundled with various supporting features and tooling to help with everything needed to create robust and usable applications, once the application itself has been written. This includes a testing framework to ensure the application continues to function as expected, and a documentation system to make it easier for others to learn how to use the application, and is supported by the nature of the language itself, which makes it easy to deploy. Let's get started!

This part contains the following chapters:

- *Chapter 14, Testing*
- *Chapter 15, Documenting Code*
- *Chapter 16, Deploying Code*
- *Chapter 17, Automation*
- *Appendix A, Tooling Setup*
- *Appendix B, The Future of Crystal*

Index

Crystal Programming

A project-based introduction to building efficient, safe, and readable web and CLI applications

George Dietrich

Guilherme Bernal

BIRMINGHAM—MUMBAI

Crystal Programming

Copyright © 2022 Packt Publishing

Group Product Manager: Alok Dhuri

Publishing Product Manager: Shweta Bairoliya

Senior Editor: Nisha Cleetus

Content Development Editor: Nithya Sadanandan

Technical Editor: Maran Fernandes

Copy Editor: Safis Editing

Project Coordinator: Deeksha Thakkar

Proofreader: Safis Editing

Indexer: Subalakshmi Govindhan

Production Designer: Vijay Kamble

Marketing Coordinator: Sonakshi Bubbar

First published: July 2022

Production reference: 1130522

Published by Packt Publishing Ltd.

Livery Place

35 Livery Street

Birmingham

B3 2PB, UK.

ISBN 978-1-80181-867-4

www.packt.com

To the future of Crystal; may it be as bright as a diamond.

– George Dietrich

To my beloved wife, who supports me all the way.

– Guilherme Bernal

Contributors

About the authors

George Dietrich is a software engineer, open-source aficionado, and Crystal community moderator. He holds a Master of Science degree in internet information systems and a Bachelor of Science degree in information sciences.

Guilherme Bernal is the chief technology officer at Cubos Tecnologia. He holds a bachelor's degree in IT management. Guilherme co-founded a software development company and several tech start-ups, including one that focused on teaching programming skills to a new generation of developers. He is also a two-time world finalist in the coding competition ACM ICPC.

About the reviewer

Brian Cardiff has been building software for others to use for over 20 years. He has been able to play many roles along the development process: requirement gathering, prototype validation, coding, deployment, and maintenance. During his 15 years in Manas.Tech, he joined Ary Borenszweig and Juan Wajnerman to give shape to Crystal. He enjoys building tools for tech and non-tech people. Mainly through Crystal, he became a collaborator in the open source community. He has also reviewed *Programming Crystal: Create High-Performance, Safe, Concurrent Apps*, by Ivo Balbaert and Simon St. Laurent. While working full-time in the industry, he tries to keep in touch with academia and research programming languages and formal methods.

> *I'd like to thank my wife and daughter for their continuous support in all the various projects that I keep committing to.*
>
> *– Brian Cardiff*

Table of Contents

3

Object-Oriented Programming

Part 2: Learning by Doing – CLI

4

Exploring Crystal via Writing a Command-Line Interface

5

Input/Output Operations

6

Concurrency

7

C Interoperability

Part 3: Learn by Doing – Web Application

8

Using External Libraries

9

Creating a Web Application with Athena

Part 4: Metaprogramming

10

Working with Macros

11

Introducing Annotations

12
Leveraging Compile-Time Type Introspection

13
Advanced Macro Usages

Part 5: Supporting Tools

14
Testing

15
Documenting Code

16
Deploying Code

17
Automation

Appendix A
Tooling Setup

Appendix B
The Future of Crystal

Index

Other Books You May Enjoy

Preface

The Crystal programming language is designed with both humans and computers in mind. It provides highly readable syntax that compiles to efficient code.

In this book, we are going to explore all that Crystal has to offer. We will start by introducing the language, including its core syntactical and semantic features. Next, we will dive into how to create a new Crystal project by walking through how to create a CLI-based application, which will involve making use of more advanced features such as IOs, concurrency, and C bindings.

In the third part of this book, we will learn how to make use of external libraries in the form of Crystal Shards. We will then make use of this knowledge by walking through the process of creating a web application using the Athena Framework.

The fourth part of the book covers one of Crystal's most powerful features: metaprogramming. Here, we will learn how to leverage macros, annotations, and compile-time-type introspection. We will then learn how these can be combined to implement some pretty powerful features.

We will wrap things up by introducing some of Crystal's supporting features, such as how to document, test, and deploy Crystal programs, as well as how to automate these processes by introducing CI into your workflow.

> **Important Note:**
> This book is intended for Crystal version 1.4.x. Future versions should also work but will not cover newly added features.

Who this book is for

Developers who want to learn Crystal programming or anyone else looking to improve their ability to solve real-world problems using the language will find this book helpful. Experience in application development using any other programming language is expected. However, prior knowledge of Crystal is not required.

What this book covers

Chapter 1, *An Introduction to Crystal*, provides a brief introduction to Crystal, including its history, key concepts, and goals. This chapter will also include information about setting up Crystal as well as information on the conventions that'll be used throughout the book.

Chapter 2, *Basics Semantics and Features of Crystal*, introduces you to writing Crystal code, starting from the very basics and advancing to the most common techniques. It also explores common types and operations from the standard library.

Chapter 3, *Object-Oriented Programming*, goes deeper into using the object-oriented features of the language by teaching you about creating new types with custom functionality, the basic tool of every non-trivial program.

Chapter 4, *Exploring Crystal via Writing a Command-Line Interface*, explores setting up a CLI project and walking through the initial implementation.

Chapter 5, *Input/Output Operations*, builds on the previous chapter by introducing I/O operations as a means of handling input and output instead of hard-coded strings.

Chapter 6, *Concurrency*, starts off by going over Crystal's concurrency features and later uses what was learned earlier to make the CLI program concurrent.

Chapter 7, *C Interoperability*, demonstrates how C libraries can be leveraged within a Crystal program by binding libnotify to make the CLI program notification aware.

Chapter 8, *Using External Libraries*, introduces the shards command and how to find it.

Chapter 9, *Creating a Web Application with Athena*, walks through creating a simple blog web application using Athena Framework, making use of many of its features.

Chapter 10, *Working with Macros*, provides an introduction to the world of metaprogramming by exploring Crystal macros.

Chapter 11, *Introducing Annotations*, talks about how to define, include data within, and read annotations.

Chapter 12, *Leveraging Compile-Time Type Introspection*, demonstrates how to iterate instance variables, types, and methods at compile time.

Chapter 13, *Advanced Macro Usages*, shows off some of the powerful things that can be created using macros and annotations, along with a little bit of creativity.

Chapter 14, *Testing*, introduces the Spec module and walks you through unit and integration testing in the context of CLI and web applications.

Chapter 15, Documenting Code, shows off how best to document, generate, host, and version Crystal code documentation.

Chapter 16, Deploying Code, talks about how to release new versions of a shard as well as how best to build and distribute the production version of an application.

Chapter 17, Automation, provides example workflows and commentary on enabling continuous integration for Crystal projects.

Appendix A, Tooling Setup, provides a hands-on explanation of how to set up Visual Studio Code for Crystal programming using the official plugin.

Appendix B, The Future of Crystal, gives a short overview of the work currently being done behind the scenes for the future of the language and shows you how to participate and contribute.

To get the most out of this book

This book requires some form of text editor as well as access to a terminal. Using macOS or Linux is suggested, but Windows with WSL should also work fine. Finally, you may need to install some additional system libraries for some code examples to function properly.

Software/hardware covered in the book	Operating system requirements
Crystal	Windows (with WSL), macOS, or Linux
libnotify	gcc (or other C compiler)
jq	libpcre2

> **Note**
>
> If you are using the digital version of this book, we advise you to type the code yourself or access the code from the book's GitHub repository (a link is available in the next section). Doing so will help you avoid any potential errors related to the copying and pasting of code.

Download the example code files

You can download the example code files for this book from GitHub at `https://github.com/PacktPublishing/Crystal-Programming/`. If there's an update to the code, it will be updated in the GitHub repository.

We also have other code bundles from our rich catalog of books and videos available at `https://github.com/PacktPublishing/`. Check them out!

Download the color images

We also provide a PDF file that has color images of the screenshots and diagrams used in this book. You can download it here: `https://static.packt-cdn.com/downloads/9781801818674_ColorImages.pdf`.

Conventions used

There are a number of text conventions used throughout this book.

`Code in text`: Indicates code words in text, database table names, folder names, filenames, file extensions, pathnames, dummy URLs, user input, and Twitter handles. Here is an example: "In our context, the types of `STDIN`, `STDOUT`, and `STDERR` are actually instantiations of `IO::FileDescriptor`."

A block of code is set as follows:

```
require "./transform"

STDOUT.puts Transform::Processor.new.process STDIN.gets_to_end
```

When we wish to draw your attention to a particular part of a code block, the relevant lines or items are set in bold:

```
require "./transform"

STDOUT.puts Transform::Processor.new.process STDIN.gets_to_end
```

Any command-line input or output is written as follows:

```
---
- id: 2
  name: Jim
```

```
- id: 3
  name: Bob
```

Bold: Indicates a new term, an important word, or words that you see onscreen. For instance, words in menus or dialog boxes appear in **bold**. Here is an example: "Open Windows PowerShell and select **Run as Administrator**."

> **Tips or Important Notes**
> Appear like this.

Get in touch

Feedback from our readers is always welcome.

General feedback: If you have questions about any aspect of this book, email us at customercare@packtpub.com and mention the book title in the subject of your message.

Errata: Although we have taken every care to ensure the accuracy of our content, mistakes do happen. If you have found a mistake in this book, we would be grateful if you would report this to us. Please visit www.packtpub.com/support/errata and fill in the form.

Piracy: If you come across any illegal copies of our works in any form on the internet, we would be grateful if you would provide us with the location address or website name. Please contact us at copyright@packt.com with a link to the material.

If you are interested in becoming an author: If there is a topic that you have expertise in and you are interested in either writing or contributing to a book, please visit authors.packtpub.com.

Share Your Thoughts

Once you've read *Crystal Programming*, we'd love to hear your thoughts! Scan the QR code below to go straight to the Amazon review page for this book and share your feedback.

https://packt.link/r/1801818673

Your review is important to us and the tech community and will help us make sure we're delivering excellent quality content.

Part 1: Getting Started

As with any programming book, we need to start by introducing the language, including how to use it, its basic features and semantics, as well as touching on some commonly used patterns it makes use of. This part focuses on just that, getting started with Crystal, but with a bias toward readers with knowledge of some other programming language, but no previous contact with Crystal itself.

This part contains the following chapters:

- *Chapter 1, An Introduction to Crystal*
- *Chapter 2, Basics Semantics and Features of Crystal*
- *Chapter 3, Object-Oriented Programming*

1
An Introduction to Crystal

Crystal is a safe, performant, general-purpose, and object-oriented language. It was heavily inspired by Ruby's syntax and Go's and Erlang's runtimes, enabling a programmer to be very productive and expressive while creating programs that run efficiently on modern computers.

Crystal has a robust type system and can compile to native programs. Consequently, most programming errors and mistakes can be identified at compile time, giving you, among other things, null safety. Having types doesn't mean you have to write them everywhere, however. Crystal relies on its unique type interference system to identify the types of almost every variable in the program. Rare are the situations where the programmer has to write an explicit type somewhere. But when you do, union types, generics, and metaprogramming help a lot.

Metaprogramming is a technique where a structured view of the written program is accessed and modified by the program itself, producing new code. This is a place where Ruby shines with all its dynamism and built-in reflection model, and so does Crystal, in its own way. Crystal is capable of modifying and generating code during compilation time with macros and a zero-cost static reflection model. It feels like a dynamic language in every way, but it will compile the program down to pure and fast machine code.

Code written in Crystal is expressive and safe, but it's also fast – really fast. Once built, it goes head to head with other low-level languages such as C, C++, or Rust. It beats pretty much any dynamic language and some compiled languages too. Although Crystal is a high-level language, it can consume C libraries with no overhead, the lingua franca of system programming.

You can use Crystal today. After 10 years of intense development and testing, a stable and production-ready version was released in early 2021. Alongside it, a complete set of libraries (called "shards") are available, including web frameworks, database drivers, data formats, network protocols, and machine learning.

This chapter will introduce a brief history of the Crystal language and present some of its characteristics regarding performance and expressiveness. After that, it will bring you up to speed by explaining how to create and run your first Crystal program. Finally, you will learn about some of the challenges for the future of the language.

In particular, we will cover the following topics:

- A bit of history

- Exploring Crystal's expressiveness

- Crystal programs are also FAST

- Creating our first program

- Setting up the environment

This should get you started on what Crystal is, understanding why it should be used, and learning how to execute your first program. This context is essential for learning how to program in Crystal, going from small snippets to fully functional and production-ready applications.

Technical requirements

As part of this chapter, you will install the Crystal compiler on your machine and write some code with it. For this, you will need the following:

- A Linux, Mac, or Windows computer. In the case of a Windows computer, the **Windows Subsystem for Linux** (**WSL**) needs to be enabled.

- A text editor such as Visual Studio Code or Sublime Text. Any will do, but these two have good Crystal plugins ready to use.

You can fetch all source code used in this chapter from the book's GitHub repository at `https://github.com/PacktPublishing/Crystal-Programming/tree/main/Chapter01`.

A bit of history

Crystal was created in mid 2011 at Manas Technology Solutions (`https://manas.tech/`), an Argentinian consulting company that worked a lot with creating Ruby on the Rails applications at that time. Ruby is an enjoyable language to work with but has always been questioned for its lacking performance. Crystal came to life when Ary Borenszweig, Brian Cardiff, and Juan Wajnerman started experimenting with the concept of a new language similar to Ruby. It would be a statically typed, safe, and compiled language with pretty much the same elegant syntax as Ruby but taking advantage of global type inference to remove runtime dynamism. Much has changed since then, but these core concepts remain the same.

The result? Today, Crystal is a stable and production-ready, 10-year-old language with over 500 contributors and a growing community. The team behind it successfully implemented a language with a fast concurrent runtime and a unique type inference system that looks at the entire program in one go while retaining Ruby's best features.

The initial motiving factor for the creators was performance. They enjoyed programming in Ruby and using Ruby's vast ecosystem, but the performance wasn't there. Ruby has improved a lot since then, but even today, there is a sensible gap compared to other dynamic languages such as Python or JavaScript.

It began with a simple idea – what if we could have the same expressiveness as Ruby, infer the types of all variables and arguments based on the call sites, and then generate native machine code similar to the C language? They began prototyping it as a side project in 2011, and it worked. Early on, it was adopted as a Manas project, allowing the trio to work on it during paid hours.

Crystal has been developed in the open since its very beginning in a public repository on GitHub at `https://github.com/crystal-lang/crystal`. It brought a community of users, contributors, and also sponsors banking on Crystal's success. The initial interest came from the Ruby community, but it quickly expanded beyond that. You can see in the following figure the growth in people interested in Crystal, measured by the number of GitHub "stars" on the main repository.

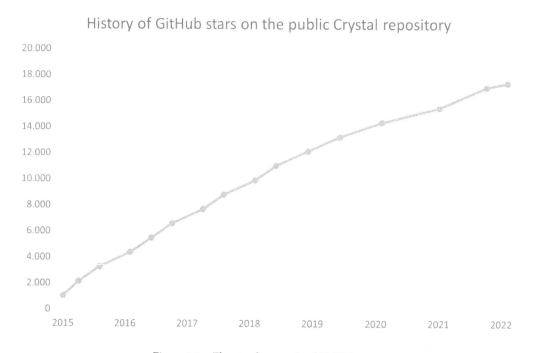

Figure 1.1 – The steady growth of GitHub stars

At the time of writing, the latest version is 1.2.2, and it can be installed from Crystal's official website, at `https://crystal-lang.org/`.

Much inspiration came from Ruby, but Crystal evolved into a different language. It kept the best pieces of Ruby but changed, improved, and removed some of its legacies. Neither language aim to be compatible with the other.

Understanding this history gives you the perspective to follow what motivated Crystal to be created and to evolve into what it is today. Crystal has grown to be very performant but also very expressive. Now, let's see what empowers this expressiveness.

Exploring Crystal's expressiveness

It is often said that Crystal is a language for humans and computers. This is because Crystal strives for a balance of being a surprisingly enjoyable language for programmers while also being very performant for machines. One cannot go without the other, and in Crystal, most abstractions come with no performance penalties. It has features and idioms such as the following:

- **Object-oriented programming**: Everything is an object. Even classes themselves are objects, that is, instances of the `Class`. Primitive types are objects and have methods, too, and every class can be reopened and extended as needed. In addition, Crystal has inheritance, method/operator overloading, modules, and generics.

- **Static-typed**: All variables have a known type at compile time. Most of them are deduced by the compiler and not explicitly written by the programmer. This means the compiler can catch errors such as calling methods that are not defined or trying to use a value that could be null (or `nil` in Crystal) at that time. Variables can be a combination of multiple types, enabling the programmer to write dynamic-looking code.

- **Blocks**: Whenever you call a method on an object, you can pass in a block of code. This block can then be called from the method's implementation with the `yield` keyword. This idiom allows all sorts of iterations and control flow manipulation and is widespread among Ruby developers. Crystal also has closures, which can be used when blocks don't fit.

- **Garbage collection**: Objects are stored in a heap, and their memory is automatically reclaimed when they are no longer in use. There are also objects created from a struct, allocated in the stack frame of the currently executing method, and they cease to exist as soon as the method finishes. Thus, the programmer doesn't have to deal with manual memory management.

- **Metaprogramming**: Although Crystal isn't a dynamic language, it can frequently behave as if it were, due to its powerful compile-time metaprogramming. The programmer can use macros and annotations, together with information about all existing types (static reflection) to generate or mutate code. This enables many dynamic-looking idioms and patterns.

- **Concurrent programming**: A Crystal program can spawn new fibers (lightweight threads) to execute blocking code, coordinating with channels. Asynchronous programming becomes easy to reason and follow. This model was heavily inspired by Go and other concurrent languages such as Erlang.

- **Cross-platform**: Programs created with Crystal can run on Linux, macOS, and FreeBSD, targeting x86 or ARM (both 32-bit and 64-bit). This includes the new Apple Silicon chips. Support for Windows is experimental, it isn't ready just yet. The compiler can also produce small static binaries on each platform without dependencies for ease of distribution.

- **Runtime safety**: Crystal is a safe language – this means there are no undefined behaviors and hidden crashes such as accessing an array outside its bounds, accessing properties on `null`, or accessing objects after they have already been freed. Instead, these become either runtime exceptions, compile-time errors, or can't happen due to runtime protections. The programmer has the option of weaving safety by using explicitly unsafe features of the language when necessary.

- **Low-level programming**: Although Crystal is safe, using unsafe features is always an option. Things such as working with raw pointers, calling into native C libraries, or even using assembly directly are available to the brave. Many common C libraries have safe wrappers around them ready to use, allowing them to use their features from a Crystal program.

At first glance, Crystal is very similar to Ruby, and many syntactic primitives are the same. But Crystal took its own road, taking inspiration from many other modern languages such as Go, Rust, Julia, Elixir, Erlang, C#, Swift, and Python. As a result, it keeps most of the good parts of Ruby's slick syntax while providing changes to core aspects, such as metaprogramming and concurrency.

Crystal programs are also FAST

From its very start, Crystal was designed to be fast. It follows the same principles as other fast languages such as C. The compiler can analyze the source code to know every variable's exact type and memory layout before execution. Then, it can produce a fast and optimized native executable without having to guess anything during runtime. This process is commonly known as **ahead-of-time compilation**.

Crystal's compiler is built upon LLVM, the same compiler infrastructure that powers Rust, Clang, and Apple's Swift. As a result, Crystal benefits from the same level of optimizations available to these languages, making it well suited for computationally intensive applications such as machine learning, image processing, or data crushing.

But not all applications are CPU-bound. Most of the time, there are other resources at stake, such as network communications or a local disk. Those are collectively known as *I/O*. Crystal has a concurrency model similar to Go's goroutines or Erlang's processes, where multiple operations can be performed behind an event loop without blocking the process or delegating too much work to the operating system. This model is ideal for applications such as web services or file manipulation tools.

Using an efficient language such as Crystal will help you reduce hardware costs and improve perceived responsiveness from your users. In addition, it means you can run smaller and fewer instances of your application to address the same processing volume.

Let's take a look at a simple implementation of the selection sort algorithm written in Crystal:

```
def selection_sort(arr)
  # For each element index...
  arr.each_index do |i|
    # Find the smallest element after it
    min = (i...arr.size).min_by { |j| arr[j] }

    # Swap positions with the smallest element
    arr[i], arr[min] = arr[min], arr[i]
  end
end


# Produce a reversed list of 30k elements
list = (1..30000).to_a.reverse


# Sort it and then print its head and tail
selection_sort(list)
p list[0...10]
p list[-10..-1]
```

This example already shows some neat things about Crystal:

- First of all, it is relatively small. The main algorithm has a total of four lines.

- It's expressive. You can iterate over lists with specialized blocks or use ranges.

- There isn't a single type notation. Instead, the compiler deduces every type, including the method argument.

Surprisingly, this same code is also valid in Ruby. Taking advantage of that, if we take this file and run it as `ruby selection_sort.cr` (note that Ruby doesn't care about file extensions), it will take about 30 seconds to finish. On the other hand, executing this program after it has been compiled with Crystal in optimized mode takes about 0.45 seconds, *60x* less. Of course, this difference isn't the same for any program. It varies depending on what kind of workload you are dealing with. It's also important to note that Crystal takes time to analyze, compile, optionally optimize and produce a native executable.

The following graph shows a comparison of this selection sort algorithm written for a variety of languages. Here, you can see that Crystal competes near the top, losing to C and coming very close to Go. It is important to note that Crystal is a safe language: it has full exception handling support, it tracks bounds on arrays to avoid unsafe access, and it checks for overflow on integer math operations. C, on the other hand, is an unsafe language and won't check any of that. Having safety comes at a slight performance cost, but Crystal remains very competitive despite that:

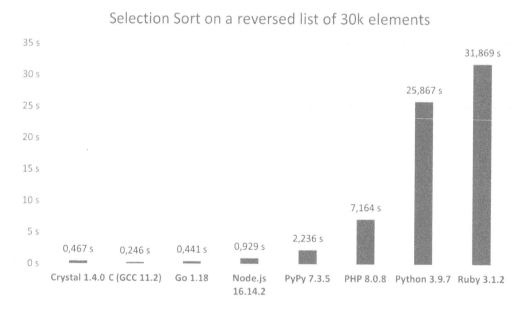

Figure 1.2 – A comparison of a simple selection sort implementation among different languages

> **Note**
>
> Comparing different languages and runtimes in a synthetic benchmark such as this isn't representative of real-world performance. Proper performance comparisons require a problem more realistic than selection sort and a broad coding review from experts on each language. Still, different problems might have very different performance characteristics. So, consider benchmarking for your use case. As a reference for a comprehensive benchmark, consider looking into the TechEmpower Web Framework Benchmarks (`https://www.techempower.com/benchmarks`).

A web server comparison

Crystal isn't only great for doing computation on small cases but also performs well on larger applications such as web services. The language includes a rich standard library with a bit of everything, and you will learn about some of its components in *Chapter 4, Exploring Crystal via Writing a Command-Line Interface*. For example, you can build a simple HTTP server, such as this:

```
require "http/server"

server = HTTP::Server.new do |context|
  context.response.content_type = "text/plain"
  context.response.print "Hello world, got #{context
    .request.path}!"
end

puts "Listening on http://127.0.0.1:8080"
server.listen(8080)
```

The first line, `require "http/server"`, imports a dependency from the standard library, which becomes available as `HTTP::Server`. It then creates the server with some code to handle each request and starts it on port `8080`. This is a simple example, so it has no routing.

Let's compare this against some other languages to see how well it performs. But, again, this isn't a complex real-world scenario, just a quick comparative benchmark:

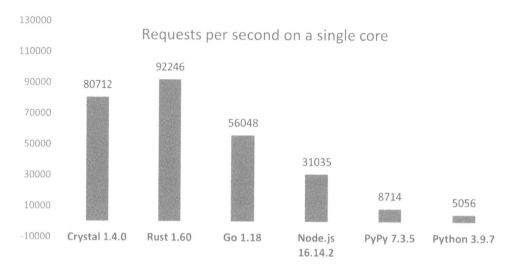

Figure 1.3 – A comparison of the request per second rate of
simple HTTP servers among different languages

Here we see that Crystal is well ahead of many other popular languages (very close to Rust and Go) while also being very high-level and developer-friendly to code. Many languages achieve performance by using low level code, but it doesn't have to cost expressiveness or expose abstractions. Crystal code is simple to read and evolve. The same trend happens in other kinds of applications as well, not only web servers or microbenchmarks.

Now, let's get hands-on with using Crystal.

Setting up the environment

Let's prepare ourselves to create and run Crystal applications, which we will begin in the *Creating our first program* section. For this, the two most important things you will need are a text editor and the Crystal compiler:

- **Text editor:** Any code editor will get the job done, but using one with good plugins for Crystal will make life much easier. Visual Studio Code or Sublime Text are recommended. You can find more details about the editor setup in *Appendix A*.

- **Crystal compiler:** Please follow the installation instructions on Crystal's website at `https://crystal-lang.org/install/`.

After installing a text editor and the compiler, you should have a working Crystal installation! Let's check it: open up your terminal and type the following: `crystal eval "puts 1 + 1"`:

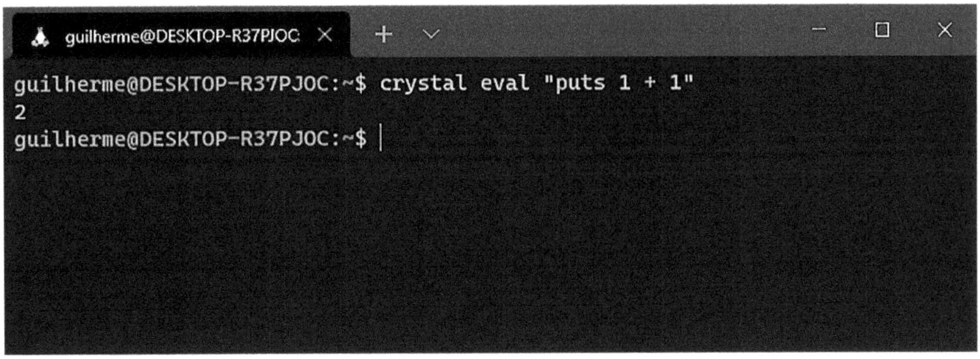

Figure 1.4 – Evaluating 1 + 1 using Crystal

This command will compile and execute the `puts 1 + 1` Crystal code, which writes the result of this computation back to the console. If you see 2 then all is set and we can move forward to writing actual Crystal code.

Creating our first program

Now let's experiment with creating our first program using Crystal. This is the basis for how you will write and execute code for the remainder of this book. Here is our first example:

```
who = "World"
puts "Hello, " + who + "!"
```

After that, perform the following steps:

1. Save this on a file called `hello.cr`.
2. Run it with `crystal run hello.cr` on your terminal. Note the output.
3. Try changing the `who` variable to something else and running again.

There is no boilerplate code such as creating a static class or a "main" function. There is also no need to import anything from the standard library for this basic example. Instead, you can just start coding right away! This is good for quick scripting but also makes applications simpler.

Note that the `who` variable doesn't need to be declared, defined, or have an explicit type. This is all deduced for you.

Calling a method in Crystal doesn't require parentheses. You can see `puts` there; it's just a method call and could have been written as `puts("Hello, " + who + "!")`.

String concatenation can be done with the + operator. It's just a method defined on strings, and you'll learn how to define your own in later chapters.

Let's try something else, by reading a name inputted by the user:

```
def get_name
  print "What's your name? "
  read_line
end


puts "Hello, " + get_name + "!"
```

After that, we'll do this:

1. Save the above code on a file called "hello_name.cr".

2. Run it with `crystal run hello_name.cr` on your terminal.

3. It will ask you for your name; type it and press *Enter*.

4. Now, run it again and type a different name. Note the output changing.

In this example, you created a `get_name` method that interacts with the user to obtain a name. This method calls two other methods, `print` and `read_line`. Note that as calling a method doesn't require parentheses, a method call without arguments looks precisely like a variable. That's fine. Also, a method always returns its last expression. In this case, the result of `get_name` is the result of `read_line`.

This is still simple, but will get you started on writing more complex code later on. Here, you can already see some console interaction and the use of methods for code reusability. Next let's see how you can make a native executable out of this code.

Creating an executable

When you need to ship your application, either to your end user's computer or to a production server, it isn't ideal to send the source code directly. Instead a better approach is to compile the code down to a native binary executable. Those are more performant, hard to reverse-engineer, and simpler to use.

So far, you have been using `crystal run hello.cr` to execute your programs. But Crystal has a compiler, and it should also produce native executables. This is possible with another command; try `crystal build hello.cr`.

As you will see, this won't run your code. Instead, it will create a "`hello`" file (without an extension), which is a truly native executable for your computer. You can run this executable with `./hello`.

In fact, `crystal run hello.cr` works mostly as a shorthand for `crystal build hello.cr && ./hello`.

You can also use `crystal build --release hello.cr` to produce an optimized executable. This will take longer, but will apply several code transformations to make your program run faster. For more details on how to deploy a final version of your application, take a look at *Appendix B, The Future of Crystal*.

Summary

Crystal delivers very well on performance, stability, and usability. It is a complete language with a growing community and ecosystem that can be used in production today. Crystal is highly innovative and has all the components of a successful programming language.

Knowing how to create and run Crystal programs will be fundamental in the following chapters, as there will be many code examples for you to try.

Now that you know about Crystal's origins and the significant characteristics of the language (namely its expressiveness and performance), let's move forward to learn the basics of programming in Crystal and get you started and productive in the language.

2

Basic Semantics and Features of Crystal

In this chapter, you will learn the basics of Crystal programming to bring you up to speed even if you don't know yet how to write a single line of Crystal code. Here you will learn about things common to many other programming languages, such as variables, functions, and control structures, and features particular to Crystal, such as the type system and passing blocks. It is expected that you have prior basic experience with some other programming language.

This chapter will cover the following main topics:

- Values and expressions
- Controlling the execution flow with conditionals
- Exploring the type system
- Organizing your code in methods
- Data containers
- Organizing your code in files

Technical requirements

To perform the tasks in this chapter, you will need the following:

- A working installation of Crystal
- A text editor configured to use Crystal

You can refer to *Chapter 1, An Introduction to Crystal*, for instructions on getting Crystal set up and to *Appendix A, Tooling Setup*, for instructions on configuring a text editor for Crystal.

Every example in the chapter (and in the rest of the book as well) can be run by creating a text file with the `.cr` extension for the code and then using the `crystal file.cr` command in a terminal application. The output or any errors will be shown on the screen.

You can fetch all the source code used in this chapter from the book's GitHub at `https://github.com/PacktPublishing/Crystal-Programming/tree/main/Chapter02`.

Values and expressions

Programming is the art of transforming and moving data. We want to receive information, maybe from the user typing on a keyboard, from an IoT sensor on the roof of your house, or even from an incoming network request sent to your server. Then, we want to interpret and understand that information, representing it in a structured way in our program. Finally, we want to process and transform it, applying algorithms and interfacing with external sources (things such as querying a database or creating a local file). Pretty much all computer programs follow this structure, and it's essential to understand that it's all about data.

Crystal has many primitive data types used to express values. For example, you can write integer numbers using digits, as in 34. You can also store data in variables. They act as named containers to store values and can change at any time. To do so, simply write the name of the variable, followed by an *equals* symbol, and the value you want to store. Here is an example of a Crystal program:

```
score = 38
distance = 104
score = 41

p score
```

You can execute this Crystal program by writing it into a file and using `crystal file.cr` on your terminal. If you do so, you'll see `41` on your screen. See that last line? It's using the p method to show the value of a variable on the screen.

If you are coming from other languages such as Java, C#, Go, or C, note that this is a complete program. In Crystal, you don't need to create a main function, declare variables, or specify types. Instead, creating a new variable and changing its value uses the same syntax.

A single line can assign multiple values to multiple variables by specifying them separated by commas. Multi-assignment is commonly used to swap the values of two variables. See this, for example:

```
# Assign two variables at once
emma, josh = 19, 16


# This is the same, in two lines
emma = 19
josh = 16


# Now swap their values
emma, josh = josh, emma


p emma # => 16
p josh # => 19
```

This example starts with a comment line. Comments are meant to add explanations or extra details in the source code and always start with the # character. Then, we have a multi-assignment creating the variables named emma and josh with the values 19 and 16, respectively. It is exactly the same as if the variables were created one at a time in two lines. Another multi-assignment is then used to swap the values of the two variables by giving emma the value of the josh variable and josh the value of the emma variable at the same time.

Variable names are always lower-cased using the convention of separating words with underscores (known as snake_case). Although uncommon, uppercase letters and non-English letters can also be used for variable names.

If the values you are using aren't going to change, you can use constants instead of variables. They must start with a capital letter and are usually written in all caps, words being separated with underscores, and can't be modified later. See this, for example:

```
FEET   = 0.3048 # Meters
INCHES = 0.0254 # Meters


my_height = 6 * FEET + 2 * INCHES   # 1.87960 meters


FEET = 20 # Error: already initialized constant FEET
```

This code shows two constants being defined: FEET and INCHES. Unlike variables, they can't be reassigned to a different value later. Constants can be accessed and used in expressions in place of their values and are useful when giving names to special or repetitive values. They can hold any kind of data, not only numbers.

Now, let's explore some of the most common primitive data types.

Numbers

Like other languages, numbers come in many flavors; here is a table describing them:

Type	Range	Suffix
Int8	Integers from -128 to 127	i8
Int16	Integers from -32,768 to 32,767	i16
Int32	Integers from -2,147,483,648 to 2,147,483,647	i32
Int64	Integers from -9,223,372,036,854,775,808 to 9,223,372,036,854,775,807	i64
UInt8	Integers from 0 to 255	u8
UInt16	Integers from 0 to 65,535	u16
UInt32	Integers from 0 to 4,294,967,295	u32
UInt64	Integers from 0 to 18,446,744,073,709,551,615	u64
Float32	Floating-point numbers with about 7 decimal significant digits of precision	f32
Float64	Floating-point numbers with about 15 decimal significant digits of precision	f64

Table 2.1 – Types of numbers and their limits

When writing a number, the most appropriate type will be used according to the value: if it's an integer, it will be either Int32, Int64, or UInt64, whichever is most suitable. If it's a floating-point value, it will always be Float64. You can also add a suffix to force one specific type. Finally, underscores can be used freely to improve legibility. Here are a few examples of how numbers can be expressed:

```
small_number = 47              # This is of type Int32
larger_number = 8795656243     # Now this is of type Int64
very_compact_number = 47u8     # Type is UInt8 because of the
   # suffix
other_number = 1_234_000       # This is the same as 1234000
negative_number = -17          # There are also negative
   # values
invalid_number = 547_u8        # 547 doesn't fit UInt8's
   # range
pi = 3.141592653589            # Fractional numbers are
   # Float64
imprecise_pi = 3.14159_f32     # This is a Float32
```

As expected, you can also do math operations with numbers. It works similarly to math in most languages. There are many operators, and they can be rearranged according to their precedence. In any case, parentheses can help organize a larger expression. Let's see an example:

```
hero_health_points = 100
hero_defense = 7
enemy_attack = 16

damage = enemy_attack - hero_defense # The enemy causes 9
   # damage
hero_health_points -= damage # Now the hero health points
   # is 91

healing_factor = 0.05 # The hero heals at a rate of 5% per
   # turn
recovered_health = hero_health_points * healing_factor
```

```
hero_health_points += recovered_health # Now the health is
  # 95.55

# This same calculation can also be done in a single line:
result = (100 - (16 - 7)) * (1 + 0.05) # => 95.55
```

Some of the most common operations with numbers are the following:

Operation	Description
num + num	Returns the sum of two numbers. For example, 2 + 3 is 5.
num - num	Returns the subtraction of two numbers. For example, 2 - 3 is -1.
num * num	Returns the product of two numbers. For example, 2 * 3 is 6 and 0.5 * 3 is 1.5.
num / num	Returns the division of two numbers. The result is always a floating-point number. For example, 3 / 2 is 1.5 and 12 / 3 is 4.0.
num // num	Returns the integer division of two numbers. If the division is imprecise, the result will be rounded down to an integer (floor division). For example, 3 // 2 is 1 and -3 // 2 is -2.
num % num	Returns the remainder of an integer division between the two numbers. For example, 3 % 2 is 1 and 3.5 % 1.2 is 1.1.
num ** num	Returns the number raised to a power. For example, 2 ** 5 is 32 and 2 ** (1 / 2) is 1.41421.
num.ceil num.floor num.round	Rounds a floating-point number into an integer. num.ceil returns a larger integer, num.floor returns a smaller and num.round returns the closest integer. For example, 1.7.floor is 1, 1.7.ceil is 2, 1.7.round is 2, and -1.7.round is -2.
num.abs	Returns the absolute value of the number. If it's negative, returns the positive equivalent. For example, -3.abs is 3.

Table 2.2 – Operations applicable to numbers

There are other types of numbers to express larger or more precise quantities:

- BigInt: Arbitrarily large integer

- BigFloat: Arbitrarily large floating-point numbers

- BigDecimal: Precise and arbitrarily numbers in base 10, especially useful for currencies

- `BigRational`: Expresses numbers as a numerator and a denominator
- `Complex`: Holds a number with a real part and an imaginary part

All these act as numbers and have similar functionality to the integers and floats we already introduced.

The primitive constants – true, false, and nil

There are three primitive constants in Crystal, each with its own meaning. The following specifies the types and uses:

Value	Description
True	Expresses truthiness. For example, the result of `5 == 5` is `true`. This value is of type `Bool`.
False	The opposite of `true`. This value is also of type `Bool`. For example, the result of `4 < 3` is `false`.
Nil	Expresses the lack of value. It is important to note that `nil` is still a value of type `Nil`. This type is detected and checked by the compiler, avoiding the common runtime "null exception" from other languages.

Table 2.3 – Primitive constants and descriptions

The `true` and `false` values are the result of comparison expressions and can be used with conditionals. Multiple conditionals can be combined with the `&&` (and) or `||` (or) symbols. For example, `3 > 5 || 1 < 2` evaluates to `true`.

Not every piece of data is composed of numbers only; we frequently have to deal with textual data. Let's see how we can handle those.

String and Char

Textual data can be represented with the `String` type: it can store arbitrary amounts of UTF-8 text, providing many utility methods to process and transform it. There is also the `Char` type, capable of storing a single Unicode code point: a **character**. Strings are expressed using text between double quotes, and characters use single quotes:

```
text = "Crystal is cool!"
name = "John"
single_letter = 'X'
kana = 'あ' # International characters are always valid
```

Inside a string, you can use interpolation to embed other values into the text. This is useful to create a string from data in other variables. Although you can interpolate any expression, try to keep it simple. Here are some examples of how this is done:

```
name = "John"
age = 37
msg = "#{name} is #{age} years old" # Same as "John is 37
   years old"
```

You can also use escape sequences inside a string to denote some special characters. For example, `puts "a\nb\nc"` will show three output lines. They are as follows:

Escape sequence	Description
`"\""`	A literal double quote character.
`"\\"`	Backslash, produces a single "\".
`"\a"`	Alert sound on interactive terminals.
`"\b"`	Backspace, moving the cursor back on interactive terminals.
`"\e"`	The start of special escape sequences on interactive terminals.
`"\f"`	The form feed control character, rarely used.
`"\n"`	Represents a line break. The string `"first\nsecond\nthird"` has three lines of text.
`"\r"`	Moves the cursor to the start of the line. On Microsoft Windows, a line break is usually represented as \r\n, instead of a single \n.
`"\t"`	Horizontal tab, produces some consistent spacing.
`"\v"`	Vertical tab control character, rarely used.
`"\123"`	Any three octal digits, represents a character of that code. `"\141"` is the same as `"a"`.
`"\xFF"`	Two hexadecimal digits, represents a character on the ASCII table. `"\x61"` is the same as `"a"`.
`"\uFFFF"` or `"\u{FFFF}"`	Represents any Unicode character with hexadecimal digits. `"\u0061"` and `"\u{61}"` are both the same as `"a"`.

Table 2.4 – Special escape sequences inside strings or chars

It's essential to keep in mind that Crystal strings are immutable after they are created, so any operation on them will produce a new string as a result. Many operations can be performed with strings; they will be used in examples throughout the entire book. Here are some common operations you can do with strings:

Operation	Description
`str.size`	Obtains the number of characters in a string. For example, `"hello".size` is 5.
`str + str`	Joins two strings together. For example, `"he" + "llo"` is `"hello"`.
`str * num`	Repeats the same string a given number of times. For example, `"hello" * 3` is `"hellohellohello"`.
`str.upcase` `str.downcase`	Transforms all characters into their upper-case variant or lower-case variant. For example, `"hello".upcase` is `"HELLO"`.

`str.starts_with?(str)`
`str.ends_with?(str)`
`str.includes?(str)`
`str.in?(str)`
	Verifies whether the string starts, ends, or includes some other given string or character. For example, `email.includes?('@')`.

`str.sub(pattern, str)` `str.gsub(pattern, str)`	Searches for and replaces occurrences of a given pattern. The sub variant does it only once, while the gsub one replaces every occurrence. For example, `"hi there".gsub("h", "jj")` is `"jji tjjere"`.
`str.lines` `str.split(str)`	Splits the string into many strings either by lines or by a given separator. For example, `"apples / oranges / grapes".split(" / ")` is `["apples", "oranges", "grapes"]`.
`str.reverse`	Returns a backward string. For example, `"hello".reverse` is `"olleh"`.
`str.strip`	Returns a new string with spaces and line breaks from the start and end removed. For example, `" hello\n".reverse` is `"hello"`.
`str.to_i` `str.to_f`	Converts a textual representation of a number into the actual number. For example, `"3".to_i` is 3 and `"1.05".to_f` is 1.05.

Table 2.5 – Common operations on string values

Strings and numbers are the usual representation for most data, but there are a few more structures we can study to make data easier to reason about.

Ranges

Another useful data type is `Range`; it allows representing an interval of values. Use two or three dots separating the values:

- `a..b` expresses an interval starting at a and ending with b, inclusive.

- `a...b` expresses an interval starting at a and ending immediately before b, excluding it.

The following are some examples of ranges:

```
1..5        # => 1, 2, 3, 4, and 5.
1...5       # => 1, 2, 3, and 4.
1.0...4.0   # => Includes 3.9 and 3.999999, but not 4.'
'a'..'z'    # => All the letters of the alphabet
"aa".."zz"  # => All combinations of two letters
```

You can also omit either the start or the end to create an open range. Here are some examples:

```
1..         # => All numbers greater than 1
...0        # => Negative numbers, not including zero
..          # => A range that includes everything, even itself
```

Ranges can be applied to different types as well; think about time intervals, for example.

There are many operations that can be done with ranges. In particular, `Range` implements both `Enumerable` and `Iterable`, making it act as a data collection. Here are some utility methods:

Operation	Description

`range.includes? value`
`range.covers? value`
`value.in? range`
	Verifies whether a given value is covered by the range. For example, `(1...10).includes? 10` is `false` and `(1..4).includes? Math::PI` is `true`.

`range.each do |value|`
  `p value`
`end`
	Iterates over each value of the range. For example, `(1..10).each { |num| puts num }` shows the numbers from 1 to 10.

Operation	Description
`range.sample`	Picks a random number on the interval. For example, `(1...100).sample` or `(3..3.5).sample` would return numbers in that range.
`range.sum`	Computes the sum of every element of this range. For example, `(1..10).sum` is 55 and `("a".."z").sum` is a string containing the entire alphabet.

Table 2.6 – Common operations on Range values

You can already express some data using literal values and variables in your code. This is enough for some basic computation; try to use it for some string transformations or math formulas. Some kinds of values can be declared first to be used later; enumerations are the simplest of these.

Enums and symbols

Strings are used to represent arbitrary text, usually regarding some interaction with the user, when the set of all possible texts is not known in advance. `String` offers operations to slice, interpolate, and transform text. There are cases where the value is not meant to be manipulated at all but just needs to represent one state out of some known possibilities.

For example, say you are interacting with some user in a multi-user system. This particular user may be either a guest, a regular authenticated user, or an admin. Each one of these has different capabilities and should be distinguished. This could be done using a numeric code to represent each kind of user, maybe 0, 1, and 2. Or, it could be done using the `String` type having "guest," "regular," and "admin" kinds of users.

The better alternative is to declare a proper enumeration of the possible kinds of users by using the `enum` keyword to create a brand-new data type. Let's see the syntax:

```
enum UserKind
  Guest
  Regular
  Admin
end
```

A variable holding a kind of user can be assigned by referring to the type name and then one of the declared kinds:

```
user_kind = UserKind::Regular
puts "This user is of kind #{user_kind}"
```

The type of the user_kind variable is UserKind, just like the type of 20 is Int32. In the next chapter, you will learn how to create more advanced custom types. Different enumerations can be created for each need; they won't mix together.

The enum value can be checked using a method generated from each alternative. You can use user_kind.guest? to check whether this user_kind holds the Guest kind or not. Likewise, the regular? and admin? methods can be used to check for the other kinds.

Declaring and using enumerations is the preferred way to handle a set of known alternatives. They will make sure you are never misspelling a user's kind, for example. Either way, enums are not the only option. Crystal also has the Symbol type.

A symbol is like a program-wise anonymous enum that doesn't need to be declared. You can simply refer to symbols by prepending a colon to the symbol name. They may look and feel very similar to strings, but their name isn't meant to be inspected and manipulated like a string; instead they are optimized for comparison and can't be created dynamically:

```
user_kind = :regular
puts "This user is of kind #{user_kind}"
```

Symbols are like tags and are uniquely identified by their name. Comparing symbols is more efficient than comparing strings, they will match if their name is the same. The compiler will scan all symbols used in the entire source code and merge the ones with the same name for this to work. They are quicker to write than a proper enum but must be used with care since a misspelling won't be detected by the compiler and will be simply treated as a different symbol.

Now we have seen how to express a multitude of types of data, but this isn't enough. Making code non-linear with conditionals and loops is fundamental for more complex programs that must make decisions based on computation. Now it's time to add logic to your code.

Controlling the execution flow with conditionals

Crystal, like most imperative languages, has a top-to-bottom line-by-line flow of execution. After the current line is executed, the line below that will be the next one. But you are empowered to control and redirect this flow of execution based on any conditional expression you can think of. The first kind of flow control we will cover is precisely that, reacting to conditionals.

if and unless

An `if` statement can be used to check a conditional; if it's truthy (that is, not `nil` nor `false`), then the statement inside it is executed. You can use `else` to add an action in case the conditional isn't `true`. See this, for example:

```
secret_number = rand(1..5) # A random integer between 1 and 5

print "Please input your guess: "
guess = read_line.to_i

if guess == secret_number
  puts "You guessed correctly!"
else
  puts "Sorry, the number was #{secret_number}."
end
```

The conditional doesn't need to be an expression that evaluates to a Bool (`true` or `false`). Any value other than `false`, `nil`, and null pointers (more about pointers in *Chapter 7, C Interoperability*) will be considered truthy. Note that zero and empty strings are also truthy.

The opposite of `if` is `unless`. It can be used when you want to react when the conditional is either `false` or `nil`. See this, for example:

```
unless guess.in? 1..5
  puts "Please input a number between 1 and 5."
end
```

An `unless` can also contain an `else` block, but in this case, it is always better to reverse the order and use an `if-else` sequence.

Both `if` and `unless` can be written as a single line by inserting it after the action. In some cases, this is more readable. The previous example is the same as this:

```
puts "Please input a number between 1 and 5." unless
  guess.in? 1..5
```

You can chain together several `if` statements using one or more `elsif` blocks. This is unique to `if` and can't be used with `unless`. See this, for example:

```
if !guess.in? 1..5
   puts "Please input a number between 1 and 5."
elsif guess == secret_number
   puts "You guessed correctly!"
else
   puts "Sorry, the number was #{secret_number}."
end
```

As you will frequently see in Crystal, these statements can also be used as expressions; they will produce the last statement of the selected branch. You can even use an `if` block in the middle of a variable assignment:

```
msg = if !guess.in? 1..5
         "Please input a number between 1 and 5."
      elsif guess == secret_number
         "You guessed correctly!"
      else
         "Sorry, the number was #{secret_number}."
      end

puts msg
```

This can be useful to avoid repetition or to perform complicated logic inside another expression. There is also the condensed version of `if` using the `condition ? truthy-statement : falsy-statement` structure. This is often known as **ternary**:

```
puts "You guessed #{guess == secret_number ? "correctly" :
   "incorrectly"}!"
```

Often you are not looking at checking conditionals but instead picking between multiple choices. This is where the `case` statement comes in, merging what would be a long sequence of `if` statements.

case

case is like an `if` statement but lets you define multiple possible outcomes depending on the given value. You specify a `case` statement with some value and one or more when alternatives checking for different possibilities. Here is the structure:

```
case Time.local.month
when 1, 2, 3
  puts "We a on the first quarter"
when 4, 5, 6
  puts "We a on the second quarter"
when 7, 8, 9
  puts "We a on the third quarter"
when 10, 11, 12
  puts "We a on the fourth quarter"
end
```

This is the direct equivalent of this much longer and less readable sequence of `if` statements:

```
month = Time.local.month
if month == 1 || month == 2 || month == 3
  puts "We a on the first quarter"
elsif month == 4 || month == 5 || month == 6
  puts "We a on the second quarter"
elsif month == 7 || month == 8 || month == 9
  puts "We a on the third quarter"
elsif month == 10 || month == 11 || month == 12
  puts "We a on the fourth quarter"
end
```

The `case` statement can also be used with ranges:

```
case Time.local.month
when 1..3
  puts "We a on the first quarter"
when 4..6
  puts "We a on the second quarter"
when 7..9
```

```
    puts "We a on the third quarter"
  when 10..12
    puts "We a on the fourth quarter"
  end
```

It can also be used with data types instead of values or ranges:

```
int_or_string = rand(1..2) == 1 ? 10 : "hello"
case int_or_string
when Int32
  puts "It's an integer"
when String
  puts "It's a string"
end
```

Thus, it is interesting to use a `case` statement to check for things other than direct equality as well. It works because, behind the scenes, `case` uses the `===` operator to compare the target value with each when clause. Instead of strict equality, the `===` operator checks for either equality or compatibility with a given set and is more relaxed.

Just like an `if` statement, a `case` statement can also have an `else` branch if none of the options match:

```
case rand(1..10)
when 1..3
  puts "I am a cat"
when 4..6
  puts "I am a dog"
else
  puts "I am a random animal"
end
```

You have learned to use variables, call methods, and diverge execution with conditionals so far. But it's also very useful to repeat execution until some condition is true, like when searching data or transforming elements. Now you will learn about the primitives to do just that.

while and until loops

The while statement is similar to the if statement, but it repeats until the condition is false. See this, for example:

```
secret_number = rand(1..5)

print "Please input your guess: "
guess = read_line.to_i

while guess != secret_number
  puts "Sorry, that's not it. Please try again: "
  guess = read_line.to_i
end

puts "You guessed correctly!"
```

Likewise, the until statement is the opposite of while, just as unless is the opposite of if:

```
secret_number = rand(1..5)

print "Please input your guess: "
guess = read_line.to_i

until guess == secret_number
  puts "Sorry, that's not it. Please try again: "
  guess = read_line.to_i
end

puts "You guessed correctly!"
```

Inside a looping structure, you can use these additional keywords:

- break – Aborts and exits the loop immediately, without rechecking the conditional
- next – Aborts the loop's current execution and starts again from the beginning, checking the conditional

Here is an example using `break` and `next` to control the flow further:

```
secret_number = rand(1..5)

while true
  print "Please input your guess (zero to give up): "
  guess = read_line.to_i

  if guess < 0 || guess > 5
    puts "Invalid guess. Please try again."
    next
  end

  if guess == 0
    puts "Sorry, you gave up. The answer was
      #{secret_number}."
    break
  elsif guess == secret_number
    puts "Congratulations! You guessed the secret number!"
    break
  end

  puts "Sorry, that's not it. Please try again."
end
```

These form the basis of controlling the execution flow, using conditionals, and looping structure. Later in this chapter, you will also learn about blocks, the most common way of looping in Crystal, especially with data containers. But before that, let's dive into the type system.

Exploring the type system

Crystal is a statically typed language; the compiler knows the types of every variable and expression before execution. This enables several correctness checks on your code, such as validating that the invoked methods exist and that the passed arguments match the signature, or ensuring that you are not trying to access nil properties.

A single type isn't enough in every situation: a single variable can be reassigned to values of different types, and thus the type of the variable can be any of the types of each value. This can be expressed with a union type, a type made from joining all the possible types. With it, the compiler knows that the variable can hold a value from any of those types at runtime.

You can use the `typeof(x)` operator to discover the type of any expression or variable as seen by the compiler. It might be a union of multiple types. You can also use `x.class` to discover the runtime type of a value; it will never be a union. Finally, there is the `x.is_a?(Type)` operator to check whether something is of a given type, which is helpful for branching and performing actions differently. The following are some examples:

```
a = 10
p typeof(a) # => Int32


# Change 'a' to be a String
a = "hello"
p typeof(a) # => String


# Maybe change 'a' to be a Float64
if rand(1..2) == 1
  a = 1.5
  p typeof(a) # => Float64
end


# Now the variable 'a' could be either a String or a Float64
p typeof(a) # => String | Float64


# But we can know during runtime what type it is
if a.is_a? String
  puts "It's a String"
  p typeof(a) # => String
else
  puts "It's a Float64"
  p typeof(a) # => Float64
end
```

```
# The type of 'a' was filtered inside the conditional, but
   # didn't change
p typeof(a) # => String | Float64


# You can also use .class to get the runtime type
puts "It's a #{a.class}"
```

In Crystal, every value is an object, even primitive types such as integers. Objects have a type and that type can respond to method calls. All operations you do on an object go through invoking some method. Even `nil` is an object of type `Nil` and can respond to methods. For example, `nil.inspect` returns `"nil"`.

All variables have a type or possibly a union of multiple types. When it's a union, it will store an object of one of the types at runtime. The actual type can be identified with the `is_a?` operator.

The methods available to a given type are always known to the compiler. Therefore, attempting to invoke a method that doesn't exist will result in a compile-time error rather than a runtime exception.

Fortunately, Crystal has a tool to help us visualize the types as they are deduced. The following section will walk you through it.

Experimenting with the crystal play command

The `crystal play` command launches the Crystal playground to play with the language using your browser. It will show the result produced by every line, along with the deduced type:

1. Open your terminal and type `crystal play`; it will show the following message:

    ```
    Listening on http://127.0.0.1:8080
    ```

2. Keep the terminal open, and then launch this URL in your favorite web browser. This will give you a neat interface to start coding in Crystal:

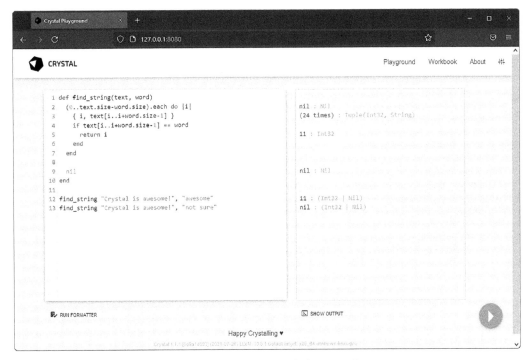

Figure 2.1 – The Crystal playground

3. On the left side, you have a text editor with some Crystal code. You can try changing the code to some of the code from this book for an interactive way of learning.

4. On the right side, there is a box with some annotations for your code. For example, it will show you the result of each line alongside the value type as seen by the compiler.

When in doubt about some examples or corner cases, try them out with the Crystal playground.

Moving forward to a more practical view of how types are used, we need to learn about storing and manipulating data in collections. These are always typed to ensure safety.

Organizing your code in methods

When writing applications, code needs to be structured in such a way that it can be reused, documented, and tested. The base of this structure is creating methods. In the next chapter, we will expand to object-oriented programming with classes and modules. A method has a name, can receive parameters, and always returns a value (`nil` is also a value). See this, for example:

```
def leap_year?(year)
    divides_by_4 = (year % 4 == 0)
    divides_by_100 = (year % 100 == 0)
    divides_by_400 = (year % 400 == 0)

    divides_by_4 && !(divides_by_100 && !divides_by_400)
end


puts leap_year? 1900 # => false
puts leap_year? 2000 # => true
puts leap_year? 2020 # => true
```

Method definitions start with the `def` keyword followed by the method name. In this case, the method name is `leap_year?`, including the interrogation symbol. Then, if the method has parameters, they will come between parentheses. A method will always return the result of its last line, in this example, the conditional result. Types don't need to be specified explicitly and will be deduced from usage.

When calling a method, the parentheses around the arguments are optional and are frequently omitted for legibility. In this example, `puts` is a method just like `leap_year?` and its argument is the result of the latter. `puts leap_year? 1900` is the same as `puts(leap_year?(1900))`.

Method names are like variables and follow the convention of using only lower-case letters, numbers, and underscores. Additionally, method names can end in interrogation or exclamation mark symbols. These don't have a special meaning in the language but are usually applied according to this convention:

- A method ending in ? may indicate that the method is checking for some condition and will return a `Bool` value. It is also commonly used for methods that return a union of some type and `Nil` to indicate a failure condition.

- A method ending in ! indicates that the operation it performs is "dangerous" somehow and the programmer must be careful when using it. Sometimes a "safer" variant of the method might exist with the same name, without the ! symbol.

Methods can build upon other methods. See this, for example:

```
def day_count(year)
  leap_year?(year) ? 366 : 365
end
```

Methods can be overloaded by the number of arguments. See this, for example:

```
def day_count(year, month)
  case month
  when 1, 3, 5, 7, 8, 10, 12
    31
  when 2
    leap_year?(year) ? 29 : 28
  else
    30
  end
end
```

In this case, the method will be selected depending on how you arrange the arguments to call it:

```
puts day_count(2020)    # => 366
puts day_count(2021)    # => 365
puts day_count(2020, 2) # => 29
```

Inside methods, the return keyword can be used to exit the method execution early, optionally delivering a value to the method's caller. The last expression in a method body behaves as an implicit return. It is mostly used inside conditionals for exceptional paths. See this, for example:

```
def day_count(year, month)
  if month == 2
    return leap_year?(year) ? 29 : 28
  end

  month.in?(1, 3, 5, 7, 8, 10, 12) ? 31 : 30
end
```

As types can be omitted when declaring a method, the parameter types are determined when the method is called. See this, for example:

```
def add(a, b) # 'a' and 'b' could be anything.
  a + b
end


p add(1, 2)          # Here they are Int32, prints 3.
p add("Crys", "tal")   # Here they are String, prints
  # "Crystal".


# Let's try to cause issues: 'a' is Int32 and 'b' is
  # String.
p add(3, "hi")
    # => Error: no overload matches 'Int32#+' with type
      # String
```

Every time the method is called with a different type, a specialized version of it is generated. In this example, the same method can be used to add numbers and to concatenate strings. It can't be confused with dynamic typing: the a parameter has a well-known type in each variation of the method.

In the third call, it tries to call add with Int32 and String. Again, a new specialized version of add is generated for those types, but now it will fail because a + b doesn't make sense when mixing numbers and text.

Not specifying types allows for the **duck typing** pattern. It is said that *if it walks like a duck and it quacks like a duck, then it must be a duck.* In this context, if the types passed as arguments support the a + b expression, then they will be allowed because this is all the implementation cares about, even if they are of a type never seen before. This pattern can be helpful to provide more generic algorithms and support unexpected use cases.

Adding type restrictions

Not having types isn't always the best option. Here are a few of the advantages of specifying types:

- A method signature with types is easier to understand, especially in the documentation.

- Overloads with different implementations can be added for different types.

- When you make a mistake and call some method with the wrong type, the error message will be cleaner when the parameters are typed.

Crystal has special semantics for specifying types: it's possible to restrict what types a parameter can receive. When the method is called, the compiler will check whether the argument type respects the parameter type restriction. If it does, then a specialized version of the method will be generated for that type. Here are some examples:

```
def show(value : String)
  puts "The string is '#{value}'"
end

def show(value : Int)
  puts "The integer is #{value}"
end

show(12)       # => The integer is 12
show("hey")    # => The string is 'hey'
show(3.14159) # Error: no overload matches 'show' with type
  # Float64

x = rand(1..2) == 1 ? "hey" : 12
show(x)  # => Either "The integer is 12" or "The string is
  # 'hey'"
```

A parameter can be restricted to a type by writing it after a colon symbol. Note that a space character before and after the colon is required. Types will be checked whenever the method is called to ensure correctness. If an attempt is made to call a method with an invalid type, it will be detected at compile time, giving a proper error message.

In this example, you also see the Int type. It is a union of all integer types and is particularly useful in restrictions. You can also use other unions as well.

The last line shows the concept of multi-dispatch in Crystal: if a call argument is a union type (Int32 | String in this case) and the method has multiple overloads, the compiler will generate code to check the actual type at runtime and pick the correct method implementation.

Multi-dispatch will also happen in a type hierarchy, if the argument expression is of an abstract parent type and there is a method defined for each possible concrete type. You will learn more about defining type hierarchies in the next chapter.

A type restriction is similar to type annotations in most other languages, where you specify the actual type of the parameter. But Crystal doesn't have type annotations. The word "restriction" is important here: a type restriction serves to restrict which possible types are acceptable. The actual type still comes from the call site. See this, for example:

```
def show_type(value : Int | String)
  puts "Compile-time type is #{typeof(value)}."
  puts "Runtime type is #{value.class}."
  puts "Value is #{value}."
end
```

```
show_type(10)
# => Compile-time type is Int32.
# => Runtime type is Int32.
# => Value is 10.
```

```
x = rand(1..2) == 1 ? "hello" : 5_u8
show_type(x)
# => Compile-time type is (String | UInt8).
# => Runtime type is String.
# => Value is hello.
```

It's interesting to see that the method body is always specialized to the types used at the call site without requiring runtime checks or any dynamism. This is part of what makes Crystal a very fast language.

You can also apply type restrictions to the return type of a method; this will ensure that the method is behaving as expected and producing the correct data. See this, for example:

```
def add(a, b) : Int
  a + b
end
```

```
add 1, 3     # => 4
add "a", "b" # Error: method top-level add must return Int
  # but it is returning String
```

Here the string variation will fail to compile because a + b will produce String, but the method is restricted to return Int. Besides a type, parameters can also have default values.

Default values

Methods can have default values to their arguments; this is a way of marking them as optional. To do so, specify a value after the parameter name, using the equals symbol. See this, for example:

```
def random_score(base, max = 10)
   base + rand(0..max)
end
```

```
p random_score(5)      # => Some random number between 5
   # and 15.
p random_score(5, 5) # => Some random number between 5
   # and 10.
```

You can use a default value when the method has a *most common value*, but you still want to allow different values to be passed if necessary. If there are many parameters with default values, it becomes a good practice to name them.

Named parameters

When a method is called with many arguments, it can sometimes be confusing as to what each one means. To improve on this, parameters can be named at the call site. Here is an example:

```
# These are all the same:
p random_score(5, 5)
p random_score(5, max: 5)
p random_score(base: 5, max: 5)
p random_score(max: 5, base: 5)
```

All four calls do the same thing, but the more verbose the call is, the easier it becomes to reason about what each 5 means. Additionally, you can reorder the arguments when using named parameters.

In some cases, it makes sense to force some parameters to always be named. For example, let's say we have a method that returns the opening time of a store. It needs to know if the day is a holiday and if it is part of the weekend:

```
def store_opening_time(is_weekend, is_holiday)
   if is_holiday
      is_weekend ? nil : "8:00"
```

```
    else
      is_weekend ? "12:00" : "9:00"
    end
  end
```

There's nothing unusual with this implementation. But if you start to use it, it becomes very confusing quickly:

```
  p store_opening_time(true, false) # What is 'true' and
    # 'false' here?
```

You can call the same method while specifying the name of each parameter for clarity:

```
  p store_opening_time(is_weekend: true, is_holiday: false)
```

To force some parameters to be named, add an * symbol before them. Everything to the left of the * will be positional parameters, and everything to the right will always be named parameters. They can also have default values:

```
  def store_opening_time(*, is_weekend, is_holiday)
    # ...
  end
```

```
  p store_opening_time(is_weekend: true, is_holiday: false)
  p store_opening_time(is_weekend: true, is_holiday: false)
```

```
  p store_opening_time(true, false) # Invalid!
```

Keep in mind that named parameters can always be used, even when they are not mandatory.

External and internal names for parameters

Sometimes a parameter can have a name that makes a lot of sense as the argument description for the caller, but can sound strange when used as a variable in the method implementation body. Crystal lets you define an external name (visible to the caller) and an internal name (visible to the method implementation). By default, they are the same, but they don't have to be. See this, for example:

```
  def multiply(value, *, by factor, adding term = 0)
    value * factor + term
```

```
  end
```

```
  p multiply(3, by: 5)                 # => 15
  p multiply(2, by: 3, adding: 10) # => 16
```

This method takes two or three parameters. The first is called `value` and is a positional parameter, meaning that it can be called without specifying the name. The next two parameters are named because of the `*` symbol. The second parameter has an external name of `by` and an internal name of `factor`. The third and final parameter has the external name `adding` and the internal name `term`. It also has a default value of `0`, so it is optional. This feature can be used to make calling methods with named parameters more natural.

Passing blocks to methods

Methods are the basis for organizing and reusing code. But to further improve this, reusability methods can also receive blocks of code when being called. Inside the method, you can use the `yield` keyword to invoke the received block, as many times as required.

Defining a method that receives a block is simple; just use `yield` inside it. See this, for example:

```
  def perform_operation
    puts "before yield"
    yield
    puts "between yields"
    yield
    puts "after both yields"
  end
```

This method can then be called, passing the block of code either around `do ... end` or curly braces `{ ... }`:

```
  perform_operation {
    puts "inside block"
  }
```

```
  perform_operation do
    puts "inside block"
  end
```

Executing this code will produce the following output:

```
before yield
inside block
between yields
inside block
after both yields
```

You can see that the inside block message happens in between statements of the method body. It appears twice because the code inside the block was executed on each `yield` of the main method.

But the code inside a block might need some context to work well. Because of this, blocks can also receive arguments and return values. Here is an example of a method that will transform the elements of an array into something else:

```
def transform(list)
  i = 0
  # new_list is an Array made of whatever type the block
    # returns
  new_list = [] of typeof(yield list[0])
  while i < list.size
    new_list << yield list[i]
    i += 1
  end
  new_list
end


numbers = [1, 2, 3, 4, 5]

p transform(numbers) { |n| n ** 2 } # => [1, 4, 9, 16, 25]
p transform(numbers) { |n| n.to_s } # => ["1", "2", "3",
  # "4", "5"]
```

The `yield` keyword behaves like a method call: you can pass arguments to it, and it will return the result of the block invocation. Block parameters are specified between a pair of pipe (|) symbols, separated with commas if there are more than one.

The aforementioned `transform` method is equivalent to the `map` method available for arrays:

```
numbers = [1, 2, 3, 4, 5]

p numbers.map { |n| n ** 2 }    # => [1, 4, 9, 16, 25]
p numbers.map { |n| n.to_s }    # => ["1", "2", "3", "4",
  # "5"]
```

There are many other methods already defined in Crystal that use blocks; the most common are the ones used to iterate over the elements of a data collection.

Just like `while` and `until`, the `next` and `break` keywords can also be used within blocks.

Using next inside a block

Use `next` to stop the current execution of the block and return to the `yield` statement that invoked it. If a value is passed to `next`, `yield` will receive it. See this, for example:

```
def generate
    first = yield 1    # This will be 2
    second = yield 2    # This will be 10
    third = yield 3    # This will be 4

    first + second + third
  end

  result = generate do |x|
    if x == 2
      next 10
    end

    x + 1
  end
  p result
```

The `generate` method invokes the received block three times and then computes the sum of the results. Finally, this method is called, passing a block that might finish earlier with the `next` call. A good analogy is that if blocks were methods, the `yield` keyword acts like a call to the method, and `next` would be equivalent to `return`.

Another way to exit the execution of a block is with the `break` keyword.

Using break inside a block

Use `break` to stop the method that is invoking the block, acting as if it returned. Expanding from the same example as before, look at the following:

```
result = generate do |x|
  if x == 2
    break 10    # break instead of next
  end

  x + 1
end
p result
```

In this case, `yield 1` will evaluate to 2, but `yield 2` will never return; instead, the `generate` method will be finalized right away and `result` will receive the value `10`. The `break` keyword causes the method that is invoking the block to finish.

Returning from inside a block

Lastly, let's see how `return` behaves when used inside a block. The **Collatz conjecture** is an interesting mathematical problem that predicts that a sequence where the next value is half the previous one if it's even or three times it plus one if it's odd will always reach 1 eventually, no matter what starting number is chosen.

The following `collatz_sequence` method implements this sequence by calling the block for each element endlessly. This implementation doesn't have a stop condition and might either run forever or be finished earlier by its caller.

Then follows an implementation of a method that starts `collatz_sequence` with some initial value and counts how many steps it takes to reach 1:

```
def collatz_sequence(n)
  while true
    n = if n.even?
```

```ruby
      n // 2
    else
      3 * n + 1
    end
    yield n
  end
end

def sequence_length(initial)
  length = 0
  collatz_sequence(initial) do |x|
    puts "Element: #{x}"
    length += 1
    if x == 1
      return length        # <= Note this 'return'
    end
  end
end

puts "Length starting from 14 is: #{sequence_length(14)}"
```

The `sequence_length` method keeps track of the number of steps, and as soon as it reaches 1, it returns. In this case, note that `return` occurs inside a block of the `collatz_sequence` method. The `return` keyword stops the block invocation (like `next`), stops the method that invoked the block with `yield` (like `break`), but then also stops the method where the block is written. A quick reminder is that return always finalizes the execution of the def it is inside.

This example code prints `Length starting from 14 is: 17`. In fact, the Collatz conjecture states that this code will always find a solution for any positive integer. It's an unsolved mathematical problem, however.

Data containers

Crystal has many built-in data containers to help you manipulate and organize non-trivial information. The most common by far is the **array**. Here's a quick overview of the most commonly used data containers in Crystal:

- `Array` – A linear and mutable list of elements. All values will share a single type, possibly a union.

- `Tuple` – A linear and immutable list of elements where the exact type of each element is preserved and known at compile time.

- `Set` – A unique and unordered group of elements. Values never repeat, and when enumerated, it shows the values in the order they were inserted (without duplicates).

- `Hash` – A unique collection of key-value pairs. Values can be obtained by their keys and can be overwritten, ensuring unique keys. Like `Set`, it is enumerated in insertion order.

- `NamedTuple` – An immutable collection of key-value pairs where every key is known at compile time, as well as the type of each value.

- `Deque` – A mutable and ordered list of elements meant to be used either as a stack (**FIFO**, or **First In First Out**) or as a queue (**FILO**, or **First In Last Out**) structure. It is optimized for fast insertion and deletion at both ends.

Next, let's study more details about some of these container types.

Arrays and tuples

You can express some simple data with numbers and text, but you will quickly need to pack more information together in lists. For this, you can use arrays and tuples. An array is a dynamic container that can grow, shrink, and be modified during program execution. A tuple, on the other hand, is static and immutable; its size and element types are known and fixed at compile time:

```
numbers = [1, 2, 3, 4]      # This is of type Array(Int32)
numbers << 10
puts "The #{numbers.size} numbers are #{numbers}"
   # => The 5 numbers are [1, 2, 3, 4, 10]
```

With arrays, you can't mix different types unless they were specified when the array was created. These errors are detected at build time; they are not runtime exceptions. See this, for example:

```
numbers << "oops"
  # Error: no overload matches 'Array(Int32)#<<' with type
     # String
```

By leveraging union types, you can have arrays that mix more than one type, either by initializing it with multiple types or by explicitly specifying them. Here's an example:

```
first_list = [1, 2, 3, "abc", 40]
p typeof(first_list)    # => Array(Int32 | String)
first_list << "hey!"    # Ok


# Now all elements are unions:
element = first_list[0]
p element          # => 1
p element.class    # => Int32
p typeof(element)  # => Int32 | String


# Types can also be explicit:
second_list = [1, 2, 3, 4] of Int32 | String
p typeof(second_list)    # => Array(Int32 | String)
second_list << "hey!"    # Ok


# When declaring an empty array, an explicit type is
   # mandatory:
empty_list = [] of Int32
```

Inside an array, all values have the same type; values of different types are expanded into a type union or a common ancestor if necessary. This is important because arrays are mutable, and a value at a given index can be freely replaced by something else.

The Array type implements the standard modules Indexable, Enumerable, and Iterable, providing several useful methods to explore and manipulate a collection.

A tuple is like an array in the sense that it stores a number of elements in an ordered fashion. The two major differences are that tuples are immutable after they are created and that the original type of each element is preserved without the need for unions:

```
list = {1, 2, "abc", 40}
p typeof(list)     # => Tuple(Int32, Int32, String, Int32)

element = list[0]
p typeof(element) # => Int32

list << 10    # Invalid, tuples are immutable.
```

Because tuples are immutable, they aren't used as frequently as arrays.

Both arrays and tuples have several useful methods. Here are some of the most common ones:

Operation	Description
list[index]	Reads the element at the given index. Raises a runtime error if this index is out of bounds. If the list is a tuple and the index is a literal integer, the out-of-bounds error will be detected at compile time.
list[index]?	Similar to list[index] but will return nil if the index is out of bounds.
list.size	Returns the number of elements inside the tuple or array.
array[index] = value	Replaces the value at a given index or raises if the index is out of bounds. As tuples are immutable, this is only available for arrays.
array << value array.push(value)	Adds a new value to the end of an array, increasing its size by one.
array.pop array.pop?	Removes and returns the last element of the array. Depending on the variant, it might raise or return nil on empty arrays.
array.shift array.shift?	Similar to pop but removes and returns the first element of the array, reducing its size by one.
array.unshift(value)	Adds a new value to the beginning of the array, increasing its size by one. It is the opposite of shift.

Operation	Description
`array.sort` `array.sort!`	Reorganizes the elements of the array to ensure they are ordered. Another useful variant is the `sort_by` method, which takes a block to receive the sorting criteria. The first variant returns a sorted copy of the array, and the second one sorts in place.
`array.shuffle` `array.shuffle!`	Reorganizes the elements of the array randomly. All permutations have the same probability. The first variant returns a shuffled copy of the array; the second one shuffles in place.

`list.each do |el|`
`    puts el`
`end`
	Iterates over the elements of the collection. Order is preserved.

`list.find do |el|`
`    el > 3`
`end`
	Returns the first element of the array or tuple that matches the given condition. If none matches, `nil` is returned.

`list.map do |el|`
`    el + 1`
`end`
	Transforms each element of the list by applying the block on it, returning a new collection (array or tuple) with the new elements in the same order. `Array` also has a `map!` method that modifies the elements in place.

`list.select do |el|`
`    el > 3`
`end`
	Returns a new array filtered by the condition in the block. If no elements match, the array will be empty. There is also `reject`, which performs the opposite operation by filtering the elements that don't match. In-place variants are available for arrays by adding a `!` to the method name.

Table 2.7 – Common operations on Array and Tuple containers

Not all data is ordered or sequential. For those, there are other data containers, such as the hash.

Hash

The `Hash` type represents a dictionary mapping keys to values. Keys can have any type, and the same goes for values. The only restriction is that each key can only have a single value, although the value can itself be another data container, such as an array.

A literal hash is created as a list of key-value pairs inside curly braces ({ . . . }). The key is separated from the value with a => symbol. For example, here are the largest populations in the world by country, according to Worldometer:

```
population = {
  "China"         => 1_439_323_776,
  "India"         => 1_380_004_385,
  "United States" => 331_002_651,
  "Indonesia"     => 273_523_615,
  "Pakistan"      => 220_892_340,
  "Brazil"        => 212_559_417,
  "Nigeria"       => 206_139_589,
  "Bangladesh"    => 164_689_383,
  "Russia"        => 145_934_462,
  "Mexico"        => 128_932_753,
}
```

The population variable is of type Hash (String, Int32) and it has 10 elements. Key and value types are deduced from usage, but if you need to declare an empty hash, the types will need to be explicitly specified, just like arrays:

```
population = {} of String => Int32
```

Hashes are mutable collections and have a handful of operators to query and manipulate them. Some common examples are as follows:

Operation	Description
hash[key]	Reads the value at a given key. If the key doesn't exist, it will raise a runtime error. For example, populations["India"] is 1380004385.
hash[key]?	Reads the value at a given key, but if the key doesn't exist, it returns nil instead of raising an error. For example, populations["India"]? is 1380004385 and populations["Mars"]? is nil.
Hash[key] = value	Replaces the value at a given key if it exists. Otherwise, adds a new key-value pair to the hash.

Operation	Description
`hash.delete(key)`	Locates and deletes the pair identified by the given key. If it was found, it returns the removed value; otherwise, it returns `nil`.

`hash.each { |k, v| p k, v }`
 	
`hash.each_key { |k| p k }`
 	
`hash.each_value { |v| p v }`
	Iterates over the elements stored in the hash. The enumeration follows the order in which the keys were inserted. Here is an example:
	
	`population.each do |country, pop|`
	`    puts "#{country} has #{pop}`
	`people."`
	`End`

`hash.has_key?(key)`
 	
`hash.has_value?(val)`
	Verifies whether a given key or value exists in the hash structure.

`hash.key_for(value)`
 	
`hash.key_for?(value)`
	Locates a pair with the given value and returns its key. This operation is expensive as it has to search all the pairs one by one.

`hash.keys`
 	
`hash.values`
	Creates an array of all keys or an array of all values from the hash.

Table 2.8 – Common operations on hash containers

As an interesting problem, let's see how to obtain the total population of all countries combined. We can use the `values` method to obtain an array of the population counters and then call the `sum` method on that array to aggregate it:

```
puts "Total population: #{population.values.sum}"
```

If you try this code, you will see it fail with the following error message:

```
Unhandled exception: Arithmetic overflow (OverflowError)
```

The problem is that `populations` is a `Hash(String, Int32)` instance, and thus calling `values` on it will produce an `Array(Int32)` instance. Adding together those values would result in 4,503,002,371, but let's remind ourselves that an `Int32` instance can only represent integers from -2,147,483,648 to 2,147,483,647. The result is outside that range and can't fit into an `Int32` instance. In these cases, Crystal will fail the operation instead of automatically promoting the integer type or giving wrong results.

One solution would be to store the population counters as `Int64` right from the start by specifying the type as we would do with an empty hash:

```
population = {
  "China"          => 1_439_323_776,
  "India"          => 1_380_004_385,
  # ...
  "Mexico"         => 128_932_753,
} of String => Int64
```

Another solution is to give an initial value to the `sum` method using the right type:

```
puts "Total population: #{population.values.sum(0_i64)}"
```

Now, let's see how we can iterate over these collections.

Iterating collections with blocks

When calling a method, it is possible to pass a block of code delimited by do...end. Several methods receive a block and operate on it, many of them allowing you to perform loops somehow. The first example is the `loop` method. It is simple – it just loops forever by calling the passed-in block:

```
loop do
  puts "I execute forever"
end
```

It's a direct equivalent of using `while true`:

```
while true
  puts "I execute forever"
end
```

Two other very useful methods that take blocks are `times` and `each`. Calling `times` on an integer will repeat the block that number of times, and calling `each` on a collection will invoke the block for each element:

```
5.times do
  puts "Hello!"
end
```

```
(10..15).each do |x|
  puts "My number is #{x}"
end
```

```
["apple", "orange", "banana"].each do |fruit|
  puts "Don't forget to buy some #{fruit}s!"
end
```

The preceding example shows how blocks can be used for iterating over some kind of collection. When writing Crystal code, this is preferred over iterating with a `while` loop. Several methods from the standard library take a block: we have seen `each`, but there is also map for transforming each element into something else, `select` or `reject` to filter elements based on some condition, and `reduce` to compute a value based on each element.

Short block syntax

A very common occurrence is to call a method passing a block that has only a single argument, and then call a method on this argument. For example, let's assume we have an array of strings, and we want to convert all of them to upper-case letters. Here are three ways to write it:

```
fruits = ["apple", "orange", "banana"]

# (1) Prints ["APPLE", "ORANGE", "BANANA"]
p(fruits.map do |fruit|
  fruit.upcase
end)

# (2) Same result, braces syntax
p fruits.map { |fruit| fruit.upcase }

# (3) Same result, short block syntax
p fruits.map &.upcase
```

The first snippet (1) used the map method together with a `do ... end` block. The map method iterates over the array, yielding to the block on each element and composing a new array with the block result. Parentheses are required in this first example because `do ... end` blocks connect to the outermost method, p in this case.

The second snippet (2) uses the { ... } syntax and can drop the parentheses because this block connects to the closest method call. Usually, the { ... } syntax is written in a single line, but that's not mandatory.

Finally, we see the short block syntax in the third snippet (3). Writing &.foo is the same as using { |x| x.foo }. It could also be written as p fruits.map(&.upcase), as if the block were a common argument of the method call.

Only the syntax differs; the behavior and semantics of all three snippets is the same. It is common to use the short block syntax whenever possible.

The Tuple container also shows up from method definitions, when using splat parameters.

Splat parameters

A method can be defined to accept an arbitrary number of arguments using splat parameters. This is done by adding an * symbol before a parameter name: it will now refer to a tuple of zero or more argument values when the method is called. See this, for example:

```
def get_pop(population, *countries)
  puts "Requested countries: #{countries}"
  countries.map { |country| population[country] }
end

puts get_pop(population, "Indonesia", "China", "United
    States")
```

This code will produce the following result:

```
Requested countries: {"Indonesia", "China", "United
    States"}
{273523615, 1439323776, 331002651}
```

Using splat will always produce tuples with the correct types as if the method had that number of normal positional parameters. In this example, typeof(countries) will be Tuple(String, String, String); the type will change for every usage. Splat parameters are the most common use case for tuples.

Organizing your code in files

Writing code in a single file is fine for some quick tests or very small applications, but anything else will eventually need to be organized in multiple files. There is always the main file, which is the one you pass to the crystal run or the crystal build command, but this file can reference code in other files with the require keyword. Compilation will always begin by analyzing this main file and then analyzing any file it references, and so on, recursively.

Let's analyze an example:

1. First, create a file named factorial.cr:

```
def factorial(n)
    (1..n).product
end
```

2. Then, create a file named program.cr:

```
require "./factorial"

(1..10).each do |i|
    puts "#{i}! = #{factorial(i)}"
end
```

In this example, require "./factorial" will search for a file named factorial. cr in the same folder as program.cr and import everything it defines. There is no way to select only part of what the required files define; require imports everything consistently. Run this example with crystal run program.cr.

The same file can't be imported twice; the Crystal compiler will check for and ignore such attempts.

There are two kinds of files you might require: it's either a file from your project – in that case, a relative path is used to refer to it, starting with a . – or it is a library file, coming from the standard library or from a dependency you installed. In that case, the name is used directly, without the relative path.

require "./filename"

The starting ./ tells Crystal to look for this file in the current directory, relative to the current file. It will search for a file named `filename.cr` or for a directory named `filename` with a file named `filename.cr` inside it. You can also use ../ to refer to the parent directory.

Glob patterns are also supported to import all files from a given directory, as here:

```
require "./commands/*"
```

This imports all Crystal files inside the `commands` directory. Importing everything from the current directory is also valid:

```
require "./*"
```

This notation is used primarily to refer to files from your own project. When referring to files from an installed library or from Crystal's standard library, the path doesn't start with a ..

require "filename"

If the path doesn't start with either ./ or ../, then it must be a library. In this case, the compiler will search for the file in the standard library and in the `lib` folder where the project dependencies are installed. See this, for example:

```
require "http/server"  # Imports the HTTP server from
   # stdlib.

Server = HTTP::Server.new do |context|
   context.response.content_type = "text/plain"
   context.response.print "Hello world, got
   #{context.request.path}!"
end

puts "Listening on http://127.0.0.1:8080"
server.listen(8080)
```

For anything larger than a couple of hundred lines, prefer splitting the code and organizing it in files, each with some objective or domain. This way, it is easier to find any particular part of the application.

Summary

This chapter has introduced several new concepts to get you started on writing real-world Crystal applications. You have learned about the basic types of values (numbers, text, ranges, and bools), how to define variables to store and manipulate data, and how to control the execution flow using conditionals and loops. You looked at creating methods to reuse code in a variety of ways. Finally, you learned about data collections with `Array` and `Hash`, together with using blocks and splat parameters. This is the toolbox you will use for the rest of this book.

The subsequent chapters begin applying this knowledge to practical projects. Next, let's embrace the object orientation features of Crystal to produce scalable software.

Further reading

Some of the language details were omitted to keep things short and focused. However, you can find documentation and reference materials on everything explained here in greater detail on Crystal's website, at `https://crystal-lang.org/docs/`.

3
Object-Oriented Programming

Like many others, Crystal is an **object-oriented language**. As such, it has objects, classes, inheritance, polymorphism, and so on. This chapter will introduce you to the features of Crystal for creating classes and handling objects while guiding you through those concepts. Crystal is largely inspired by Ruby, which itself borrows a lot from the Small Talk language, which is famous for its powerful object model.

In this chapter, we will cover the following main topics:

- The concept of objects and classes
- Creating your own classes
- Working with modules
- Values and references – using structs
- Generic classes
- Exceptions

Technical requirements

To complete the tasks in this chapter, you will need the following:

- A working installation of Crystal

- A text editor configured to use Crystal

Please refer to *Chapter 1, An Introduction to Crystal*, for instructions on getting Crystal set up and *Appendix A, Tooling Setup*, for instructions on configuring a text editor for Crystal.

You can find all the source code for this chapter in this book's GitHub repository at `https://github.com/PacktPublishing/Crystal-Programming/tree/main/Chapter03`.

The concept of objects and classes

Objects have some amount of data inside themselves and govern the access and behaviors around that data. They are like actors, communicating with other objects by calling methods and exchanging data in a very defined interface. No object is allowed to interfere with the internal state of another object directly – methods define all interaction.

Classes are the blueprints that objects are created from. Every object is an instance of some class. The class defines the data layout, the available methods, the behaviors, and the internal implementation. The class of an object is often referred to as its *type*: every object has a type.

In Crystal, everything is an object – every value you interact with has a type (that is, it has a class) and has methods you can invoke. Numbers are objects, strings are objects – even `nil` is an object of the `Nil` class and has methods. You can query the class of an object by calling the `.class` method on it:

```
p 12.class              # => Int32
p "hello".class         # => String
p nil.class             # => Nil
p true.class            # => Bool
p [1, 2, "hey"].class   # => Array(Int32 | String)
```

In the previous example, you can see that there are more complicated classes, such as the *array composed of integer and string elements*. Don't worry – we will cover those in the last section of this chapter.

Every class provides some methods to the objects that are instances of it. For example, all instances of the String class have a method called size that returns the number of characters of the string as an object of the Int32 type. By the same token, objects of the Int32 type have a method named + that takes another number as a single argument and returns their sum, as shown in the following example:

```
p "Crystal".size + 4      # => 11
```

It is the same as the more explicit form:

```
p("Crystal".size().+(4))      # => 11
```

This shows that all common operators and properties are just method calls.

Some classes don't have a literal representation and objects need to be created using the class name directly. The following is an example:

```
file = File.new("some_file.txt")
puts file.gets_to_end
file.close
```

Here, file is an object of the File type and it shows how you can open a file, read all its contents, and then close it. The new method is called on File to create a new instance from the class. This method receives a string as an argument and returns a new File object by opening the referred file. From here, the internal implementation of this file in memory is hidden away and you can only interact with it by calling other methods. gets_to_end is then used to obtain the contents of the file as a string and the close method is used to close the file and free some resources.

The previous example can be simplified by using a block variant that closes the file automatically after it has been used:

```
File.open("some_file.txt") do |file|
   puts file.gets_to_end
end
```

In the previous snippet, a block is being passed to the open method, which receives a file as an argument (the same that new would return). The block is executed and then the file is closed afterward.

You may have noticed that just like this code calls the `gets_to_end` method on the `file` object, it also calls the `open` method on the `File` class. Previously, you learned that methods are how we talk to objects, so why is it being used here to interact with a class as well? This is a very important detail to be aware of: in Crystal, everything is an object, even classes. All classes are objects of the `Class` type, and they can be assigned to variables just like plain values:

```
p 23.class             # => Int32
p Int32.class          # => Class

num = 10
type = Int32
p num.class == type # => true

p File.new("some_file.txt")          # =>
  #<File:some_file.txt>
file_class = File
p file_class.new("some_file.txt")   # =>
  #<File:some_file.txt>
```

Now, you know that primitive values are objects, instances of more complex types from the standard library's classes are objects, and that classes themselves are objects too. Every object has an internal state and exposes behavior thought methods. Variables are used to hold these objects.

Although Crystal comes with many useful classes and you can install more from external dependencies, you can create your own classes for anything you need. We'll look at this in the next section.

Creating your own classes

Classes describe the behavior of objects. It is nice to learn that the standard types that come with Crystal are, for the most part, just ordinary classes you could have implemented on your own. Also, your application will need some more specialized classes, so let's create them.

New classes are created with the `class` keyword, followed by the name and then the definition of the class. The following a minimal example:

```
class Person
end


person1 = Person.new
person2 = Person.new
```

This example creates a new class named `Person` and then two instances of this class – two objects. This class is empty – it doesn't define any method or data, but Crystal classes come with some functionality by default:

```
p person1          # You can display any object and
   # inspect it
p person1.to_s    # Any object can be transformed into
   # a String
p person1 == person2     # false. By default, compares
   # by reference.
p person1.same?(person2) # Also false, same as above.
p person1.nil?            # false, person1 isn't nil.
p person1.is_a?(Person)  # true, person1 is an instance
   # of Person.
```

Inside a class, you can define methods the same way you can define top-level methods. One such method is special: the `initialize` method. It is called whenever a new object is created to initialize it to its initial state. The data that's stored inside an object is held in instance variables; they are like local variables, but they are shared among all the methods of a class and start with the @ character. Here is a more complete `Person` class:

```
class Person
  def initialize(name : String)
    @name = name
    @age = 0
  end


  def age_up
    @age += 1
```

```
    end

    def name
        @name
    end

    def name=(new_name)
        @name = new_name
    end
end
```

Here, we have created a more realistic `Person` class with an internal state composed of a `@name`, a `String`, an `@age`, and an `Int32`. The class has a few methods that interact with this data, including the `initialize` method, which will create a new baby person.

Now, let's use this class:

```
jane = Person.new("Jane Doe")
p jane    # => #<Person:0x7f97ae6f3ea0 @name="Jane Doe",
   # @age=0>
jane.name = "Mary"
5.times { jane.age_up }
p jane    # => #<Person:0x7f97ae6f3ea0 @name="Mary", @age=5>
```

This example creates an instance of `Person` by passing a string to the new method. This string is used to initialize the object and ends up assigned to the `@name` instance variable. By default, objects can be inspected with the p top-level method, and it shows the class name, the address in memory, and the value of the instance variables. The following line calls the `name=(new_name)` method – it could do anything, but conveniently, it updates the `@name` variable with a new value. Then, we go ahead and call `age_up` five times and inspect the object again. Here, you should see the new name and age of the person.

Note that in the `initialize` method, we explicitly specify the type of the `name` argument instead of letting the compiler deduce it from usage. This is required here because the types of the instance variables must be known from the class alone and can't be inferred from usage. This is why it can't be said that Crystal has a global type inference engine.

Now, let's dive deeper into how methods and instance variables can be defined.

Manipulating data using instance variables and methods

All the data inside an object is stored in instance variables; their names always start with an @ symbol. There are multiple ways to define an instance variable for a class, but one rule is fundamental: their type must be known. The type can either be explicitly specified or deduced syntactically by the compiler.

The initial value of an instance variable can be given either inside the `initialize` method or directly in the class body. In the latter case, it behaves as if the variable were initialized at the beginning of the `initialize` method. If an instance variable isn't assigned in any `initialize` method, then it is implicitly assigned to `nil`.

The type of the variable will be inferred from every assignment to it in the class, from all methods. But keep in mind that their type can only depend on literal values or typed arguments and nothing else. Let's see some examples:

```
class Point
   def initialize(@x : Int32, @y : Int32)
   end
end
origin = Point.new(0, 0)
```

In this first case, the `Point` class specifies that its objects have two integer instance variables. The `initialize` method will use its arguments to provide the initial value to them:

```
class Cat
   @birthday = Time.local

   def adopt(name : String)
      @name = name
   end
end

my_cat = Cat.new
my_cat.adopt("Tom")
```

Now, we have a class describing a cat. It doesn't have an `initialize` method, so it behaves as if it had an empty one. The `@birthday` variable is assigned to `Time.local`. This happens inside this empty `initialize` method when a new instance of the object is created. The type is inferred to be a `Time` instance, as `Time.local` is typed to always return it. The `@name` variable receives a string value from a typed argument but doesn't have an initial value anywhere, so its type is `String?` (this can also be represented as `String | Nil`).

Note that deducing the instance variable from an argument only works when the parameter is explicitly typed, and the instance variable is assigned directly to the value. The following example is invalid:

```
class Person
  def initialize(first_name, last_name)
    @name = first_name + " " + last_name
  end
end


person = Person.new("John", "Doe")
```

In this example, the `@name` variable is constructed by concatenating two arguments with whitespace between them. Here, the type of this variable can't be inferred without a deeper analysis of the types of the two parameters and the result of the + method call. Even if the arguments were explicitly typed as `String`, it still wouldn't be enough information as the + method for strings can be redefined somewhere in the code to return some other arbitrary type. In cases like this, the instance variable type must be declared:

```
class Person
  @name : String
  def initialize(first_name, last_name)
    @name = first_name + " " + last_name
  end
end
```

Alternatively, a literal string interpolation can be used, as it is guaranteed to always produce a string:

```
class Person
  def initialize(first_name, last_name)
    @name = "#{first_name} #{last_name}"
  end
end
```

In any situation, it is allowed to declare the type of an instance variable explicitly, maybe for clarity.

> **Note**
> You may be wondering, why doesn't the compiler go ahead and analyze the entire program and every method call to discover the types of every instance variable by itself, like it already does for local variables? The compiler did just that in the early days, but this feature was removed as this analysis was too expensive performance-wise and it would make incremental compilation infeasible in the future. The existing rules about deducing instance variables are successful in most cases and they rarely need to be typed.

Instance variables represent the private state of an object and should only be manipulated from methods inside the class. They can be exposed through getters and setters. Instance variables can be accessed externally with the `obj.@ivar` syntax, but that isn't encouraged.

Creating getters and setters

Crystal doesn't have a special concept of a getter or a setter for object properties; instead, they are constructed from features we have already learned about. Let's say we have a person that has a `name` instance variable:

```
class Person
  def initialize(@name : String)
  end
end
```

We can already create a new person and inspect it:

```
person = Person.new("Tony")
p person
```

But it would be nice to be able to write something like the following as if `@name` were accessible:

```
puts "My name is #{person.name}"
```

`person.name` is just the invocation of a method called `name` on the `person` object. Remember that parentheses are optional for method calls. We can go ahead and create exactly this method:

```
class Person
  def name
    @name
  end
end
```

Now, calling `person.name` is valid as if the instance variable were accessible externally. As an added benefit, future refactoring can change the internal structure of the object and reimplement this method without affecting users. This is so common that there is a utility macro just for it:

```
class Person
  getter name
end
```

The previous two snippets have the same behavior. The `getter` macro produces a method exposing the instance variable. It can also be combined with a `type` declaration or an initial value:

```
class Person
  getter name : String
  getter age = 0
  getter height : Float64 = 1.65
end
```

Multiple getters can be created in a single line:

```
class Person
  getter name : String, age = 0, height : Float64 = 1.65
end
```

For setters, the logic is very similar. Crystal method names can end with a = symbol to denote a setter. When it has a single parameter, it can be called with a convenient syntax:

```
class Person
  def name=(new_name)
    puts "The new name is #{new_name}"
  end
end
```

This name= method can be called like this:

```
person = Person.new("Tony")
person.name = "Alfred"
```

The last line is just a method call and doesn't change the value of the @name instance variable. It is the same as writing person.name=("Alfred"), as if = were any other letter. We can take advantage of this to write a setter method:

```
class Person
  def name=(new_name)
    @name = new_name
  end
end
```

Now, it will behave as if name were a publicly accessible property of the object. As a form of shorthand, the setter macro can produce these methods for you, similar to the getter macro we just saw:

```
class Person
  setter name
end
```

It can also be used with a type declaration or an initial value.

We frequently need to expose an instance variable with both a getter and a setter. Crystal has the property macro for that:

```
class Person
  property name
end
```

This is the same as writing the following:

```
class Person
  def name
    @name
  end

  def name=(new_name)
    @name = new_name
  end
end
```

As usual, type declarations or initial values can be used for a very convenient syntax. There are other useful macros, such as the `record` macro, as you will see later in this chapter. In the following chapters, you will also learn how to create your own macros to automate code generation. Next, you will learn about a core concept from object-oriented programming: classes that inherit from other classes.

Inheritance

Classes can build upon other classes to provide more specialized behavior. When a class inherits from another, it gets all the existing methods and instance variables and can add new ones or overwrite existing ones. For example, let's extend the previously defined `Person` class:

```
class Person
  property name : String
  def initialize(@name)
  end
end

class Employee < Person
  property salary = 0
end
```

An instance of `Employee` can be in any place where an instance of `Person` is required as for all intents and purposes, an employee is a person:

```
person = Person.new("Alan")
employee = Employee.new("Helen")
```

```
employee.salary = 10000
p person.is_a? Person      # => true
p employee.is_a? Person    # => true
p person.is_a? Employee    # => false
```

In this example, `Person` is the parent class and `Employee` is the child class. More classes can be created to produce a hierarchy of classes. When you're inheriting from an existing class, the child can not only extend but also override parts of its parent. Let's see this in practice:

```
class Employee
  def yearly_salary
    12 * @salary
  end
end

class SalesEmployee < Employee
  property bonus = 0

  def yearly_salary
    12 * @salary + @bonus
  end
end
```

In this example, we can see the `Employee` class that was previously defined being reopened to add a new method. When reopening a class, its parent class should not be specified (`Person`, in this case). The `yearly_salary` method is added to `Employee` and then a new specialized type of `Employee` is created, inheriting from it (and, in turn, also inheriting from `Person`). A new property is added and `yearly_salary` is redefined to take it into account. The redefinition only affects objects of the `SalesEmployee` type, not those of the `Employee` type.

When you're inheriting from a class and overriding a method, the `super` keyword can be used to call the overridden definition, from the parent class. `yearly_salary` could have been written like this:

```
def yearly_salary
  super + @bonus
end
```

As the `initialize` method is used to prepare the initial state of an object, it is always expected to be executed before anything else. Thus, it is common practice to use the `super` keyword to call the parent class constructor when you're inheriting from an existing class.

Now that we have defined multiple classes and subclasses, we can take advantage of another powerful concept: objects of the type of a subclass can be stored in a variable typed to hold one of its base classes.

Polymorphism

`SalesEmployee` inherits from `Employee` to define a more specialized kind of employee, but it doesn't change the fact that a sales employee is an employee and can be treated as such. This is called **polymorphism**. Let's see an example of this in action:

```
employee1 = Employee.new("Helen")
employee1.salary = 5000
employee2 = SalesEmployee.new("Susan")
employee2.salary = 4000
employee2.bonus = 20000
employee3 = Employee.new("Eric")
employee3.salary = 4000
employee_list = [employee1, employee2, employee3]
```

Here, we have created three different employees and then created an array holding all of them. This array is of the `Array(Employee)` type, even though it holds a `SalesEmployee` as well. This array can be used to call methods:

```
employee_list.each do |employee|
  puts "#{employee.name}'s yearly salary is $#{employee.
    yearly_salary.format(decimal_places: 2)}."
end
```

This will produce the following output:

```
Elen's yearly salary is $60,000.00.
Susan's yearly salary is $68,000.00.
Eric's yearly salary is $48,000.00.
```

As this example has shown, Crystal will call the correct method based on the real runtime type of the object, even when it is statically typed as the parent class.

Creating a class hierarchy isn't useful only to reuse code, but to allow polymorphism to happen. You can even introduce incomplete classes to your program just to tighten up similar concepts together. Some of those will need to be abstract classes, as we will see next.

Abstract classes

Sometimes, we are writing a hierarchy of classes and it doesn't make sense to allow an object to be created from some of them because they don't represent concrete concepts. This is the moment to mark a class as **abstract**. Let's look at an example:

```
abstract class Shape
end

class Circle < Shape
  def initialize(@radius : Float64)
  end
end

class Rectangle < Shape
  def initialize(@width : Float64, @height : Float64)
  end
end
```

Both circles and rectangles are kinds of shapes, and they can be understood by themselves. But Shape itself is something abstract and was made to be inherited from. When a class is abstract, instantiating it into an object is not allowed:

```
a = Circle.new(4)
b = Rectangle.new(2, 3)
c = Shape.new # This will fail to compile; it doesn't make
    # sense.
```

An abstract class doesn't only impose a restriction but also allows us to describe characteristics that every subclass must implement. Abstract classes can have abstract methods, and methods without definitions must be overridden:

```
abstract class Shape
   abstract def area : Number
end

class Circle
   def area : Number
     Math::PI * @radius ** 2
   end
end

class Rectangle
   def area : Number
     @width * @height
   end
end
```

By defining the abstract area method on the parent class, we ensure that all the subclasses will have to define it while following the same signature (no arguments, returning some kind of number). If we have a list of shapes, for example, we can ensure that we can compute the area of every single one of them.

The abstract class isn't limited to abstract methods – it can also define normal methods and instance variables.

Class variables and class methods

Objects are instances of a specific class and store values for its instance variables. Although the names and types of the variables are the same, each instance (each object) can have different values for them. If the instance variable type is a union of more than one type, then different objects can store values of different types in them. The class describes the skeleton, while the objects are the live things.

But classes are objects too! Shouldn't they have *instance* variables and methods? Yes, of course.

When you're creating a class, you can define class variables and class methods. Those live in the class itself, not in any particular object. Class variables are denoted with the @@ prefix, just like instance variables have a @ prefix. Let's see this in practice:

```
class Person
  @@next_id = 1
  @id : Int32
  def initialize(@name : String)
    @id = @@next_id
    @@next_id += 1
  end
end
```

Here, we have defined a class variable called @@next_id. It exists for the whole program at once. We also have the @name and @id instance variables, which exist on each Person object:

```
first = Person.new("Adam")   # This will have @id = 1
second = Person.new("Jess")  # And this will have @id = 2
# @@next_id inside Person is now 3.
```

Be aware that these class variables act as global variables and their values are shared with the whole program. While this is useful for some global states, it is also not thread-safe on programs with parallelism enabled as there can be race conditions. The previous example isn't thread-safe if Person instances are created from different threads. Crystal isn't multi-threaded by default.

Similar to class variables, class methods can be defined on the class itself by prefixing its name with self. Take a look:

```
class Person
  def self.reset_next_id
    @@next_id = 1
  end
end
```

Now, you can call Person.reset_next_id to perform this action, operating on the class directly. From this, it's clear that classes are indeed objects as they have data and methods. All of this works as expected with inheriting subclasses as well.

As a class method is called on a class and not on an instance of the class, there is no object in play and the `self` keyword refers to the class itself. You can't access instance variables or call instance methods without referring to some object.

Similar to instance variables, there are helper macros to help with exposing class variables with class methods – that is, `class_getter`, `class_setter`, and `class_property`:

```
class Person
  class_property next_id
end
```

Now, it's possible to do `Person.next_id` = 3 or x = `Person.next_id`.

Working with modules

Modules, like abstract classes, don't represent concrete classes that you can create objects from. Instead, modules are fragments of the implementation class that can be included in a class when you're defining it. Modules can define instance variables, methods, class variables, class methods, and abstract methods, all of which get injected into the class that includes them.

Let's explore an example of a module that defines a `say_name` method based on some existing `name` method:

```
module WithSayName
  abstract def name : String

  def say_name
    puts "My name is #{name}"
  end
end
```

This can be used with your `Person` class:

```
class Person
  include WithSayName
  property name : String

  def initialize(@name : String)
  end
end
```

Here, the name method that's expected by WithSayName is produced by the property macro. Now, we can create a new instance of Person and call say_name on it.

Modules can be used on type restrictions and for the type of variables. When this is done, it indicates *any class that includes this module*. Given the previously defined code, we can do the following:

```
def show(thing : WithSayName)
   thing.say_name
end
show Person.new("Jim")
```

As usual, type restrictions are optional, but they may help with legibility and documentation.

Modules are frequently used for the same purpose as interfaces from other languages, where a common set of characteristics is defined, and many different classes implement the same module. Also, a single class can include as many modules as necessary.

The standard library includes some useful modules to indicate the characteristics of some classes:

- Comparable: This implements all the comparison operators, given that you have correctly implemented the <=> operator. Classes that represent values with a natural order that can be sorted inside a container usually include this module.

- Enumerable: This is used for collections whose elements can be listed one by one. The class must implement the each method, yielding each element to a block. This module, in turn, implements several helper methods to manipulate the collection.

- Iterable: This indicates that it is possible to lazily iterate over the including collection. The class must implement the each method without receiving a block and return an Iterator instance. The module will add many useful methods to transform this iterator.

- Indexable: This is meant for collections whose elements have a numerical position in some strict order and can be counted from 0 to the collection size. The class is expected to provide a size and an unsafe_fetch method. Indexable includes Enumerable and Iterable and provides all their methods, along with some additions for operating with indexes.

You can read more about each of these modules in the official documentation at https://crystal-lang.org/docs.

We have discussed modules being used as *mixins* when their primary focus is being included in another existing class. Instead, a module can be used simply as a namespace or act as a holder of variables and methods. The `Base64` module from the standard library is an example of this – it just provides some utility methods and isn't meant to be included in a class:

```
# Prints "Crystal Rocks!":
p Base64.decode_string("Q3J5c3RhbCBSb2NrcyE=")
```

Here, `Base64` is just a group of related methods to be directly accessed from the module. This is a common pattern that helps you organize methods and classes.

More about different use cases for modules will be covered later in this book. We have learned a lot about classes and objects, but not every object behaves the same. Next, let's learn the difference between values and references.

Values and references – using structs

By default, Crystal objects are allocated into memory and are managed by a garbage collector. This means that you don't have to worry about where each object is in memory and how long it should live – the runtime will take care of accounting for which objects are still referred to by some variables and will release all others, automatically freeing resources. Variables will not store the object per se – it will store a reference pointing to the object. It all works transparently and there is no need to worry about it.

The aforementioned is true for all objects that are created from classes; the types of these objects are reference types. But there is another kind of object: value types.

In the following diagram, you can see the inheritance chain of some types. The ones that are references inherit from the `Reference` class, while the ones that are values inherit from the `Value` struct. All of them inherit from the special `Object` base type:

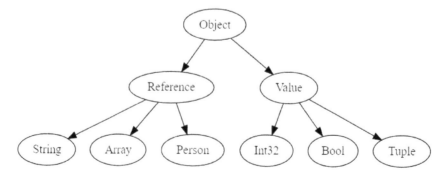

Figure 3.1 – Hierarchy of types showing how references relate to values

References are managed by the garbage collector and live in the heap, a special region of memory. Variables point to them, and multiple variables can refer to the same object. Value objects, on the other hand, live in the variables themselves and are usually small. They are created from structs.

You can create your own structs. They are very similar to classes in that they also have instance variables and methods:

```
struct Address
  property state : String, city : String
  property line1 : String, line2 : String
  property zip : String

  def initialize(@state, @city, @line1, @line2, @zip)
  end
end
```

Structs and classes are all types of objects and they can be used to type any variable, including type unions. For example, let's store an address inside the Person class:

```
class Person
  property address : Address?
end
```

Here, the @address instance variable is of the Address? type, a shorthand for Address | Nil. As there is no initial value and this variable is not assigned in the initialize method, it starts as nil. Using the struct is straightforward:

```
address = Address.new("CA", "Los Angeles", "Some fictitious
  line", "First house", "1234")
person1 = Person.new
person2 = Person.new
person1.address = address
address.zip = "ABCD"
person2.address = address
puts person1.address.try &.zip
puts person2.address.try &.zip
```

We started this example by creating an address and two persons – a total of three objects: one `Value` object and two `Reference` objects. Then, we assigned the address from the local `address` variable to the `@address` instance variable of `person1`. Since `Address` is a `Value`, this operation copies the data. We go to modify it and assign `@address` of `person2`. Note that modifying it does not affect `person1` – the values are always copied over. Finally, we show the ZIP code in each address. We need to use the `try` method to only access the `zip` property when the union is not `nil` at this point, as there is no way for the compiler to tell on its own.

Experiment with changing `Address` to a class and running the previous code again. This time, both people will have the same ZIP code. This happens because references are not copied over on assignments, so all the variables will refer to the same address object.

Struct values are always copied when you're assigning them from one variable to another, when you're passing them as arguments to a method call, or when you're receiving them from the return value of a method call. This is known as "by-value" semantics; thus, it is recommended that structs are kept small in terms of their memory size. There is an interesting and useful exception to this rule: when the method body simply returns an instance variable directly, then the copy is elided, and the value is accessed directly. Let's look at an example:

```
struct Location
  property latitude = 0.0, longitude = 0.0
end

class Building
  property gps = Location.new
end

building = Building.new
building.gps.latitude = 1.5
p store
```

In the preceding example, we created a `Location` struct type that has two properties and a `Building` class that has a single property. The `property gps` macro will generate a method called `def gps; @gps; end` for the getter – notice how this method simply returns an instance variable directly, matching the rule about copy elision. If this method were anything else, this example wouldn't work.

The `building.gps.latitude = 1.5` line calls the `gps` method and grabs the result, then calls the `latitude=` setter with `1.5` as an argument. If the `gps` return value were copied, then the setter would operate on a copy of the struct and wouldn't affect the value stored inside the `building` variable. Try to experiment with adding a custom definition for the `gps` method.

Now that you know how to create both classes and structs, we will take a step forward and learn about generics and how this new concept can help you write more malleable types.

Generic classes

A **generic class** (or **struct**) is constructed on top of one or more unknown types that are only determined later when you're creating an instance of said class. This sounds complex, but you have already used some generic classes before. `Array` is the most common one: have you noticed that we always need to specify the type of data the array holds? It isn't enough to say that a given variable is an array – we must say it is an array of strings, or `Array(String)`. The `Hash` generic class is similar, but this one has two type parameters – the types of the keys and the types of the values.

Let's look at a simple example. Say you want to create a class that holds a value in one of its instance variables, but the value can be of any type. Let's look at a way we can do this:

```
class Holder(T)
  def initialize(@value : T)
  end

  def get
    @value
  end

  def set(new_value : T)
    @value = new_value
  end
end
```

Generic parameters are, by convention, single capital letters – T, in this case. In this example, Holder is a generic class, and Holder(Int32) would be a generic instantiation of this class: a normal class that can construct objects. The @value instance variable is typed as T, whatever T happens to be later. Here is how this class can be used:

```
num = Holder(Int32).new(10)
num.set 40
p num.get  # Prints 40.
```

In this example, we create a new instance of the Holder(Int32) class. It is as if you had a Holder abstract class and a Holder_Int32 class that inherits from it, generated on demand for T=Int32. The object can be used like any other. Methods are invoked and they interact with the @value instance variable.

Note that the T type doesn't have to be explicitly specified in these cases. As the initialize method takes an argument of the T type, the generic parameter can be deduced from usage. Let's create a Holder(String):

```
str = Holder.new("Hello")
p str.get  # Prints "Hello".
```

Here, T is deduced to be a String because Holder.new is called with a string-typed argument.

The container classes from the standard library are generic classes just like the Holder class we defined. Some examples are Array(T), Set(T), and Hash(K, V). You may play with creating your own container classes using generics.

Next, let's learn about how to cause and handle exceptions.

Exceptions

There are many ways code can fail. Some failures are detected at analysis time, such as a method not being implemented or a nil value in a variable that shouldn't contain nil. Some other failures happen during the program's execution and are described by special objects: exceptions. An **exception** represents a failure on the happy path, and it holds the exact location where the error was detected, along with details to understand it.

An exception can be raised at any point using the raise top-level method. This method won't return anything; instead, it will begin walking back on all the method calls as if they all had an implicit return. If nothing captures the exception higher in the method chain, then the program will abort, and the exception's details will be presented to the user. The nice aspect of raising an exception is that it doesn't have to stop the program's execution; instead, it can be captured and handled, resuming normal execution.

Let's look at an example:

```
def half(num : Int)
  if num.odd?
    raise "The number #{num} isn't even"
  end


  num // 2
end

p half(4) # => 2
p half(5) # Unhandled exception: The number 5 isn't even
  # (Exception)
p half(6) # This won't execute as we have aborted the
  # program.
```

In the preceding snippet, we defined a `half` method that returns half of the given integer but only for even numbers. If an odd number is given, it will raise an exception. There is nothing in this program to capture and handle this exception, so the program will abort with an `Unhandled exception` message.

Note that `raise "error description"` is the same as `raise Exception.new("error description")`, so an exception object will be raised. `Exception` is a class, with the only thing special about it being that the `raise` method only accepts its objects.

To show the difference between compile-time and runtime errors, try adding `p half("hello")` to the previous example. It is now an invalid program (because of the type mismatch) and won't even build, so it cannot run. Runtime errors are only detected and reported during the program's execution.

Exceptions can be captured and handled using the `rescue` keyword. It is more common on `begin` and `end` expressions but can be used at method bodies or block bodies directly. Here is an example:

```
begin
  p half(3)
rescue
  puts "can't compute half of 3!"
end
```

If any exception happens to be raised inside the `begin` expression, regardless of how deep in the method call chain it happens to be, the exception will be recovered to the `rescue` code. It is neat to be able to handle all kinds of exceptions in one go, but you can also get access to which exception it is by specifying a variable:

```
begin
  p half(3)
rescue error
  puts "can't compute half of 3 because of #{error}"
end
```

Here, we captured the exception object, and we can inspect it. We could even raise it again using `raise error`. The same concept can be applied to method bodies:

```
def half?(num)
  half(num)
rescue
  nil
end

p half? 2 # => 1
p half? 3 # => nil
p half? 4 # => 2
```

In this example, we have a no-raising version of the `half` method called `half?`. This one will return a union of `Int32 | Nil`, depending on the input number.

Finally, the `rescue` keyword can also be used inline to guard a single line of code against any exception and replace its value. The `half?` method could be implemented like this:

```
def half?(num)
  half(num) rescue nil
end
```

In the real world, it is common practice to go the other way around and first implement a method that returns `nil` in the unhappy path and then create a variant that raises an exception on top of the first implementation.

The standard library has many types of predefined exceptions, such as `DivisionByZeroError`, `IndexError`, and `JSON::Error`. Each represents different kinds of errors. They are plain classes that inherit from the `Exception` class.

Custom exceptions

As exceptions are just usual objects and `Exception` is a class, you can define new types of exceptions by inheriting from them. Let's see this in practice:

```
class OddNumberError < Exception
  def initialize(num : Int)
    super("The number #{num} isn't even")
  end
end


def half(num : Int32)
  if num.odd?
    raise OddNumberError.new(num)
  end


  num // 2
end
```

In this example, we created a class called `OddNumberError` that inherits from `Exception`. Thus, its objects can be raised and rescued. Then, we proceed to rewrite the `half` method to use this more specific error class. These objects can have instance variables and methods as usual.

Now that we have defined an error class, we can capture errors just from one particular class instead of every exception possible. Handling only the known set of errors you can handle is the advised way to go. This can be done by specifying a type restriction to the `rescue` keyword:

```
def half?(num)
  half(num)
rescue error : OddNumberError
  nil
end
```

You can repeat multiple `rescue` blocks to capture and handle multiple different types of exceptions. The only situation where you can't be picky is with the inline `rescue` as it will always handle and replace all exceptions.

Summary

In this chapter, you learned how to create classes and structs, understanding their differences. It became clear that every single value is an object – even classes themselves are objects: objects hold data and can be manipulated with methods. You saw how to inherit and extend classes and how to create reusable modules to organize your code. Finally, you learned about exceptions and how to use classes to create a custom type of error. As a heavily object-oriented language, you will interact with objects on pretty much every line of code. Knowing how to define your own classes is an essential skill for writing Crystal programs.

In the next chapter, we'll jump into solving more practical problems using the Crystal language by writing some tools for the **command-line interface** (**CLI**).

Part 2: Learning by Doing – CLI

This part will introduce the first *Learn by Doing* project by walking through everything needed to create a CLI application. This includes various Crystal features such as I/Os, fibers, and C bindings. This part will also cover the basics of scaffolding a new Crystal project.

This part contains the following chapters:

- *Chapter 4, Exploring Crystal via Writing a Command-Line Interface*
- *Chapter 5, Input/Output Operations*
- *Chapter 6, Concurrency*
- *Chapter 7, C Interoperability*

4

Exploring Crystal via Writing a Command-Line Interface

Now that you are familiar with the basics of Crystal, we're ready to put those skills to use. This part will guide you through creating a **command-line interface** (**CLI**) that'll make use of the concepts from *Chapter 1, An Introduction to Crystal*, as well as some new ones.

This chapter will be an introduction to what this part of the book entails, focusing on setting up the project and the first pass at the CLI implementation. The idea is that this chapter does the initial implementation, and then future chapters expand/improve upon it.

The goal of the CLI is to create a program that allows using **YAML** data with **jq**, a popular CLI application that allows structured **JSON** data to be sliced, filtered, mapped, and transformed using a filter to describe that process. This chapter will serve as the starting point of our project, which will cover the following topics:

- Project introduction
- Scaffolding the project
- Writing the basic implementation

By the end of this chapter, you should be able to create your own Crystal projects, including understanding what each file and folder within a project is used for. You will also be introduced to how to work with multi-file/folder projects. Both of these are important parts of any Crystal application.

Technical requirements

You'll need the following software for running the code in this chapter:

- A working installation of Crystal
- A working installation of jq

You can refer to *Chapter 1*, *An Introduction to Crystal*, for instructions on getting Crystal set up. jq can most likely be installed using the package manager on your system, but can also be installed manually by downloading it from `https://stedolan.github.io/jq/download`.

All of the code examples used in this chapter can be found in the `Chapter 4` folder on GitHub: `https://github.com/PacktPublishing/Crystal-Programming/tree/main/Chapter04`.

Project introduction

Before we get into our CLI application, it would help to understand a bit about how jq works given it's a core part of our application's desired functionality. As previously mentioned, jq allows for the creation of filters that are used to describe how the input JSON data should be transformed.

A filter consists of a string of various characters and symbols, some of which have special meaning. The most basic filter is ., also known as the *Identity Filter*. This filter leaves the input data unchanged, which can be useful in cases where you just want to format the input data given jq will pretty print all output by default. The identity filter also represents the input data as it travels through multiple filters. More on this soon.

jq includes various other filters whose purpose is to access specific portions of the input data or to control how the filter is executed, the most common ones being the following:

- **Object identifier-index**
- **Array index**
- **Comma**
- **Pipe**

The object identifier-index filter allows accessing the value at a specific key, assuming the input data is an object, and producing an error if it is not. This filter will return `null` if the desired key is not present within the object. For example, using the filter .name on the input data {"id":1,"name":"George"} would produce the output "George". The Array Index filter works much like the object identifier-index filter, but for array inputs. Given the input data [1, 2, 3] using the filter . [1] would produce the output 2.

While the first two examples focus on accessing data, the Comma and Pipe filters are intended to control how the data flows through the filter. If multiple filters are separated by a comma, the input data is passed to each filter independently. For example, using the input object from earlier, the .id, .name filter produces the output 1 and "George", each on their own line. A pipe, on the other hand, will pass the output of the filter on its left as the input to the filter on its right. Again, using the same input as before, the .id | . + 1 filter would produce the output 2. Take note that in this example, we are using the identity filter to reference the output value of the previous filter, which, in this example, was 1, which originally came from the input object.

Accessing specific values from the input data is only half the story when it comes to transforming the data. jq provides a way to build new objects/arrays using the JSON syntax. Using the trusty input object we've been using, the filter { "new_id": (.id+2) } produces a new object that looks like { "new_id":3}. Similarly, an array can be created via the [] syntax and [(.id), (.id*2), (.id)] produces the array [1, 2, 1]. In both of the latter examples, we are using parentheses in order to control the order of operations of how the filter is evaluated.

Let's combine all of these features into a more complex example, given the following input data:

```
[
    {
        "id": 1,
        "author": {
            "name": "Jim"
        }
    },
    {
        "id": 2,
        "author": {
            "name": "Bob"
        }
    }
]
```

We can use the filter `[.[] | {"id": (.id + 1), "name": .author.name}]` to produce the following output, the full command being `jq '[.[] | {"id": (.id + 1), "name": .author.name}]' input.json`:

```
[
    {
        "id": 2,
        "name": "Jim"
    },
    {
        "id": 3,
        "name": "Bob"
    }
]
```

If you want to learn more about the features of jq, check out its documentation at `https://stedolan.github.io/jq/manual` as there are plenty of options, methods, and features outside the scope of this book.

Now that you are familiar with the syntax of jq, let's move on to applying that to create our own application, starting with the basic organizational structure of it.

Scaffolding the project

The first thing we need to do is initialize a new project that'll contain the code for the application. Crystal offers an easy way to do this via the `crystal init` command. This command will create a new folder, scaffold out a basic set of files, and initialize an empty **Git** repository. The command supports creating both **app** and **lib** type projects, with the only difference being that lib projects also have the `shard.lock` file ignored via `.gitignore`, with the reason being the dependencies will be locked via the application using the project. Given we won't have any external shared dependencies and we'll eventually want to allow the project to be included in other Crystal projects, we're going to create a lib project.

Start by running `crystal init lib transform` within your terminal. This will initialize a library project called `transform`, with the following directory structure (Git-related files omitted for brevity):

```
.
├── .editorconfig
├── LICENSE
├── README.md
├── shard.yml
├── spec
│   ├── transform_spec.cr
│   └── spec_helper.cr
├── src
    └── transform.cr
```

Let's take a closer look at what these files/directories represent:

- `.editorconfig` – An `https://editorconfig.org` file that allows some IDEs (if configured correctly) to automatically apply Crystal code style to `*.cr` files.

- `LICENSE` – The license the project uses. The default is MIT, which is fine for us. See `https://docs.github.com/en/github/creating-cloning-and-archiving-repositories/creating-a-repository-on-github/licensing-a-repository` for more information.

- `README.md` – Should be used for general documentation regarding the application, such as installation, usage, and contributing information.

- `shard.yml` – Contains metadata about this Crystal shard. More on this in *Chapter 8*, *Using External Libraries*.

- spec/ – The folder where all of the specs (tests) related to the application live. More on this in *Chapter 14, Testing*.

- src/ – The folder where the source code for the application lives.

- src/transform.cr – The main entry point into the application.

While this project structure provides a good starting point, we are going to make a couple of changes by creating another file: src/transform_cli.cr. Also, add the following to the shard.yml file:

```
targets:
  transform:
    main: src/transform_cli.cr
```

This will allow us to run shards build, and have our CLI binary built and output to the ./bin directory.

It's a good practice to split up code into multiple files, both for organizational reasons and to provide more *specialized* entry points into your application. For example, the **transform** project could be utilized both via the command line or within another Crystal application. Because of this, we can have src/transform.cr serve as the main entry point, while src/transform_cli.cr requires src/transform.cr, but also includes some CLI-specific logic. We'll get back to this file later in the chapter.

For now, we have all the required files we'll need for our application and can move on to the initial implementation.

Writing the basic implementation

Before we jump right into writing code, let's take a minute to plan out what our code needs to do exactly. The goal for our CLI is to create a program that allows using YAML with jq. Ultimately, this boils down to three **requirements**:

1. Transform the input YAML data into JSON.
2. Pass the transformed data to jq.
3. Transform the output JSON data into YAML.

It is important to keep in mind that the end goal of this exercise is to demonstrate how various Crystal concepts can be applied to create a functional and usable CLI application. As such, we're not going to focus too much on trying to make it 100% robust for every use case, but instead, focus more on the various tools/concepts used as part of the implementation.

With that in mind, let's move on to writing the initial implementation, starting with something simple and iterating on it until we have a complete working implementation. Let's start with the simplest case: invoke jq with hardcoded JSON data just to show how that part is going to work. Fortunately for us, Crystal's standard library includes the `https://crystal-lang.org/api/Process.html` type that'll allow invoking the jq process currently installed directly. This way, we can utilize all of its features without needing to port it into Crystal.

Open up `src/transform.cr` in your IDE of choice and update it so that it looks like this:

```
module Transform
  VERSION = "0.1.0"

  # The same input data used in the example at the
    # beginning of the chapter.
  INPUT_DATA = %([{"id":1,"author":{"name":"Jim"}},{"id":2,
    "author":{"name":"Bob"}}])

  Process.run(
    "jq",
    [%([.[] | {"id": (.id + 1), "name": .author.name}])],
    input: IO::Memory.new(INPUT_DATA),
    output: :inherit
  )
end
```

We first define a constant with the example input data used in the earlier example. `Process.run` will execute a process and wait for it to finish. We then call it using jq as the command along with an array of arguments (just the filter in this case). We pass a memory IO as the input to the command. Don't pay much attention to this; it'll be covered more in-depth in the next chapter. Finally, we set the output of the command to `:inherit`, which makes the program inherit the output of its parent, which is our terminal.

Executing this file via `crystal src/transform.cr` results in the same output as the earlier jq example, which handles the second requirement of our CLI. However, we still need to handle requirements 1 and 3. Let's start on this next.

Transforming the data

Following along with the earlier recommendation, I'm going to create a new file that'll contain the logic for the transformation. To begin, create `src/yaml.cr` with the following content:

```
require "yaml"
require "json"

module Transform::YAML
  def self.deserialize(input : String) : String
    ::YAML.parse(input).to_json
  end

  def self.serialize(input : String) : String
    JSON.parse(input).to_yaml
  end
end
```

Also, be sure to require this file within `src/transform.cr` by adding `require "./yaml"` to the top of the file.

Crystal comes with a fairly robust standard library of common/helpful features. A good example of this are the `https://crystal-lang.org/api/YAML.html` and `https://crystal-lang.org/api/JSON.html` modules that'll make writing the transformation logic easy. I defined two methods, one for handling YAML => JSON and the other for handling JSON => YAML. Notice that I'm using `::YAML` to reference the standard library's module. This is because the method is already defined within a YAML namespace. Without `::`, Crystal will look for a `.parse` method within its current namespace instead of considering the standard library. This syntax also works with methods, which can come in handy if you happen to define your own `#raise` method and then want to invoke the standard library's implementation as well, for example.

I then updated `src/transform.cr` to look like this:

```
require "./yaml"

module Transform
  VERSION = "0.1.0"
```

```
INPUT_DATA = <<-YAML
---
- id: 1
  author:
    name: Jim
- id: 2
  author:
    name: Bob
YAML


output_data = String.build do |str|
  Process.run(
    "jq",
    [%([.[] | {"id": (.id + 1), "name": .author.name}])],
    input: IO::Memory.new(
      Transform::YAML.deserialize(INPUT_DATA)
    ),
    output: str
  )
end

puts Transform::YAML.serialize(output_data)
end
```

The code is largely the same, but now it is supplying YAML input data and has
our transformation logic integrated. It is worth pointing out that we are now leveraging
`String.build` to build a string in code as you will have seen on your terminal
previously. The main reason for this is we need the string in order to transform it back
into **YAML** before printing it to our terminal's output.

At this point, we have a working basic implementation that meets our goals, but the code
isn't really reusable as it's all defined at the top level of our `transform` namespace.
We should fix that before we can call it done.

Improving reusability

This is the point where we'll start to make use of the `src/transform_cli.cr` file.
The plan to resolve this reusability challenge is to define a `Processor` type that'll contain
the logic related to invoking jq and transforming the data.

Let's start off by creating `src/processor.cr`, being sure to require it within `src/transform.cr`, with the following content:

```
class Transform::Processor
  def process(input : String) : String
    output_data = String.build do |str|
      Process.run(
        "jq",
        [%([.[] | {"id": (.id + 1), "name": .author.name}])],
        input: IO::Memory.new(
          Transform::YAML.deserialize input
        ),
        output: str
      )
    end

    Transform::YAML.serialize output_data
  end
end
```

Having this class makes our code much more flexible/reusable. We're able to create a `Transform::Processor` object and call its #process method multiple times with various input strings. Next, let's make use of this new type within `src/transform_cli.cr`:

```
require "./transform"

INPUT_DATA = <<-YAML
  ---
  - id: 1
    author:
      name: Jim
  - id: 2
    author:
      name: Bob
  YAML


puts Transform::Processor.new.process INPUT_DATA
```

Finally, `src/transform.cr` should now look like this:

```
require "./processor"
require "./yaml"


module Transform
  VERSION = "0.1.0"
end
```

Running `src/transform_cli.cr` still produces the same output it did before, but now it's possible to reuse our conversion logic for different inputs. However, the purpose of a CLI is to allow the consumption of arguments from the terminal and use the values within the CLI. Given we currently have the input filter hardcoded into the processor type, I think that is something we should address before calling the initial implementation complete.

The arguments passed to a CLI program are exposed via the `ARGV` constant in the form of `Array(String)`. The actual code to make use of this is quite straightforward given the arguments to jq already accept an array of strings that we currently have hardcoded. We can simply replace that array with the `ARGV` constant and that will take care of that. `src/processor.cr` now looks like this:

```
class Transform::Processor
  def process(input : String) : String
    output_data = String.build do |str|
      Process.run("jq",
        ARGV,
        input: IO::Memory.new(Transform::YAML.deserialize
          input
        ),
        output: str
      )
    end

    Transform::YAML.serialize output_data
  end
end
```

Also, because the filter is no longer hardcoded, we will need to manually pass it in. Running `crystal src/transform_cli.cr '[.[] | {"id": (.id + 1), "name": .author.name}]'` once again produces the same output, but in a much more flexible manner.

If you prefer using `crystal run`, the command will need to be slightly altered to account for the different semantics of each variant. In this case, the command would be `crystal run src/transform_cli.cr -- '[.[] | {"id": (.id + 1), "name": .author.name}]'`, where the `--` option tells the `run` command that future arguments should be passed to the file being executed, not as arguments to the `run` command itself.

Crystal's standard library also includes the `OptionParser` type, which provides a DSL that allows a description of the arguments a CLI accepts, handles parsing them from `ARGV`, and generates help information based on those options. We will be making use of this type in a later chapter, so stay tuned!

Summary

At this point, our CLI meets all of our requirements. We are able to transform multiple hardcoded YAML data inputs into JSON and have them be processed via a jq filter with the output being transformed back into YAML and output for us to see, all the while accepting the jq filter as a CLI argument. However, our implementation is still lacking in terms of flexibility and performance. The next chapter will introduce how to use input/output (IO) types to improve the application in regard to both of those criteria.

While what we did in this chapter may seem pretty basic, it is important to remember these concepts are common to *every* future Crystal project you will create as well. Proper application design, both in terms of the organizational structure and the code itself, are important parts of developing readable, testable, and maintainable applications.

5
Input/Output Operations

This chapter will expand upon the CLI application started in the last chapter with a focus on **input/output (IO)** operations. It will cover the following topics:

- Supporting terminal-based IO such as **STDIN/STDOUT/STDERR**
- Supporting additional IO
- Performance testing
- Explaining IO behavior

By the end of this chapter, you should have a working understanding of IO operations, including how to use them and how they behave. With these concepts, you will be able to build interactive, efficient stream-based algorithms that could be used in a variety of applications. Knowing how IO behaves will also set you up for understanding more advanced concepts that will be covered in future chapters, such as *Chapter 6, Concurrency.*

Technical requirements

You'll need the following software for running the code in this chapter:

- A working installation of Crystal

- A working installation of jq

- A means of measuring memory usage, such as `https://man7.org/linux/man-pages/man1/time.1.html` with the `-v` option

You can refer to *Chapter 1, An Introduction to Crystal*, for instructions on getting Crystal set up. jq can most likely be installed using the package manager on your system but can also be installed manually by downloading it from `https://stedolan.github.io/jq/download`.

All of the code examples used in this chapter can be found in the `Chapter 5` folder on GitHub: `https://github.com/PacktPublishing/Crystal-Programming/tree/main/Chapter05`.

Supporting terminal input/output

In the previous chapter, we left off with our `Processor` type having a `def process(input : String) : String` method that handles transforming the input string, processing it via jq, and then transforming and returning the output data. We then call this method with static input. However, a CLI application is not very useful if it needs to be recompiled every time you want to change the input data.

The more *proper* way to handle this is by leveraging terminal-based IO, namely, **Standard In (STDIN)**, **Standard Out (STDOUT)**, and **Standard Error (STDERR)**. These will allow us to consume data, output data, and output errors, respectively. In fact, you have already been using STDOUT without even knowing it! The Crystal method `puts` writes the content passed to it to STDOUT, followed by a newline. STDOUT's type inherits from the abstract IO type, which also defines a `puts` method on the IO instance. Basically, this allows you to do the same thing as the top-level `puts`, but for any IO. For example, notice how these two variations of `puts` produce the same output:

```
puts "Hello!"          # => Hello!
STDOUT.puts "Hello!" # => Hello!
```

But wait – what *is* IO exactly? In Crystal, IO is technically anything that inherits from the abstract `IO` type.

However, in practice, IO usually represents something that can have data written and/ or read off of it, such as files or HTTP request/response bodies. IO is also usually implemented so that not all of the data being read/written needs to be in memory at once in order to support the "streaming" of data. Custom IO can also be defined for more specialized use cases.

In our context, the types of STDIN, STDOUT, and STDERR are actually instantiations of `IO::FileDescriptor`.

Crystal provides some commonly helpful IO types that we have actually already been making use of. Remember how we also used `IO::Memory` as a means to pass our transformed input data to jq? Or how we leveraged `String.build` to create a string of data after jq transformed it? `IO::Memory` is an IO implementation that stores the written data within the memory of the application as opposed to an external store such as a file. The `String.build` method yields IO that data can be written to, and then returns the written content as a string. The yielded IO can be thought of as an optimized version of `IO::Memory`. An example of this in action would look like this:

```
io = IO::Memory.new

io << "Hello"
io << " " << "World!"

puts io # => Hello World!

string = String.build do |io|
  io << "Goodbye"
  io << " " << "World"
end

puts string # => Goodbye World!
```

Crystal's standard library also includes some mixins that can be used to enhance the behavior of IO. For example, the `IO::Buffered` module can be included in an IO type to possibly improve performance by adding input/output buffering to the IO type. Or in other words, you can make it so that data is not written immediately to the underlying IO in case that is a heavy process. A file is an example of buffered IO.

Crystal also provides some additional specialized IO types that can be used as building blocks for making other IO types. A few worth noting include the following:

- `Delimited` – IO that wraps another IO, only reading up to the beginning of a specified delimiter. Can be useful for exporting only a part of a stream to a client.

- `Hexdump` – IO that prints a hexadecimal dump of all transferred data. Can be useful for debugging binary protocols to better understand when/how data is sent/received.

- `Sized` – IO that wraps another IO, setting a limit on the number of bytes that can be read.

Refer to the API documentation for the full list: `https://crystal-lang.org/api/IO.html`.

Now that we have been introduced to IO, let's get back to updating our CLI to make better use of terminal-based IO. The plan for this is to update `src/transform_cli.cr` to read directly from STDIN and output directly to STDOUT. This will also allow us to remove the need for the `INPUT_DATA` constant. The file now looks like this:

```
require "./transform"


STDOUT.puts Transform::Processor.new.process STDIN.gets_to_end
```

The main thing that changed is that we replaced the `INPUT_DATA` constant with `STDIN.gets_to_end`. This will read in all of the data within `STDIN` as a string, passing it as an argument to the `#process` method. We also replaced `puts` with `STDOUT.puts`, which are semantically equivalent, but it just makes it a bit clearer where the output is going.

The rest of the logic within our processor type remains as it was, including `String.build` in order to return the output of jq as a string so that we can transform it back into YAML before outputting it to the terminal. However, the next section will introduce some refactors that will make this unnecessary.

We can validate that our change is working by running echo `$'---\n- id: 1\n author:\n    name: Jim\n- id: 2\n  author:\n    name: Bob\n'` | `crystal src/transform_cli.cr '[.[] | {"id": (.id + 1), "name": .author.name}]'`, which should output as it did before:

```
---
- id: 2
  name: Jim
- id: 3
  name: Bob
```

While we are now reading in input from STDIN, it would also be a good improvement if we allowed passing an input file to read the input data from. Crystal defines an **ARGF** constant that allows reading in from a file and falling back onto STDIN if no files are provided. ARGF is also an IO, so we can just replace STDIN with ARGF within `src/transform_cli.cr`. We can test this change by writing the output of the last invocation to a file, say `input.yaml`. Next, run the application, passing the file as the second argument after the filter. The full command would be `crystal src/transform_cli.cr . input.yaml`. However, upon running this, you will notice that it errors: `Unhandled exception: Error reading file: Is a directory (IO::Error)`. You may wonder why this is, but the answer is how ARGF works.

ARGF will first check whether ARGV is empty. If it is, then it will fall back on reading from STDIN. If ARGV is *not* empty, then it assumes each value in ARGV represents a file to be read. In our case, ARGV is not empty as it contains `[".", "input.yaml"]`, so it tries reading from the first *file*, which in this case is a dot, which represents the current folder. Because a folder cannot be read like a file, the exception we saw is raised. In order to work around this, we need to ensure that ARGV *only* contains the file we wish to read *before* calling `ARGF#gets_to_end`. The simplest way to handle this is by calling the `#shift` method on ARGV, which works because it is an `Array`. This method removes the first item in the array, and returns it, which would then leave only the file in ARGV.

However, there is another problem we also need to solve. Since we are using ARGV directly to provide the input arguments to jq, we will need to do some refactoring to be able to access the filter before the `#gets_to_end` call. We can accomplish this by moving some of the logic from `src/transform_cli.cr` into `src/processor.cr`! Update `src/processor.cr` so that it looks like this:

```
class Transform::Processor
  def process : Nil
    filter = ARGV.shift
    input = ARGF.gets_to_end

    output_data = String.build do |str|
      Process.run(
        "jq",
        [filter],
        input: IO::Memory.new(
          Transform::YAML.deserialize input
        ),
```

```
      output: str
    )
  end


    STDOUT.puts Transform::YAML.serialize output_data
  end
end
```

The key addition here is the introduction of `filter = ARGV.shift`, which ensures the rest of ARGV *only* contains the file we want to use as input. We are then using our variable as the sole element in the array representing the arguments we are passing to jq, replacing the hardcoded ARGV reference.

Also notice that we removed the `input` argument from the `#process` method. The reason for this is that all input data is now obtained from within the method itself, and as such, there's no reason to accept external input. Another noteworthy change was altering the return type of the method to `Nil` given we are outputting it directly to STDOUT. This does reduce the flexibility of the method a bit, but that will also be addressed in the next section.

There is one last thing we need to handle before we can call the refactor complete: what happens if an invalid filter (or data) is passed to jq? Currently, it'll raise a not-so-friendly exception. What we really should do is check whether jq executed successfully and, if not, write the error message to STDERR and exit the application by making the following adjustments to `src/processor.cr`:

```
class Transform::Processor
  def process : Nil
    filter = ARGV.shift
    input = ARGF.gets_to_end


    output_data = String.build do |str|
      run = Process.run(
        "jq",
        [filter],
        input: IO::Memory.new(
          Transform::YAML.deserialize input
        ),
        output: str,
        error: STDERR
```

```
    )

    exit 1 unless run.success?
  end

    STDOUT.puts Transform::YAML.serialize output_data
  end
end
```

The two main improvements are specifying that any error output that happens while jq is running should be printed to STDERR and that the program should exit early if jq did not execute successfully.

These two improvements make it clearer to the user what went wrong and prevent further execution of the application, which otherwise would result in it trying to turn an error message into YAML.

Supporting other IO

We have made quite a few improvements already during the last section: we no longer have to hardcode the input data, and we're better at handling errors coming from jq. But remember how we also wanted to support using our application in a library context? How would someone go about processing the response body of an HTTP response and outputting it to a file if our processor is tightly coupled with terminal-based concepts?

In this section, we're going to address this deficiency by refactoring things again to allow *any* IO type, not just terminal-based IO types.

The first step in accomplishing this is to re-introduce arguments to `Processor#process`: one for the input arguments, input IO, output IO, and error IO. Ultimately, this is going to look like this:

```
class Transform::Processor
  def process(input_args : Array(String), input : IO,
    output : IO, error : IO) : Nil
    filter = input_args.shift
    input = input.gets_to_end

    output_data = String.build do |str|
      run = Process.run(
```

```
        "jq",
        [filter],
        input: IO::Memory.new(
          Transform::YAML.deserialize input
        ),
        output: str,
        error: error
      )

    exit 1 unless run.success?
  end


    output.puts Transform::YAML.serialize output_data
  end
end
```

We then of course should update the related constants with their new argument variables. As mentioned earlier, having this method output directly to STDOUT made it not as flexible as it was when it just returned the final transformed data. However, now that it supports any IO type as output, someone could easily leverage `String.build` as we are to obtain a string of the transformed data. Next up, we will need to update our transformation logic to also be IO-based.

Open up `src/yaml.cr` and update the first argument to accept IO, as well as add another IO argument that will represent the output. Both of the `.parse` methods support `String | IO` inputs, so we do not need to do anything special there. The `#to_*` methods also have an IO-based overload that we will pass the new output argument to. Finally, since this method is not going to be returning the transformed data as a string anymore, we can update the return type to be `Nil`. In the end, it should look as follows:

```
require "yaml"
require "json"

module Transform::YAML
  def self.deserialize(input : IO, output : IO) : Nil
    ::YAML.parse(input).to_json output
  end

  def self.serialize(input : IO, output : IO) : Nil
```

```
      JSON.parse(input).to_yaml output
    end
  end
```

Because we added a second argument, we will of course also need to update the processor to pass in the second argument. Similarly, since we are now working solely with IOs, we will need to implement a new way of storing/moving data around. We can accomplish both of these challenges by using IO::Memory objects to store the transformed data. Plus, since they themselves are an IO type, we can pass them directly as input to jq. The final result of this refactor is the following:

```
class Transform::Processor
  def process(input_args : Array(String), input : IO,
    output : IO, error : IO) : Nil
    filter = input_args.shift

    input_buffer = IO::Memory.new
    output_buffer = IO::Memory.new

    Transform::YAML.deserialize input, input_buffer
    input_buffer.rewind

    run = Process.run(
      "jq",
      [filter],
      input: input_buffer,
      output: output_buffer,
      error: error
    )

    exit 1 unless run.success?

    output_buffer.rewind
    Transform::YAML.serialize output_buffer, output
  end
end
```

We are still shifting the filter from the input arguments. However, instead of using `#gets_to_end` to retrieve all the data in the IO, we are now instantiating two `IO::Memory` instances – the first to store the JSON data from the **deserialization transformation,** and the second to store the **JSON data** output via jq.

Basically, how this works is that the deserialization process will consume all the data in the input IO type, outputting the transformed data to the first `IO::Memory`. We then pass it as the input to jq, which is writing the processed data to the second `IO::Memory`. The second instance is then passed as the input IO type to the `serialize` method, which outputs directly to the output IO type.

Another key point worth pointing out is how we need to call `.rewind` on the buffers before/after running the transformation logic. The reason for this is due to how `IO::Memory` works. As data is written to it, it keeps appending the data to the end.

Another way to think about it would be to imagine you are writing an essay. As the essay gets longer and longer, the further and further away you get from the start. Calling `.rewind` has the same effect as if you were to move your cursor back to the start of the essay. Or, in the case of our buffer, it resets the buffer so that future reads start at the beginning. If we did not do this, jq – and our transformation logic – would start reading from the end of the buffer, which would result in incorrect output due to it being essentially *empty*.

Following along with our idea of also allowing our application to be used within someone else's project, there is one more thing we need to improve. Currently, we are exiting the process if jq's invocation fails. It would not be good if someone was using this within a web framework, for example, and we accidentally shut down their server! Fortunately, the fix is a simple one. Instead of calling `exit 1`, we should just raise an exception that we can check for within the CLI-specific entry point. Or, in other words, replace that line with `raise RuntimeError.new unless run.success?`. Then, update `src/transform_cli.cr` to the following:

```
require "./transform"

begin
  Transform::Processor.new.process ARGV, STDIN, STDOUT, STDERR
rescue ex : RuntimeError
  exit 1
end
```

By doing it this way, we will still have the proper exit code when used as a CLI but will also better allow using our application in a library context since the exception could be rescued and gracefully handled. But wait – we have been talking a lot about using our application as a library in another project, but what does that look like?

First off, users of our library would need to install our project as a shard – more on this in *Chapter 8, Using External Libraries*. Then they could require our `src/transform.cr` to have access to our processor and transformation logic. This would be much trickier if we did not use the separate entry point for the CLI context. From here, they could create a `Processor` type and use it to fit their needs. For example, say they wanted to process the response body of an HTTP request, outputting the transformed data to a file. This would look something like this:

```
require "http/client"
require "transform"

private FILTER = %({"name": .info.title, "swagger_version":
  .swagger, "endpoints": .paths | keys})

HTTP::Client.get "https://petstore.swagger.io/v2/
  swagger.yaml" do
    |response|
  File.open("./out.yml", "wb") do |file|
    Transform::Processor.new.process [FILTER],
      response.body_io, file
  end
end
```

With the resulting file being the following:

```
---
name: Swagger Petstore
swagger_version: "2.0"
endpoints:
- /pet
- /pet/findByStatus
- /pet/findByTags
- /pet/{petId}
- /pet/{petId}/uploadImage
```

- `/store/inventory`
- `/store/order`
- `/store/order/{orderId}`
- `/user`
- `/user/createWithArray`
- `/user/createWithList`
- `/user/login`
- `/user/logout`
- `/user/{username}`

This ability can be super valuable to someone else as it may mean that they do not have to implement this logic on their own.

Now that both our processor and transformation types are utilizing IO, there is another optimization we can make. The current transformation logic uses the `.parse` class method on the related format module. This method is very convenient, but has one main downside: it loads *all* of the input data into memory. This may not be a problem for the small tests we have been doing, but imagine trying to transform much larger files/inputs? It is likely that this would result in our application using a lot of (and possibly running out of) memory.

Fortunately for us, JSON, and by extension YAML, are *streamable* serialization formats. In other words, you can translate one format to another one character at a time without needing all of the data loaded in beforehand. As mentioned earlier, this is one of the major benefits of making our application IO-based. We can leverage this by updating our transformation logic to output the transformed output data while it is also parsing the input data. Let's start with the `.deserialize` method within `src/yaml.cr`. The code for this method is quite long, and can be found on Github at `https://github. com/PacktPublishing/Crystal-Programming/blob/main/Chapter05/ yaml_v2.cr`.

There is a lot going on here, so let's break down the algorithm a bit:

1. We start leveraging some new types within each format's module instead of having them both rely on the `.parse` method:

    - `YAML::PullParser` allows consumption of the YAML input token by token on demand as data is available from the input IO type. It also exposes a method that returns what kind of token it is currently parsing.

    - `JSON::Builder`, on the other hand, is used to build JSON with an object-oriented API, writing the JSON to the output IO type.

2. We use these two objects in tandem to simultaneously parse YAML and output the JSON. The algorithm basically starts reading the stream of YAML data, starting a loop that will continue until the end of the YAML document, translating the related YAML token to its JSON counterpart.

The `.serialize` method follows the same general idea, with the code also being available on Github within the same file.

However, in this case, the algorithm is essentially reversed. We're using a JSON pull parser and a YAML builder. Let's run a benchmark to see how much this helped.

Performance testing

For the benchmark, I will be using the GNU implementation of the `time` utility, with the `-v` option for verbose output. For the input data, I'll be using the `invItems.yaml` file, which can be found in this chapter's folder on GitHub. The input data does not really matter as long as it is YAML, but I chose this data because it was fairly large, coming in at 53.2 MB. To perform the benchmark, we will follow these steps:

1. Start with the old version of the code, so be sure to revert to the old code before continuing.

2. Build the binary in release mode via `shards build --release`. Since we want to test the performance of our application and not jq, we are just going to use the identity filter so as to not give jq extra work.

3. Run the benchmark via `/usr/bin/time -v ./bin/transform . invItems.yaml > /dev/null`. Given we do not care about the actual output, we are just redirecting the output to `/dev/null`. This command will output quite a bit of information, but the one line we really care about is `Maximum resident set size (kbytes)`, which represents the total amount of memory used by the process in kilobytes. In my case, this value was `1,432,592`, which means our application consumed almost 1.5 GB to transform this data!

Next, restore the new code and run through the previous steps again to see whether our changes bring about any improvement in the memory usage. This time around, I got `325,352`, which is over 4x less than before!

Up until now, there has been data within the input IO to process either from an input file or STDIN. However, what would happen if our application is expecting input data but there is no data to process? In the next section, we are going to explore how IO behaves in this scenario.

Explaining IO behavior

If you build and run the application as `./bin/transform .`, it will just hang indefinitely. The reason for this is due to how most IO works in Crystal. The majority of IO is blocking by nature, meaning it will wait for data to come through the input IO type, in this case, STDIN. This can be best demonstrated with this simple program:

```
print "What is your name? "

if (name = gets).presence
  puts "Your name is: '#{name}'"
else
  puts "No name supplied"
end
```

The `gets` method is used to read a line in from STDIN and will wait until it either receives data or the user interrupts the command. This behavior is also true for non-terminal-based IO, such as HTTP response bodies. The reasoning and benefit of this behavior will be explained in the next chapter.

Summary

We've made some fantastic progress on the application in this chapter. We not only made it actually useable by supporting terminal-based IO, but also made it even more flexible than it was before by allowing any IO to be used. We also drastically improved the efficiency of our transformation logic by streaming the conversion. Finally, we learned a little about the blocking nature of IO, setting the stage for the next chapter.

IO is a core piece of any application that is reading/writing data. Having the knowledge to know when to use it and, more importantly, how to take advantage of how to use it will ultimately lead to more efficient programs. This chapter also touched on the point of proper application design introduced in the last chapter, by giving some examples of how small changes can go a long way in improving the overall usefulness of an application.

In the next chapter, we are going to explore the concept of concurrency and how it can allow our application to process multi-file input more efficiently.

6
Concurrency

In some scenarios, a program might need to handle the processing of multiple chunks of work, such as summing the number of lines in a series of files. This is a perfect example of the type of problem that **Concurrency** can help to solve by allowing the program to execute chunks of work while waiting on others. In this chapter, we will learn how concurrency works in Crystal and cover the following topics:

- Using fibers to complete work concurrently
- Using channels to communicate data safely
- Transforming multiple files concurrently

By the end of this chapter, you should be able to understand the differences between concurrency and parallelism, how to use fibers to handle multiple concurrent tasks, and how to use channels to properly share data between fibers. Together, these concepts allow for the creation of programs that can multitask, resulting in more performant code.

Technical requirements

Before we dive into the chapter, you'll need the following installed on your system:

- A working installation of Crystal
- A working installation of jq

You can refer to *Chapter 1, An Introduction to Crystal*, for instructions on how to set up Crystal. Note that jq can most likely be installed using the package manager on your system. However, you can also install it manually by downloading it from `https://stedolan.github.io/jq/download`.

All of the code examples used in this chapter can be found in the `Chapter 6` folder on GitHub at `https://github.com/PacktPublishing/Crystal-Programming/tree/main/Chapter06`.

Using fibers to complete work concurrently

A fiber represents a chunk of work that should be executed, either concurrently with other fibers, or at some point in the future when there are some free cycles. They are similar to operating system threads, but are more lightweight and are managed internally by Crystal. Before we dive too deep, it is important to mention that concurrency is *not* the same thing as parallelism, but they are related.

In concurrent code, a little bit of time is spent on various chunks of work, with only a piece of work being executed at a given time. On the other hand, parallel code allows for multiple chunks of work to be executed at the same time. What this means in practice is that, by default, only one fiber is executed at a time. Crystal *does* have support for parallelism that would allow for more than one fiber to be executed at once, but it is still considered experimental. Because of that, we are going to focus on concurrency.

We have already been using fibers under the hood as part of all of the code we have been working with so far. All Crystal code is executed within its own **main fiber**. Additionally, we can create our own fibers via the **spawn** method, which takes a block representing the work to be done in that fiber. Take the following program as an example:

```
puts "Hello program!"

spawn do
  puts "Hello from fiber!"
end

puts "Goodbye program!"
```

If you were to run this, it would output the following:

```
Hello program!
Goodbye program!
```

But wait! What happened to the message within the fiber that we spawned? The answer can be found at the start of the chapter, within the definition of a fiber. The key words are *at some point in the future*. Spawning a fiber does *not* immediately execute the fiber. Instead, it is scheduled for execution by Crytal's scheduler. The scheduler will execute the next queued fiber when it gets a chance. In this example, a chance never arises, so the fiber never gets executed.

This is an important detail in understanding how concurrency works in Crystal as well as why the nature of IOs discussed in *Chapter 5, Input/Output Operations*, can be so helpful. Things that will cause another fiber to be executed include the following:

- The `sleep` method
- The `Fiber.yield` method
- IO-related things, such as reading/writing to a file or Socket
- Waiting to receive a value from a channel
- Waiting for a value to be sent to a channel
- When the current fiber finishes executing

All of these options will block a fiber, resulting in other fibers having a chance to execute. For example, add `sleep 1` after the spawn block and rerun the program. Notice that, this time, `Hello from fiber!` is actually printed. The sleep method tells the scheduler that it should continue executing the main fiber one second from now. In the meantime, it is free to execute the next queued fiber, which, in this case, is the one that prints our message.

The `Fiber.yield` method, or `sleep 0`, would result in the same output but means something slightly different. When using the `sleep` method with a positive integer argument, the scheduler knows it should return to that fiber at some point in the future after it has slept enough. However, using `Fiber.yield`, or `sleep 0`, would check whether there are fibers awaiting to be executed and if so, execute them. Otherwise, it would continue without switching. This behavior is most common when you are executing some logic within a tight loop but still want to give a chance for other fibers to execute. However, `Fiber.yield` just tells the scheduler *hey, you can run another fiber*, but does not guarantee when, or if, the execution will switch back to that original fiber.

In both cases, the only reason the execution switches back to the main fiber at all is that something within the fiber performs one of the actions that can cause another fiber to execute. If you were to remove `puts` and have the fiber consist only of an infinite loop, then it would block the fiber forever and the program would never exit. If you want to allow the execution of other fibers and permanently block the main fiber, you can use `sleep` without any arguments. This will keep the main fiber idle and execute other fibers as they are spawned.

Following up with the previous example, you might find yourself wanting to use variables within the fiber that were defined outside of it. However, this is a bad idea as it leads to unexpected results:

```
idx = 0

while idx < 4
  spawn do
    puts idx
  end

  idx += 1
end

Fiber.yield
```

You would expect the preceding code to print the numbers one through four, but it actually prints the number four, four times. The reason for this is two-fold:

- The fibers do not execute immediately.
- Each fiber is referencing the same variable.

Because fibers do not execute immediately, a fiber is spawned upon each iteration of the `while` loop. After four times, the value of `idx` reaches four and breaks out of the `while` loop. Then, since each fiber refers to the same variable, they all print that variable's current value, which is 4. This could be solved by moving the spawning of each fiber into its own Proc, which would create a closure, capturing the value of the variable upon each iteration. However, this is less than ideal because it is unnecessary and hurts the readability of the code. A better way to handle this is to use the alternative form of `spawn`, which accepts a call as its argument:

```
idx = 0
```

```
while idx < 4
  spawn puts idx
  idx += 1
end


Fiber.yield
```

This internally handles the creation and execution of the Proc, which allows for much more readable code. Using methods with blocks, such as `4.times { |idx| spawn { puts idx } }`, work as expected. This scenario is only an issue when referencing the same local, class, or instance variable when iterating. This is also a prime example of why sharing state directly within fibers is considered a bad practice. The proper way to do that is to make use of channels, which we are going to cover in the next section.

Using channels to communicate data safely

If sharing variables between fibers is not the proper way to communicate between fibers, then what is? The answer is channels. A channel is a way to communicate between fibers without needing to worry about race conditions, locks, semaphores, or other special structures. Let's take a look at the following example:

```
input_channel = Channel(Int32).new
output_channel = Channel(Int32).new

spawn do
  output_channel.send input_channel.receive * 2
end

input_channel.send 2

puts output_channel.receive
```

The preceding example creates two channels that contain the Int32 input and output values. Then it spawns a fiber that first receives a value from the input channel, doubles it, and sends it to the output channel. We then send the input channel an initial value of 2, and, finally, print the result we receive back from the output channel. As mentioned in the previous section, the fiber itself does not execute when we spawn it, nor when we send it a value. The key part of this example is the final receive call on the output channel. This invocation blocks the main fiber until it receives a value back, resulting in our fiber being executed and the final result of 4 being printed.

Let's look at another example that will make the behavior clearer:

```
channel = Channel(Int32).new

spawn do
  loop do
    puts "Waiting"
    sleep 0.5
  end
end

spawn do
  sleep 2

  channel.send channel.receive * 2
  sleep 1
  channel.send channel.receive * 3
end

channel.send 2

puts channel.receive

channel.send 3

puts channel.receive
```

Running the program results in the following output:

```
Waiting
Waiting
Waiting
Waiting
4
Waiting
Waiting
9
```

The first send and receive results in the second fiber are executed first. However, the first line is `sleep 2`, so it does just that. Because sleeping is a blocking operation, Crystal's scheduler will execute the next waiting fiber, that is, the one that prints `Waiting`, then waits for half a second in a loop. This message is printed four times, which matches up with the two-second sleep, followed by the expected output of `4`. Then, the execution moves back to the second fiber, but it immediately goes to the first fiber due to `sleep 1`, which prints `Waiting` twice more before sending the expected output of `9` back to the channel.

In both examples, we have been working with unbuffered channels. An unbuffered channel will continue execution on the fiber that is waiting to receive a sent value from a channel. In other words, this is why the execution of the program changes back to the main fiber to print the value instead of continuing with executing the second fiber.

On the other hand, a buffered channel will not switch to another fiber when calling `send` unless the buffer is full. A buffered channel can be created by passing the size of the buffer to the `Channel` constructor. For example, take a look at the following:

```
channel = Channel(Int32).new 2

spawn do
  puts "Before send 1"
  channel.send 1
  puts "Before send 2"
  channel.send 2
  puts "Before send 3"
  channel.send 3
  puts "After send"
```

```
end

3.times do
  puts channel.receive
end
```

This will output the following:

```
Before send 1
Before send 2
Before send 3
After send
1
2
3
```

Now, if we ran the same code with an unbuffered channel, the following would be the output:

```
Before send 1
Before send 2
1
2
Before send 3
After send
3
```

In both cases, the first value has been sent as you would expect. However, the two types of channels start to differ when the second value is sent. In the unbuffered case, there is no waiting receiver, so the channel triggers a reschedule, resulting in the execution switching back to the main fiber. After printing the first two values, the execution switches back to the fiber and sends the third value. This results in a reschedule that will be switching the execution back to the main fiber the next time there is a chance. In this specific case, that chance comes after printing the end message and when there is nothing left to execute in the fiber.

In the buffered case, the first sent value fulfills channel.receive, which originally caused the fiber to execute. The second value is added to the buffer, followed by the third value, and, finally, the end message. At this point, the fiber is done executing, so the execution switches back to the main fiber, printing all three values: these include the one from the initial receive, plus the two from the channel's buffer. Let's add one more value to the fiber by adding puts "Before send 4" and channel.send 4 before the ending message. Then, update the loop to say 4.times do. Running the program again produces the following output:

```
Before send 1
Before send 2
Before send 3
Before send 4
1
2
3
4
```

Notice that this time, the end message has not been printed. This is because the second and third values fit within the buffer size of 2. However, when the fourth value is sent, the buffer is no longer able to handle additional values, so the channel triggers a reschedule, causing the execution to switch to the main fiber again. Since the first value was sent as part of the initial channel.recieve channel, and the second, third, and fourth values are already in the channel's buffer, they are printed as you would expect. At this point, however, the main fiber has already received the four values it wanted. Therefore, it never has an opportunity to resume the execution of the fiber in order to print the end message.

In all of these examples, we have been receiving a value from a single channel. *But what if you wanted to consume the first values received from a set of multiple channels?* This is where the select keyword (not to be confused with the #select method) comes into play. The select keyword allows you to wait on multiple channels and executes some logic for whichever one receives a value first. Also, it supports running logic if all the channels are blocked and after a set amount of time has passed with no value being received. Let's start with a simple example:

```
channel1 = Channel(Int32).new
channel2 = Channel(Int32).new

spawn do
```

```
    puts "Starting fiber 1"
    sleep 3
    channel1.send 1
  end

  spawn do
    puts "Starting fiber 2"
    sleep 1
    channel2.send 2
  end

  select
  when v = channel1.receive
    puts "Received #{v} from channel1"
  when v = channel2.receive
    puts "Received #{v} from channel2"
  end
```

This example outputs the following:

```
Starting fiber 1
Starting fiber 2
Received 2 from channel2
```

Here, both fibers start executing at more or less the same time, but since the second fiber has a shorter sleep and finishes first, this causes the `select` keyword to print the value from that channel and then exit. Notice that the `select` keyword acts similarly to a single `channel.receive` channel in that it blocks the main fiber and then continues after it receives a value from any channel. Additionally, we could handle multiple iterations by putting the `select` keyword into a loop in conjunction with the `timeout` method to avoid blocking forever. Let's expand upon the previous example to demonstrate how this works. First, let's add a `channel3` variable similar to the other two we already have. Next, let's spawn another fiber that will send a value to our third channel. For example, take a look at the following:

```
  spawn do
    puts "Starting fiber 3"
    channel3.send 3
  end
```

Finally, we can move our `select` keyword into a loop:

```
loop do
  select
  when v = channel1.receive
    puts "Received #{v} from channel1"
  when v = channel2.receive
    puts "Received #{v} from channel2"
  when v = channel3.receive
    puts "Received #{v} from channel3"
  when timeout 3.seconds
    puts "Nothing left to process, breaking out"
    break
  end
end
```

This version of the `select` keyword is similar to the first, but we have added two new clauses to it. One reads a value from the third channel, and the other will break out of the loop if no data is received on any channel within three seconds. The output of this program is as follows:

```
Starting fiber 1
Starting fiber 2
Starting fiber 3
Received 3 from channel3
Received 2 from channel2
Received 1 from channel1
Nothing left to process, breaking out
```

The fibers are starting to execute in order, but they finish in a different order due to the varying amount of time they sleep. Three seconds later, the last when clause is executed due to nothing being received, and then the program exits.

The `select` keyword is not limited to just receiving values. It can also be used when sending them as well. Take this program as an example:

```
spawn_receiver = true

channel = Channel(Int32).new
```

```
if spawn_receiver
  spawn do
    puts "Received: #{channel.receive}"
  end
end

spawn do
  select
  when channel.send 10
    puts "sent value"
  else
    puts "skipped sending value"
  end
end

Fiber.yield
```

Running this as is produces the following output:

```
sent value
Received: 10
```

Flipping the spawn_receiver flag to false and rerunning it produces skipped sending value. The reason for the difference in output is due to the behavior of send in conjunction with the else clause of the select keyword. select will check each when clause for one that will not block when performed. However, in this case, send blocks because there is no fiber awaiting a value, so the else clause will execute since no other clause was able to execute without blocking. Since no receiving fiber was spawned, the latter path is executed, resulting in the skipped message. In the other scenario, there is a receiver waiting that does not allow send to block.

While using channels and fibers to signal the completion of a unit of work is one of their use cases, it is not the only use case. These two concepts, plus select, can be combined to create some pretty powerful patterns, such as only allowing a specific number of fibers to execute at a time, coordinating the state between multiple fibers and channels, or handling the processing of multiple independent chunks of work concurrently. The latter has the added benefit of most likely being set up already to handle multithreaded workflows, as each fiber can be processed on a different thread.

At this point, we have covered pretty much all of the major concepts of concurrency in Crystal. The next step is to apply these concepts, along with what was learned in previous chapters, to our CLI application to support the processing of multiple files at once concurrently.

Transforming multiple files concurrently

At present, the application supports file input, but only from a single file. A valid use case could be to provide multiple files and create a new file with the transformed data for each one. Given the transformation logic is IO-bound, doing this concurrently makes sense and should lead to better performance.

The reason why IO-bound logic and concurrency go so well together is because of the Crystal scheduler. When a fiber gets to a point in its execution where it is dependent on some piece of data from an IO, the scheduler is able to seamlessly put that fiber to the side until that data has arrived.

A more concrete example of this in action would be to look at how the standard library's HTTP::Server functions. Each request is handled in its own fiber. Because of this, if another HTTP request needs to be made during the processing of a request, such as to get data from an external API, Crystal would be able to continue to process other requests while waiting for the data to come back through the IO socket.

Concurrency does not help much if the portion of work is CPU-bound. However, in our case, the reading/writing of data to/from files is an IO-bound problem, which makes this the perfect candidate to show off some concurrency features.

Getting back to our multiple file processing logic, first, let's first create an implementation that is not concurrent and then refactor it to make use of the concurrency features covered in the last two sections.

Before we jump right into things, let's take a moment to plan out what we need to do to support this:

- Find a way to tell the CLI that it should process in multiple file mode.
- Define a new method that will handle processing each file from ARGV.

The first requirement can be satisfied by supporting a --multi CLI option that will put it in the correct mode. The second requirement is also simple, as we can add another method to the `Processor` type to also expose it for library usage. First, let's start with the `Processor` method. Open `src/processor.cr` and add the following method to it:

```
def process_multiple(filter : String, input_files :
  Array(String), error : IO) : Nil
    input_files.each do |file|
      File.open(file, "r") do |input_file|
        File.open("#{input_file.path}.transformed", "w") do
          |output_file|
          self.process [filter], input_file, output_file, error
        end
      end
    end
  end
```

This method boils down to the following steps:

1. Define a new method specific to handling multiple file inputs that accepts the filter and an array of files to process.

2. Iterate over each input file using the `File.open` method to open the file for reading.

3. Use `File.open` again to open the output file for writing using the input file path prepended with `.transformed` as the name of the output file,

4. Call the single input method, passing in our filter as the only argument and using the opened files as the input and output IOs.

Before we can test it, we need to make it so that passing the --multi option causes the CLI to invoke this method. Let's do this now. Open `src/transform_cli.cr` and update it so that it looks like the following:

```
require "./transform"
require "option_parser"


processor = Transform::Processor.new
```

```
multi_file_mode = false

OptionParser.parse do |parser|
  parser.banner = "Usage: transform <filter> [options]
    [arguments] [filename ...]"
  parser.on("-m", "--multi", "Enables multiple file input
    mode") { multi_file_mode = true }
  parser.on("-h", "--help", "Show this help") do
    puts parser
    exit
  end
end

begin

  if multi_file_mode
    processor.process_multiple ARGV.shift, ARGV, STDERR
  else
    processor.process ARGV, STDIN, STDOUT, STDERR
  end
rescue ex : RuntimeError
  exit 1
end
```

Once again, Crystal's standard library comes to the rescue in the form of the OptionParser type. This type allows you to set up logic that should run when those options are passed via ARGV. In our case, we can utilize this to define a more user-friendly interface that would also support the -h or --help options. Additionally, it allows you to react to the --multi flag without manually needing to parse ARGV. The code is pretty straightforward. If the flag is passed, we are setting the multi_file_mode variable to true, which is used to determine which processor method to call.

To test this out, I created a few simple YAML files within the root directory of the project. It does not matter too much what they are, just that they are valid YAML. Then, I built our binary and ran it with ./bin/transform --multi . file1.yml file2.yml file3.yml, asserting that the three output files were created as expected. For me, this took ~0.1 seconds. Let's see whether we can improve this by implementing the concurrent version of the process_multiple method.

Recalling what we learned in the last two sections, in order to make this method concurrent, we will want to spawn the opening of the file and process the logic inside a fiber. We will then need a channel so that we can keep track of the files that have finished. In the end, the method should look like this:

```
def process_multiple(filter : String, input_files :
  Array(String), error : IO) : Nil
  channel = Channel(Bool).new

  input_files.each do |file|
    spawn do
      File.open(file, "r") do |input_file|
        File.open("#{input_file.path}.transformed", "w")
          do |output_file|
          self.process [filter], input_file, output_file,
            error
        end
      end
    ensure
      channel.send true
    end
  end

  input_files.size.times do
    channel.receive
  end
end
```

It is essentially the same, just with the introduction of fibers to make it concurrent. The purpose of the channel is to ensure that the main fiber does not exit before all the files have finished processing. This is accomplished by sending `true` to the channel after a file has been processed and that value is received the expected number of times. The `send` command is within an `ensure` block to handle the scenario when the process fails. This implementation needs a bit more work and will be revisited in the next chapter. I ran the same test as before with the concurrent code and got between `0.03` and `0.06` seconds. I would take a 2–3 times boost in performance any day.

Summary

And there you have it: the concurrent processing of multiple file inputs! Concurrent programming can be a valuable tool for creating performant applications by allowing IO-bound workloads to be broken up so that some portion of work is always executing. Additionally, it can be used to reduce the memory footprint of an application by simultaneously processing input as it comes, without needing to wait and load all of the data into memory.

At this point, our CLI is almost complete! It is now able to efficiently handle both single and multiple file inputs. It can stream data to reduce memory usage and is set up to easily support library usages. Next up, we are going to do something a bit different: we are going to support emitting desktop notifications on various events within our CLI. To accomplish this, in the next chapter, we are going to learn about Crystal's ability to bind to C libraries.

7

C Interoperability

This chapter is going to focus on one of the more advanced Crystal features: the ability to interop with existing C libraries by writing **C Bindings**. This Crystal feature allows you to reuse highly optimized and/or robust code within Crystal without writing a line of C or taking on the non-trivial task of porting all of it to Crystal. We will cover the following topics:

- Introducing C bindings
- Binding libnotify
- Integrating the bindings

libnotify provides a way to emit desktop notifications as a means to provide non-intrusive information to the user as events occur. We are going to leverage this library to emit our own notifications.

By the end of this chapter, you should be able to write C bindings for existing libraries and understand how to best hide the implementation details of the bindings from the end user. C bindings allow Crystal code to leverage highly optimized C code, or simply allow reusing code without needing to port the whole library to Crystal beforehand.

Technical requirements

The requirements for this chapter are as follows:

- A working installation of Crystal

- A working installation of jq

- A working installation of libnotify

- A working C compiler, such as GCC

You can refer to *Chapter 1, An Introduction to Crystal,* for instructions on getting Crystal set up. The latest versions of jq, libnotify, and GCC can most likely be installed using the package manager on your system, but can also be installed manually by downloading them from `https://stedolan.github.io/jq/download`, `https://gitlab.gnome.org/GNOME/libnotify`, and `https://gcc.gnu.org/releases.html` respectively. If
you're working through this chapter on a non-Linux-based OS, for example, macOS or Windows/WSL, things may not work as expected, if at all.

All of the code examples used in this chapter can be found in the `Chapter 7` folder on GitHub: `https://github.com/PacktPublishing/Crystal-Programming/tree/main/Chapter07`.

Introducing C bindings

Writing C bindings involves using some specific Crystal keywords and concepts in order to define the API of the C library, such as what functions it has, what the arguments are, and what the return type is. Crystal is then able to use these definitions to handle how to use them. The end result is the ability to call C library functions from Crystal without needing to write any C yourself. Before we dive directly into binding libnotify, let's start off with some more basic examples to introduce the concepts and such. Take this simple C file for example:

```c
#include <stdio.h>

void sayHello(const char *name)
{
  printf("Hello %s!\n", name);
}
```

We define a single function that accepts a char pointer representing the name of a person to whom to say hello. We can then define our bindings:

```
@[Link(ldflags: "#{__DIR__}/hello.o")]
lib LibHello
    fun say_hello = sayHello(name : LibC::Char*) : Void
end


LibHello.say_hello "Bob"
```

The @[Link] annotation is used to inform the linker where to find additional external libraries it should link when creating the Crystal binary. In this case, we are pointing it at the object file created from our C code – more on this soon. Next, we are making use of the lib keyword to create a namespace that will contain all of the binding's types and functions. In this example, we only have one function. Functions are bound by using the fun keyword followed by what is essentially a normal Crystal function declaration with one difference. In a normal Crystal method, you may use the Nil return type, however, here we are using Void. Semantically they are equivalent, but Void is preferred when writing C bindings. Finally, we are able to call the methods defined within our lib namespace as if they are class methods.

Also notice that the name we are using to invoke this function is different than the name defined in the C implementation. Crystal's C bindings allow the C function name to be aliased to better fit Crystal code style suggestions. In some cases, aliasing may be required if the C function name is not a valid Crystal method name, such as if it includes periods. In this case, the function name can be put in double quotes, for example, fun ceil_f32 = "llvm.ceil.f32"(value : Float32) : Float32.

Looking at the Crystal code, you may notice some things that may seem odd. For example, why is the LibC::Char type or the string "Bob" not a pointer? Because Crystal also binds to some C libraries for the implementations in the standard library, it provides aliases to C types that handle platform differences. For example, if you were to run a program on a 32-bit machine, the C type long would be 4 bytes while on a 64-bit machine it would be 8 bytes, which would map to the Crystal types Int32 and Int64 respectively. In order to better handle this difference, you could use the LibC::Long alias, which handles setting it to the proper Int type depending on the system that is compiling the program.

Crystal also provides some abstractions that make it easier to work with the bound functions. The reason we can pass a string to a function expecting a pointer is that the `String` type defines a `#to_unsafe` method that returns a pointer to the string's contents. This method is defined on various types within the standard library but can also be defined on custom types. If this method is defined, Crystal will call it, expecting it to return the proper value that should be passed to the related C function.

As mentioned earlier, before we can run our Crystal program, we need to create the object file for the C code. This can be done with various C compilers, but I will be creating it via GCC by running the command `gcc -Wall -O3 -march=native -c hello.c -o hello.o`. We already have the link annotation referencing the newly created `hello.o` file, so all that is left to do is run the program via `crystal hello.cr`, which produces the output `Hello Bob!`.

Binding functions will not be enough to make use of libnotify; we also need a way to represent the notification object itself in the form of a C struct. These are also defined within the `lib` namespace, for example:

```c
#include <stdio.h>

struct TimeZone {
    int minutes_west;
    int dst_time;
};

void print_tz(struct TimeZone *tz)
{
    printf("DST time is: %d\n", tz->dst_time);
}
```

Here we are defining a C struct called `TimeZone` that has two `int` properties. We then define a function that will print the DST time property of a pointer to that struct. The related Crystal binding would look like the following:

```crystal
@[Link(ldflags: "#{__DIR__}/struct.o")]
lib LibStruct
  struct TimeZone
    minutes_west : Int32
    dst_time : Int32
```

```
    end

  fun print_tz(tz : TimeZone*) : Void
end


tz = LibStruct::TimeZone.new
tz.minutes_west = 1
tz.dst_time = 14


LibStruct.print_tz pointerof(tz)
```

Defining this struct allows it to be instantiated like you would any other object via .new. Unlike the previous example, however, we are not able to pass the object directly to the C function. This is because the struct is defined within the lib namespace, is expecting a pointer to it, and does not have a #to_unsafe method. The next section will cover how to best handle this.

Compiling the object file and running the Crystal program like before will output: DST time is: 14.

Another common C binding feature is supporting callbacks. The Crystal equivalent to a C function pointer is a **Proc**. This is best shown with an example. Let's write a C function that accepts a callback accepting an integer value. The C function will generate a random number then call the callback with that value. In the end, this could look something like this:

```
#include <stdlib.h>
#include <time.h>

void number_callback(void (*callback)(int))
{
    srand(time(0));
    return (*callback)(rand());
}
```

The Crystal bindings would look like this:

```
@[Link(ldflags: "#{__DIR__}/callback.o")]
lib LibCallback
  fun number_callback(callback : LibC::Int -> Void) : Void
```

```
end

LibCallback.number_callback ->(value) { puts "Generated:
  #{value}" }
```

In this example, we are passing a `Proc(LibC::Int, Nil)` as the value to the C callback argument. Normally, you would need to type the `value` Proc argument. However, since we are passing the Proc directly, the compiler is able to figure it out based on the type of the bound `fun` and type it for us. The type is required if we first assigned it to a variable, such as `callback = ->(value : LibC::Int) { ... }`.

The callback will print what random value the C code generated. Remember, before we can run the Crystal code, we need to compile the C code into an object file using this command: `gcc -Wall -O3 -march=native -c callback.c -o callback.o`. After that, you can freely run the Crystal code multiple times and assert it generates a different number each time.

While we can pass Procs as a callback function, you cannot pass a closure, such as if you tried to reference a variable defined outside of the Proc within it. For example, if we wanted to multiply the generated C value by some multiplier:

```
multiplier = 5
LibCallback.number_callback ->(value : LibC::Int) { puts
  value * multiplier }
```

Running this would result in a compile-time error: `Error: can't send closure to C function (closured vars: multiplier)`.

Passing a closure *is* possible, but it is quite a bit more involved. I'd suggest checking out this example in the Crystal API docs: `https://crystal-lang.org/api/Proc.html#passing-a-proc-to-a-c-function`. As mentioned earlier, C bindings can be a great way to make use of pre-existing C code. Now that you know how to link to the library, write the bindings, and use them within Crystal, you can now actually make use of the C library's code. Next, let's move on to writing the bindings for libnotify.

Binding libnotify

One of the benefits of writing C bindings in Crystal is that you only need to bind what you need. In other words, we do not need to fully bind libnotify if we are only going to use a small portion of it. In reality, we really only need four functions:

- `notify_init` – Used to initialize libnotify

- `notify_uninit` – Used to uninitialize libnotify

- `notify_notification_new` – Used to create a new notification

- `notify_notification_show` – Used to show a notification object

In addition to these methods, we also need to define a single struct, `NotifyNotification`, which represents a notification that can be shown. I determined this by looking at libnotify's `*.h` files on GitHub: `https://github.com/GNOME/libnotify/blob/master/libnotify`. Libnotify's HTML documentation is also included within this chapter's folder on GitHub, which can be used as an additional reference point.

Based on the information from their documentation, source code, and what we learned in the last section, the bindings we need for libnotify would look like the following:

```
@[Link("libnotify")]
lib LibNotify
  alias GInt = LibC::Int
  alias GBool = GInt
  alias GChar = LibC::Char


  type NotifyNotification = Void*


  fun notify_init(app_name : LibC::Char*) : GBool
  fun notify_uninit : Void


  fun notify_notification_new(summary : GChar*, body :
    GChar*, icon : GChar*) : NotifyNotification*
  fun notify_notification_show(notification :
    NotifyNotification*, error : Void**) : GBool
  fun notify_notification_update(notification :
```

```
      NotifyNotification*, summary : GChar*, body : GChar*,
          icon : GChar*) : GBool
end
```

Notice, unlike the other cases, we are able to just pass `"libnotify"` as an argument to the `Link` annotation. We can do this because the related library is already installed system-wide as opposed to being a custom file we created.

Under the hood, Crystal leverages `https://www.freedesktop.org/wiki/Software/pkg-config`, if available, in order to identify what should be passed to the linker in order to properly link the library. For example, if we were to inspect the full link command Crystal runs when building our binary, we would be able to see which flags are being used. In order to see this command, add the `--verbose` flag to the `build` command, which would look like `crystal build --verbose src/transform_cli.cr`. This will output a fair amount of information, but what we want to look at the very end, after the `-o` option specifying what the output binary's name is going to be. If we were to run `pkg-config --libs libnotify`, we would get `-lnotify -lgdk_pixbuf-2.0 -lgio-2.0 -lgobject-2.0 -lglib-2.0`, which we can also see in the raw link command.

If `pkg-config` is not installed or available, Crystal will try passing the `-llibnotify` flag, which may or may not work depending on the library being linked. In our case, it does not. It is also possible to explicitly provide what flags should be passed to the linker using the `ldflags` annotation field, which would be like `@[Link(ldflags: "...")]`.

The other thing to notice is that we are making use of some aliases in the lib. Aliases in this context act just like standard Crystal aliases. The reason we defined these is to make the code a bit easier to maintain by staying as close to the actual definition of the methods. If in the future the creators of the library wanted to change the meaning of `GInt`, we could also easily support that.

For representing the notification type, we are using the `type` keyword to create an opaque type backed by a void pointer, which we can get away with since we do not need to actually reference or interact with the actual internal representation of the notification in libnotify. This also serves as a good example of how not everything needs to be bound, especially if it will not be used.

The reason for making `NotifyNotification` an opaque type is because libnotify handles creating/updating the struct internally. The `type` keyword allows us to create something that we can reference in our Crystal code without needing to care about how it was created.

In the case of `notify_notification_show`, we made the second argument of type `Void` because we are going to assume everything works as expected. We also bound the function `notify_notification_update`. This method is not really required but it will help demonstrate something later on in this section, so stay tuned!

Testing the bindings

The next question we need to answer is where should we put the binding file? The ideal solution would be to create a dedicated shard and require it as a dependency. The main benefit this provides is that others could use them independently of our CLI application source. However, for the purposes of this demonstration, we are just going to add them to the source files of our CLI application.

We are going to create a `lib_notify` subdirectory to at least get some organization separation from the types related to the bindings versus our actual logic. This would also make it easier to switch to a dedicated shard if we decided to do that later on. Let's create a new `src/lib_notify/lib_notify.cr` file that will contain the binding-related code. Be sure to add `require "./lib_notify"` to the `src/transform.cr` file as well.

Given the bindings themselves have no dependencies on our CLI application, we are able to test them independently. We can do that by adding the following lines to our binding file running it, and being sure to remove this test code after running it:

```
LibNotify.notify_init "Transform"
notification = LibNotify.notify_notification_new "Hello",
  "From Crystal!", nil
LibNotify.notify_notification_show notification, nil
LibNotify.notify_uninit
```

If everything worked correctly, you should see a desktop notification appear with the title of "Hello" and a body of "From Crystal!". We are passing `nil` to the arguments we have no value for. This works out fine because these arguments are optional and Crystal handles converting it to a null pointer under the hood. It would not work however if the variable was a union of `Pointer` and `Nil`. While working with the raw bindings is functional, it is not a great user experience. It is a common practice to define standard Crystal types that wrap the C binding types. This allows the internals of the C library to be hidden behind an API that is more user-friendly and is easier to document. Let's start on this now.

Abstracting the bindings

Based on the C logic we used earlier, the two main abstractions we need are as follows:

- A better way to emit a notification to avoid needing to call the `init` and `uninit` methods

- A better way to create/edit a notification pending emission

To handle the first abstraction, let's create a new file, `src/lib_notify/notification.cr`, with the following code:

```
require "./lib_notify"

class Transform::Notification
  @notification : LibNotify::NotifyNotification*

  getter summary : String
  getter body : String
  getter icon : String

  def initialize(@summary : String, @body : String, @icon :
    String = "")
    @notification = LibNotify.notify_notification_new
      @summary, @body, @icon
  end

  def summary=(@summary : String) : Nil
    self.update
  end

  def body=(@body : String) : Nil
    self.update
  end

  def icon=(@icon : String?) : Nil
    self.update
  end
```

```
    def to_unsafe : LibNotify::NotifyNotification*
      @notification
    end

    private def update : Nil
      LibNotify.notify_notification_update @notification,
        @summary, @body, @icon
    end
  end
end
```

This class is essentially just a wrapper type around the C notification pointer. We define the #to_unsafe method that returns the wrapped pointer in order to allow providing an instance of this class to the C functions. This type is also where we will make use of notify_notification_update. The type implements setters for each of the notification's properties that both update the value within the wrapper type and also update the C structs' values.

libnotify also has various additional features we could play with, such as notification priority or setting a delay before the notification is shown. We do not really need these features for our CLI, but feel free to explore libnotify and customize things how you want! Next up, let's create a type that will help with emitting these notification instances.

Create a new file, src/lib_notify/notification_emitter.cr, with the following code:

```
require "./lib_notify"
require "./notification"

class Transform::NotificationEmitter
  @@initialized : Bool = false

  at_exit { LibNotify.notify_uninit if @@initialized }

  def emit(summary : String, body : String) : Nil
    self.emit Transform::Notification.new summary, body
  end

  def emit(notification : Transform::Notification) : Nil
    self.init
```

```
        LibNotify.notify_notification_show notification, nil
    end

    private def init : Nil
      return if @@initialized
      LibNotify.notify_init "Transform"
      @@initialized = true
    end
  end
end
```

The main method this type provides is `#emit`, which will show the provided notification, ensuring libnotify is initialized beforehand. The first overload accepts a summary and body, creates a notification, then passes it to the second overload. We are storing the initialization status of libnotify as a class variable as it is not tied to a specific `NotificationEmitter` instance. We have also registered an `at_exit` handler that will deinitialize libnotify before the program exits if it was initialized earlier.

It is also worth mentioning that handling initialization of libnotify in a multiple threaded application would be a bit more troublesome given libnotify only needs to be initialized once, not per thread or fiber. However, because Crystal's multithreading support is still considered experimental, and this topic is a bit out of scope, we are just going to skip over this scenario. For now, we will be using our application. It will not be a problem.

Now that we have our abstractions in place, we are free to move on to implementing them within our CLI.

Integrating the bindings

Because of what we did in the last section, this will be the easiest part of the chapter, with the only remaining question being: what notification do we want to emit? A good use case for it would be to emit one when there is an error during the transformation process. The notification would get the user's attention that they need to take action on something that otherwise may have gone unnoticed if it was expected to take a while.

Now you might be thinking that we just instantiate new `NotificationEmitter` instances as needed and use them for each context. However, we are going to take a slightly different approach. The plan is to add an initializer to our `Processor` type that will keep a reference to an emitter as an instance variable. This would look like `def initialize(@emitter : Transform::NotificationEmitter = Transform::NotificationEmitter.new); end`. I am going to hold off on explaining the reasoning behind this as it will be covered in *Chapter 14, Testing*.

Let's focus on handling the error context first. Unfortunately, since jq will output its error messages directly to the error IO, we will not be able to handle those. We can, however, handle actual exceptions from our Crystal code. Because we want to handle any exception that happens within our #process method, we can use the short form for defining a rescue block:

```
rescue ex : Exception
  if message = ex.message
    @emitter.emit "Oh no!", message
  end


  raise ex
```

This code should go directly below the last line in each method but before the method's end tag. This block will rescue any exception raised within the method. It will then emit a notification with the exception's message as the body of the notification. Not all exceptions have a message, so we are handling that case by ensuring it does before emitting the notification. Finally, we are re-raising the exception.

In the case of the #process_multiple method, we will need to improve our concurrency code a bit to better support exception handling. It is considered a good practice to handle any exceptions raised within a fiber within the fiber itself.

Unfortunately, at the moment, working with channels and fibers is a bit lower-level than it would ideally be. There are some outstanding proposals, such as https://github. com/crystal-lang/crystal/issues/6468, but nothing has been implemented in the standard library yet that would allow for some built-in abstractions or higher-level APIs. On the bright side, the problem we want to solve is pretty trivial.

In the last chapter, we added send using an ensure block to gracefully handle failure contexts but mentioned that this implementation is less than ideal, mainly since we want to be able to differentiate between success and failure contexts. In order to solve this, we can modify the channel to accept a union of Bool | Exception instead of just Bool. Then, using the short form of rescue again, we can send the channel the raised exception, replacing the ensure block. This would end up looking like this:

```
    channel.send true
  rescue ex : Exception
    channel.send ex
```

Similar to the other rescue blocks, this one also will go right after `channel.send true`, but before the `end` tag of the `spawn` block. We then need to update the receiving logic to handle an exception value, as at the moment we are always ignoring the received value. To do this, we will update the loop to check the type of the received value, and raise it if it is an `Exception` type:

```
input_args.size.times do

  case v = channel.receive
    in Exception then raise v
    in Bool
      # Skip
    end
end
```

Now that we are raising the exception from the fiber within the method itself, our `rescue` block on the method will now be called correctly. The full `#process_multiple` method is located within the chapter's folder on GitHub: `https://github.com/PacktPublishing/Crystal-Programming/blob/main/Chapter07/process_multiple.cr`.

I found the easiest way to test our notification emission logic is by passing a file that does not exist when in multiple file mode. For example, running `./bin/transform -m . random-file.txt` should result in a notification being displayed informing you that there was an error trying to open that file.

Summary

Alas, we have come to the end of our CLI project. Over the course of the last four chapters, we have improved the application quite a bit. We also expanded our knowledge of various Crystal concepts in the process. While this is the end of this part of the book, it does not have to be the end of the CLI. Feel free to continue on your own, adding features as you wish. Ultimately, this will help reinforce the concepts introduced along the way.

The next part of the book is going to introduce some new projects focused on web development and will utilize everything you have learned up until now. It will also spend some time demonstrating various design patterns that may come in handy in future projects of yours. So what are you waiting for? First up is learning how to use external Crystal projects, aka shards, as dependencies within your own project. Go get started!

Part 3: Learn by Doing – Web Application

This part will continue the *Learn By Doing* paradigm with another common type of application: a web framework. This part will build upon the information from the first two parts. Most commonly, a web application is created with the help of a framework. Thankfully, Crystal's ecosystem has various frameworks to choose from. While the best framework to use varies from use case to use case, we are going to focus on Athena Framework.

This part contains the following chapters:

8

Using External Libraries

Reducing duplication by sharing code is a rule of thumb in many programming languages. Doing this within the context of a single project is easy enough. However, when you want to share something between multiple projects, it becomes a bit more challenging. Fortunately for us, most languages also provide their own package managers that allow us to install other libraries in our projects as dependencies in order to make use of the code defined therein.

Most commonly, these external projects are just called **libraries** or **packages**, but a few languages have unique names for them, such as **Ruby gems**. Crystal follows the Ruby pattern and names its projects **Crystal Shards**. In this chapter, we are going to explore the world of external libraries, including how to find, install, update, and manage them. We will cover the following topics:

- Using Crystal Shards
- Finding Shards

Technical requirements

The requirements for this chapter are as follows:

- A working installation of Crystal

You can refer to *Chapter 1*, *An Introduction to Crystal*, for instructions on getting Crystal set up.

All of the code examples used in this chapter can be found in the Chapter 08 folder on GitHub: https://github.com/PacktPublishing/Crystal-Programming/tree/main/Chapter08.

Using Crystal Shards

If you remember *Chapter 4*, *Exploring Crystal via Writing a Command-Line Interface*, when we were first scaffolding out the project, there was the shard.yml file that was created as part of that process, but we did not really get into what it was for. The time has come to more fully explore what the purpose of this file is. The gist of it is that this file contains various metadata about the Shard, such as its name, version, and what external dependencies it has (if any). As a refresher, the shard.yml file from that project looked like this:

```
name: transform
version: 0.1.0

authors:
  - George Dietrich <george@dietrich.app>

crystal: ~> 1.4.0

license: MIT

targets:
  transform:
    main: src/transform_cli.cr
```

Similarly to how we have been interacting with our Crystal applications thus far using the `crystal` binary, there is a dedicated binary for interacting with Crystal Shards, aptly named `shards`. We used this a bit at the start of the CLI project to handle building the project's binary, but it can also do much more. While the `shards build` command could be replicated with multiple `crystal build` commands, the `shards` command also provides some unique features, mainly around installing, updating, pruning, or checking external dependencies. While the `shard.yml` file will most commonly be created as part of the `crystal init` command we used a few chapters ago, it may also be created by the `shards init` command, which will scaffold out only this file instead of a whole project.

Speaking of dependencies, there are two types that a project could have:

- **Runtime dependencies**

- **Development dependencies**

The core dependencies would be anything that is required for the project to run in a production environment. Development dependencies however are not required in production but are needed when developing the project itself. A good example of these would be any extra testing or static analysis tools used by the project.

Both of these types of dependencies can be specified in the `shard.yml` file via the `dependencies` and `development_dependencies` mappings respectively. An example of these mappings is as follows:

```
dependencies:
  shard1:
    github: owner/shard1
    version: ~> 1.1.0
  shard2:
    github: owner/shard2
    commit: 6471b2b43ada4c41659ae8cfe1543929b3fdb64c


development_dependencies:
  shard3:
    github: dev-user/shard3
    version: '>= 0.14.0'
```

In this example, there are two core dependencies and a single development dependency. The keys in the map represent the name of the dependency and the value of each key is another mapping that defines information on how to resolve it. Most commonly, you would be able to use one of the helper keys: `github`, `bitbucket`, or `gitlab` in the form of `owner/repo` depending on where the dependency is hosted. Extra keys on each dependency can be used to select a specific version, version range, branch, or commit that should be installed. In addition to the helper keys, a repository URL may be provided for Git, Mercurial, or Fossil via the `git`, `hg`, and `fossil` keys respectively. The `path` key could also be used to load a dependency from a specific file path, but it cannot be used with the other options, including version, branch, or commit.

It is highly suggested to specify versions on your dependencies. If you do not, then it will default to the latest release, which could silently break your application if you later update to a version that includes breaking changes. Using the `~>` operator can be helpful in this regard to allow for updates, but not past specific minor or major versions. In this example, `~> 1.1.0` would be equivalent to `>= 1.1.0 and < 1.2` while `~> 1.2` would be equivalent to `>= 1.2 and < 2`.

In some cases, however, you may want to use a change that has not yet been released. To handle this, you can also pin a dependency to a specific branch or commit. Depending on the exact context, the commit is usually preferred in order to prevent unexpected changes from being introduced on subsequent updates.

Once you have your `shard.yml` file updated with all the dependencies your project will need, you can go ahead and install them via the `shards install` command. This will resolve the version of each dependency and install them into the `lib/` folder. From here, you can require the code by doing `require "shard1"` or whatever the name of the Shard is from within your project.

You may have noticed that Crystal is able to find the Shard within the `lib/` folder when normally it would error since it is nowhere to be found within `src/`. The reason it works is due to the `CRYSTAL_PATH` environmental variable. This variable determines the location(s) Crystal will look for required files, outside of the current folder. For example, for me, running `crystal env CRYSTAL_PATH` outputs `lib:/usr/lib/crystal`. We can see here that it will first try the `lib/` folder followed by Crystal's standard library, using the standard search rules in each location.

The installation process will also create another file called shard.lock. The purpose of this file is to allow for reproducible builds by *locking* the versions of each installed dependency such that future invocations of shards install would result in the same versions being installed. This is primarily intended for end applications as opposed to libraries since the dependencies of the library will also be locked within the application's lock file. The lock file is ignored by version control systems by default for libraries as well, for example, when creating a new project via crystal init lib lib_name.

The --frozen option may also be passed to shards install, which will force it to install only what is in the shard.lock file, erroring if it does not exist. By default, running shards install will also install development dependencies. The --without-development option can be used to only install the core dependencies. The --production option may also be used to combine these two behaviors.

While most dependencies will only provide code that can be required, some may also build and provide a binary in the bin/ folder of your project. This behavior can be enabled for a library by having something similar to the following added to its shard.yml file:

```
scripts:
  postinstall: shards build

executables:
  - name_of_binary
```

The postinstall hook represents a command that will be invoked after the Shard has been installed. Most commonly this is just shards build, but we could also call into a Makefile for more complex builds. However, when using postinstall hooks and especially Makefiles, compatibility needs to be kept in mind. For example, if the hook is running on a machine without make or one of the build requirements, the entire shards install command would fail.

The executables array then represents which of the built binaries should be copied into the installing project whose names map to the name of the locally built binaries. The --skip-postinstall and --skip-executables options that can be passed to shards install also exist if you didn't want to execute one or both of these steps.

Next up, let's explore why some extra care needs to be taken when the project has dependencies on C code.

Shard dependencies on C code

Up until now, it has been assumed that the Shards being installed are pure Crystal implementations. However, as we learned earlier in *Chapter 7, C Interoperability*, Crystal can bind to and use existing C libraires. Shards do *not* handle installing the C libraries required by the Crystal bindings. It is up to the user using the Shard to install them, such as via their system's package manager.

While Shards do not handle installing them for you, it does support an informational `libraries` key within `shard.yml`. An example of this looks as follows:

```
libraries:
  libQt5Gui: "*"
  libQt5Help: "~> 5.7"
  libQtBus: ">= 4.8"
```

By looking at this, someone trying to use the Shard could find out which libraries need to be installed based on the C libraries the Shard links to. Once again, this is purely informational, but you are still encouraged to include it if your Shard binds to any C libraries.

In most projects, the installed dependencies will most likely become stale over time, which would cause an application to lose out on potentially important bug fixes or new features. Let's take a look at how to update Shards next.

Updating Shards

Software is constantly evolving and changing. Because of this, it is common for libraries to frequently release new versions of the code that include new features, enhancements, and bug fixes. While it may be tempting to blindly update your dependencies to the latest versions whenever a new version is released, some care does need to be taken. New versions of a library may not be compatible with previous versions, which could lead to breaking your application.

It is suggested that all Shards follow `https://semver.org`. It is by following this standard that we allow the ~> operator to work, given it can be assumed that no breaking changes will be introduced to a minor or patch version. Or if they are, then there will be another patch release to fix the regression.

If you did not version your dependencies and the next release of a dependency is a major bump, then you will be forced to either downgrade back to the previous version or get to work making your application compliant with the new version of the dependency. It is for this reason that I will again strongly suggest properly versioning your dependencies, as well as making sure to keep up to date and read the **changelogs** for your dependencies so you know what to expect when they are updated.

Assuming you have done that and have your dependencies versioned, you can update them by running the `shards update` command. This will go out and resolve and install the latest versions of your dependencies based on your requirements. It will also update the `shard.lock` file with the new versions.

Checking dependencies

In some cases, you may just want to ensure all the required dependencies are installed without actually installing anything new. In this case, the `shards check` command can be used. It will set a non-zero exit code if all dependencies are not installed as well as print some textual information to the terminal. Similarly, the `shards outdated` command can be used to check whether your dependencies are up to date based on your requirements.

The `shards prune` command can also be used to remove unused dependencies from the `lib/` folder. A Shard is considered to be unused when it is no longer present within the `shard.lock` file.

Going back to earlier in this chapter, how can you determine which Shards are available to install in the first place? This is precisely the topic we are going to cover in the next section. Let's get started.

Finding Shards

Unlike some dependency managers in other languages, Shards does not have a centralized repository from which they can be installed. Instead, Shards are installed from the relevant upstream source directly via checking out the Git project, or symlinking it if using the `path` option.

Because there is no central repository with the usual search and discovery features, it can be a bit harder to find Shards. Fortunately, there are various websites that either automatically scrape hosting sites for Shards or are manually curated.

As with any library, regardless of language, some libraries may be abandoned, forgotten, or become inactive. Because of this, it is worth spending some time looking into all the available Shards to determine which would be the best option versus just finding one and assuming it will work.

Following are some of the more popular/useful resources to find Shards:

- **Awesome Crystal**: `https://github.com/veelenga/awesome-crystal` is an implementation of `https://github.com/sindresorhus/awesome/blob/main/awesome.md` for Crystal. It is a manually curated list of Crystal Shards and other related resources within various categories. It is a good resource as it includes various popular Shards within the ecosystem.

- **Shardbox**: `https://shardbox.org/` is a manually curated database of Shards that is a bit more advanced than Awesome Crystal. It includes search and tagging functions, dependency information, and metrics for all the Shards in its database.

- **Shards.info**: Unlike the previous two resources, `https://shards.info/` is an automated resource that works by scraping repositories from GitHub and GitLab on a periodic basis, targeting repositories that have been active within the last year and whose language is Crystal. It is a useful resource for finding new Shards, but you may also run into some that are not production-ready.

If you are looking for something in particular, you should be able to find it using one of these resources. However, if you cannot find a Shard that suits your purpose, another option is to ask the community: `https://crystal-lang.org/community/#chat`. Asking those familiar with the language is usually an excellent source of information.

Crystal is relatively new compared to other languages, such as Ruby or Python. Because of this, the Crystal ecosystem is not as large, which could result in a Shard you need being out of date or missing entirely. In this case, either reviving the older Shard or implementing your own open source version can help the ecosystem grow and allow others to reuse the code.

Example scenario

Now that we have a pretty good understanding of how to use and find Shards, let's take some time and walk through more of a real-world example. Say you are developing an application and want to use TOML as a means of configuring it. You go and look through Crystal's API docs and see that it does not include a module to handle parsing TOML. Because of this, you will either need to write your own implementation or install someone else's implementation as a Shard.

You start off looking through the Awesome Crystal list and notice there is a `toml.cr` Shard within the Data Formats category. However, after reading through its `readme` file, you determine it will not work because you require TOML 1.0.0 support, and that Shard is for 0.4.0. In order to get a greater selection of Shards, you decide to move onto `shard.info`.

Upon searching for `TOML`, you find `toml-cr`, which provides C bindings to a TOML parsing library compatible with TOML 1.0.0, and you decide to go with this one. Looking at the releases in GitHub, you notice that the Shard is not yet 1.0.0, with the latest release being 0.2.0. In order to prevent breaking changes from causing issues from unintended updates, you decide to set the version to `~> 0.2.0` such that it would allow `0.2.x` but not `0.3.x`. You ultimately add the following to your `shard.yml` file:

```
dependencies:
  ctoml-cr:
    github: syeopite/ctoml-cr
    version: ~> 0.2.0
```

From here you can run `shards install`, then require the Shard via `require "toml-cr"` and jump right back to your own project's code.

As we saw here, Shards can be an important part of keeping up developer efficiency when it comes to writing a program. Instead of spending the time it would have taken to implement TOML parsing, you are able to easily leverage a robust existing implementation and invest that time into working on your own program instead. However, as we saw in this example and mentioned earlier, some care needs to be taken when choosing Shards. Not all of them are equal, whether that be in terms of their development status/maturity, what the underlying dependency that they are coded against supports, or the features they provide. Take some time and do some research into which Shard will meet your requirements.

Summary

Knowing how to install and manage external libraries is an incredibly helpful tool in developing any application you may find yourself working on in the future. Finding an existing Shard can dramatically speed up the development time of your projects by removing the need to implement that code yourself. It will also make your project easier to maintain since you will not need to maintain the code yourself. Be sure to keep an eye on the lists and databases we talked about for Shards that could be useful in your projects!

In the next chapter, we are going to make use of some external libraries in order to create a web application using Athena.

9
Creating a Web Application with Athena

Crystal's similarities with Ruby have made it quite popular as a web-based language hoping to entice some Ruby on Rails, among other frameworks, users to make the switch to Crystal. Crystal boasts quite a few popular frameworks, from simple routers to full stack, and everything in between. In this chapter, we are going to walk through how to create an application using one of these frameworks in the Crystal ecosystem called **Athena Framework**. While we will be making heavy use of this framework, we will also cover more general topics that can be leveraged irrespective of what framework you ultimately decide upon. By the end of the chapter, we will have covered the following topics:

- Understanding Athena's architecture
- Getting started with Athena
- Implementing database interactions
- Leveraging content negotiation

Technical requirements

The requirements for this chapter are as follows:

- A working installation of Crystal

- The ability to run a PostgreSQL server, such as via Docker

- A way to send HTTP requests, such as cURL or Postman

- An installed and working version of `https://www.pcre.org/` (`libpcre2`)

You can refer to *Chapter 1*, *An Introduction to Crystal*, for instructions on getting Crystal set up. There are a few ways to run the server, but I am going to be leveraging Docker Compose and will include the file I am using within the chapter's folder.

All of the code examples used in this chapter can be found on GitHub: `https://github.com/PacktPublishing/Crystal-Programming/tree/main/Chapter09`.

Understanding Athena's architecture

Unlike other Crystal frameworks, Athena Framework primarily takes its inspiration from non-Ruby frameworks such as PHP's Symfony or Java's Spring. Because of this, it has some unique features/concepts not found elsewhere in the ecosystem. It has been steadily maturing over time and has a solid foundation in place to support future features/concepts.

Athena Framework is the result of integrating the various components from the larger Athena ecosystem into a singular cohesive framework. Each component provides a different framework feature, such as serialization, validation, eventing, and so on. These components may also be used independently, such as if you wanted to make use of their features within another framework, or even use them to build your own framework. However, using them within Athena Framework provides the best experience/integration. Some of the highlights include the following:

- Annotation-based

- Adheres to the **SOLID** design principles:

  - S – Single responsibility principle

  - O – Open-closed principle

  - L – Liskov substitution principle

  - I – Interface segregation principle

- • D – Dependency inversion principle

- • Event-based

- • Flexible foundation

Annotations are a core part of Athena in that they are the primary way to define and configure routes, among other things. For example, they are used to specify what HTTP method and path a controller action handles, what query parameters should be read, and whatever custom logic you want via user-defined annotations. This approach keeps all the logic related to an action centralized on the action itself versus having the business logic in one file and routing logic in another. While Athena makes heavy use of annotations, we are not going to dive too deep into them as they will be covered in more depth in *Chapter 11, Introducing Annotations*.

Due to Crystal being an **object-oriented** (**OO**) language, Athena encourages following OO best practices such as that of SOLID. These principles, especially the *dependency inversion principle*, are quite helpful in developing an application that is easy to maintain, test, and customize by integrating a **dependency injection** (**DI**) service container. Each request has its own container, with its own set of services, that allows sharing state without needing to worry about the state bleeding between requests. Using the DI service container outside of Athena itself is possible by using that component on its own, however, how to best implement/leverage it in a project is a bit out of scope for this chapter.

Athena is an event-based framework. Instead of leveraging a chain of HTTP::Handler, various events are emitted during the life cycle of the request. These events, and their related listeners, are used to implement the framework itself, but custom listeners may also tap into the same events. Ultimately, this leads to a very flexible foundation. The flow of a request is depicted in the following figure:

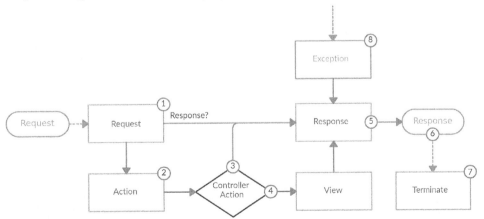

Figure 9.1 – Request life cycle diagram

Listeners on these events can be used for anything from handling CORS, returning error responses, converting objects to a response via content negotiation, or whatever else your application may need. Custom events may also be registered. See `https://athenaframework.org/components/` for a more in-depth look into each event and how they are used.

While it may seem obvious, it is important to point out that Athena Framework is a framework. In other words, its main purpose is to provide you with the building blocks used to create your application. The framework also leverages these building blocks internally to build the core framework logic. Athena tries to be as flexible as possible, by allowing you to only use the features/components you need. This allows your application to be as simple or as complex as needed.

Athena also has a few other components that are a bit out of scope for this chapter to explore in more depth. These include the following, and are linked in the *Further reading* section at the end of the chapter:

- `EventDispatcher` – Powers the listeners and the event-based nature of Athena
- `Console` – Allows creating CLI-based commands, akin to rake tasks
- `Routing` – Performant and robust HTTP routing

Also, check out `https://athenaframework.org/` in order to learn more about the framework and its features. Feel free to stop by the Athena Discord server to ask any questions, report any issues, or discuss possible improvements to the framework.

But enough talk. Let's jump into writing some code and see how everything plays out in practice. Throughout this chapter, we are going to walk through creating a simple blog application.

Getting started with Athena

Similar to what we did when creating our CLI application in *Chapter 4, Exploring Crystal via Writing a Command-Line Interface*, we are going to make use of the `crystal init` command to scaffold our application. However, unlike last time, where we scaffolded out a library, we are going to initialize an app. The main reason for this is so that we also get a `shard.lock` file to allow for reproducible installs, as we learned in the previous chapter. The full command would end up looking like `crystal init app blog`.

Now that we have our application scaffolded, we can go ahead and add Athena as a dependency by adding the following to the `shard.yml` file, being sure to run `shards install` afterward as well:

```
dependencies:
  athena:
    github: athena-framework/framework
    version: ~> 0.16.0
```

And that is all there is to installing Athena. It is designed to be non-intrusive by not requiring any external dependencies outside of Shards, Crystal, and their required system libs to install and run. There is also no need for directory structures or files that ultimately reduce the amount of boilerplate to only what is needed based on your requirements.

On the other hand, this means we will need to determine how we want to organize our application's code. For the purposes of this chapter, we are going to use simple folder grouping, for example, all controllers go in one folder, all HTML templates go in another, and so on. For larger applications, it could make sense to have folders for each feature of the application under `src/`, then group by the type of each file. This way the types are more closely related to the features that use them.

Because our application is based on creating blog articles, let's start by making it possible to create a new article. From there, we could iterate on it to actually save it to the database, update an article, delete an article, and get all or specific articles. However, before we can create the endpoint, we need to define what an article actually is.

The Article entity

Following along with our organization strategy, let's create a new folder and file, say, `src/entities/article.cr`. Our article entity will start off as a class that defines the properties that we want to keep track of. In the next section, we will look at how to reuse the article entity for interacting with the database. It could look like this:

```
class Blog::Entities::Article
  include JSON::Serializable

  def initialize(@title : String, @body : String); end

  getter! id : Int64

  property title : String
```

```
    property body : String

    getter! updated_at : Time
    getter! created_at : Time
    getter deleted_at : Time?
  end
```

This entity defines some basic data points related to the article such as its ID, title, and body. It also has some metadata such as when it was created, updated, and deleted.

We are leveraging the bang version of the `getter` macro to handle the ID and created/updated at properties. This macro creates a *nilable* instance variable and two methods, which in the case of our `ID` property, would be `#id` and `#id?`. The former raises if the value is `nil`. This works well for columns that are going to have values the majority of the time in practice but will not have one until it is saved to the database.

Because our application is going to primarily serve as an API, we are also including `JSON::Serializable` to handle (de)serialization for us. Athena's serializer component has a similar module, `ASR::Serializable`, that functions in the same way, but with additional features. At the moment, we do not really need any additional features. We can always revisit it if the need arises. See `https://athenaframework.org/Serializer/` for more information.

Returning an article

Now that we have the article entity modeled, we can move on to creating the endpoint that will handle creating it based on the request body. Just as we did for the article type, let's create our controller within a dedicated folder, such as `src/controllers/article_controller.cr`.

Athena is a **Model View Controller** (**MVC**) framework in that a controller is a class that contains one or more methods that have routes mapped to them. For example, add the following code to our controller file:

```
class Blog::Controllers::ArticleController < ATH::Controller
  @[ARTA::Post("/article")]
  def create_article : ATH::Response
    ATH::Response.new(
      Blog::Entities::Article.new("Title", "Body").to_json,
      headers: HTTP::Headers{"content-type" => "application/
      json"}
    )
```

```
    end
  end
```

Here we define our controller class, being sure to inherit from `ATH::Controller`. If so desired, custom abstract controller classes could be used in order to provide common helper logic to all controller instances. We next defined a `#create_article` instance method that returns an `ATH::Response`. This method has an `ARTA::Post` annotation applied to it that specifies this endpoint is a `POST` endpoint, as well as the path in which this controller action should handle. As for the body of the method, we are instantiating and converting a hardcoded instance of our article object to JSON to use as the body of our response. We are also setting the `content-type` header of the response. From here, let's go wire everything up and make sure it's working as expected.

Going back to the initially scaffolded `src/blog.cr` file, replace all its current content with the following:

```
require "json"

require "athena"

require "./controllers/*"
require "./entities/*"

module Blog
  VERSION = "0.1.0"

  module Controllers; end

  module Entities; end
end
```

Here, we just need Athena, Crystal's JSON module, as well as our controller and entity folders. We also defined the `Controllers` and `Entities` namespaces here such that documentation could be added to them in the future.

Next let's create another file that will serve as the entry point to our blog, say, `src/server.cr` with the following content:

```
require "./blog"

ATH.run
```

Doing it this way ensures that the server will not start automatically if we just want to require the source code elsewhere, such as within our spec code. `ATH.run` will start our Athena server on port `3000` by default.

Now that the server is running, if we were to execute the following request, using cURL like this, for example, `curl --request POST 'http://localhost:3000/article'`, we would get the following response back, as expected:

```
{
    "title": "Title",
    "body": "Body"
}
```

However, because we want our API to return JSON, there is an easier way to go about it. We can update our controller action to return an instance of our article object directly. Athena will take care of converting it to JSON and setting the required headers for us. The method now looks like this:

```
def create_article : Blog::Entities::Article
  Blog::Entities::Article.new "Title", "Body"
end
```

If you send another request, you will see the response is the same. The reason this works relates to *Figure 9.1* from earlier in the chapter. If a controller action returns an `ATH::Response`, that response is returned to the client as it is. If anything else is returned, a `view` event is emitted whose job is to convert the returned value into an `ATH::Response`.

Athena also provides some subclasses of `ATH::Response` that are more specialized. For example, `ATH::RedirectResponse` can be used to handle redirects and `ATH::StreamedResponse` can be used to stream data to the client via chunked encoding in cases where the response data would be otherwise too large to fit into memory. For more information on these subclasses, refer to the API documentation: `https://athenaframework.org/Framework/`.

Assuming our API is going to be serving a separate frontend code base, we will need to set up CORS so that the frontend can access the data. Athena comes bundled with a listener that handles it and just needs to be enabled and configured.

To keep things organized, let's create a new file, `src/config.cr`, and add the following code, being sure to require it within `src/blog.cr` as well:

```
def ATH::Config::CORS.configure : ATH::Config::CORS?
  new(
    allow_credentials: true,
    allow_origin: ["*"],
  )
end
```

Ideally, the `origin` value would be the actual domain of your application, such as `https://app.myblog.com`. However, for this chapter, we are just going to allow anything. Athena also supports the concept of parameters, which can be used to configure things in an environmentally agnostic way. See `https://athenaframework.org/components/config/` for more information.

We are also making use of a not too widely known Crystal feature in order to make our configuration logic a bit more concise. A `def` can be prefixed with a type and a period before the method name as a shortcut when defining a class method on a specific type. For example, the previous example would be equivalent to the following:

```
struct ATH::Config::CORS
  def self.configure : ATH::Config::CORS?
    new(
      allow_credentials: true,
      allow_origin: ["*"],
    )
  end
end
```

In addition to also being more concise, the shortcut syntax removes the need to figure out if the type is a struct or class. At this point, we can make a request and get back a created article but given that the article returned from this endpoint is hardcoded, it is not really useful. Let's refactor things so that we can create an article based on the body of the request.

Handling the request body

As we saw earlier, because we included `JSON::Serializable` in our entity, we can convert it to its JSON representation. We can also do the opposite: create an instance based on a JSON string or I/O. We can update our controller action to do that by updating it to look like this:

```
def create_article(request : ATH::Request) :
  Blog::Entities::Article
  if !(body = request.body) || body.peek.try &.empty?
    raise ATH::Exceptions::BadRequest.new "Request does not
      have a body."
  end

  Blog::Entities::Article.from_json body
end
```

Controller action parameters, such as those from the route's path or query parameters are provided to the action as method arguments. For example, if the path of an action was `"/add/{val1}/{val2}"`, the controller action method would be `def add(val1 : Int32, val2 : Int32) : Int32` where the two values to add are resolved from the path, converted to their expected types, and provided to the method. Action arguments may also come from default values, `ATH::Request` typed arguments, or the request's attributes.

In this example, we are making use of an `ATH::Request` typed parameter to get access to the request body in order to deserialize it. It is also technically possible for the request to not have a body, so we are making sure it exists before continuing, returning an error response if it is `nil`, or if there is no request body. We are also deserializing directly from the request body I/O, so no intermediary string needs to be created, leading to more memory-efficient code.

Error handling in Athena looks much like any other Crystal program as it leverages exceptions to represent errors. Athena defines a set of common exception types within the `ATH::Exceptions` namespace. Each of these exceptions inherits from `Athena::Exceptions::HTTPException`, which is a special type of exception used to return HTTP error responses. For example, if there was no body, this would be returned to the client, with a status code of `400`:

```
{
    "code": 400,
```

```
      "message": "Request does not have a body."
  }
```

The base type or a child type can also be inherited in order to capture additional data or add additional functionality. Any exception that is raised that is not an instance of `Athena::Exceptions::HTTPException` is treated as a `500` internal server error. By default, these error responses are JSON serialized, however, this behavior can be customized. See `https://athenaframework.org/Framework/ErrorRendererInterface/` for more information.

Now that we have ensured there is a body, we can go ahead and create our article instance via returning `Blog::Entities::Article.from_json body`. If you were to make the same request as before, but with this payload, you would see whatever you send you get back in the response:

```
{
    "title": "My Title",
    "body": "My Body"
}
```

The related cURL command would be as follows:

```
curl --request POST 'http://localhost:3000/article' \
--header 'Content-Type: application/json' \
--data-raw '{
    "title": "My Title",
    "body": "My Body"
}'
```

Great! But just like there was a better way to return the response, Athena provides a pretty slick way to make deserializing the response body easier. Athena has a unique concept called **param converters**. Param converters allow applying custom logic to convert raw data from the request into more complex types. See `https://athenaframework.org/Framework/ParamConverter/` for more information.

Example param converters include the following:

- Converting a datetime string into a `Time` instance
- Deserializing the request body into a specific type
- Converting a user's ID path parameter into an actual `User` instance

Athena provides the first two as built-in converters, but the sky is the limit when it comes to defining custom ones. Let's make use of a param converter to simplify our article creation controller action. Update the method to be the following:

```
@[ARTA::Post("/article")]
@[ATHA::ParamConverter("article", converter:
  ATH::RequestBodyConverter)]
def create_article(article : Blog::Entities::Article) :
  Blog::Entities::Article
  article
end
```

We were able to essentially condense the controller action into a single line! The main new addition here is that of the `ATHA::ParamConverter` annotation as well as updating the method to accept an article instance instead of the request. The first positional argument within the annotation represents which controller action parameter the param converter will handle. Multiple param converter annotations may be applied to convert multiple action argument parameters. We are also specifying that it should use the `ATH::RequestBodyConverter`, which is what actually deserializes the request body.

The converter infers the type it should deserialize into based on the type restriction of the related method parameter. If that type does not include `JSON::Serializable` or `ASR::Serializable`, a compile-time error is thrown. We can confirm things are still working by making another request, like the one before, and asserting we get the same response as before.

However, there is an issue with this implementation. Our API currently gladly accepts empty values for both the `title` and `body` properties. We should probably prevent this by validating the request body so we can be assured it is valid by the time it makes it to the controller action. Fortunately for us, we can make use of Athena's Validator component.

Validation

Athena's Validator component is a robust and flexible framework for validating objects and values alike. Its primary API involves applying annotations that represent the constraints you want to validate against. An instance of that object could then be validated via a validator instance that will return a possibly empty list of violations. The component has too many features to cover in this chapter, so we are going to focus on what is needed for validating our articles. See `https://athenaframework.org/Validator/` for more information.

In regards to our articles, the main thing we want to prevent is empty values. We could also enforce minimum/maximum length requirements, ensuring they do not contain certain words or phrases, or whatever else you may want to do. Either way, the first thing that needs to be done is to `include AVD::Validatable` into our `Article` type. From here, we can then apply the `NotBlank` constraint to the title and body by adding the `@[Assert::NotBlank]` annotation, for example:

```
@[Assert::NotBlank]
property title : String
```

```
@[Assert::NotBlank]
property body : String
```

If you were to try and POST blank values, a `422` error response would be returned that includes the violations along with what property they relate to. The error code UUID is a machine-readable representation of a specific violation that could be used to check for certain errors without needing to parse the message, which could be customized, for example:

```
{
    "code": 422,
    "message": "Validation failed",
    "errors": [
        {
            "property": "body",
            "message": "This value should not be blank.",
            "code": "0d0c3254-3642-4cb0-9882-46ee5918e6e3"
        }
    ]
}
```

This works out of the box because `ATH::RequestBodyConverter` will check if the deserialized object is validatable after it is deserialized, validating it if it is. The validator component comes with a slew of constraints, but custom ones can also be defined. See `https://athenaframework.org/Validator/Constraints/` and `https://athenaframework.org/components/validator/#custom-constraints` for more information respectively.

Next up on the list of things to address is that currently our endpoint to create an article essentially just returns what was provided to it. In order to make it possible to see all the articles, we need to set things up to allow persisting them to a database.

Implementing database interactions

Any application that needs to persist data such that it can be retrieved at a later time needs some form of a database. Our blog is no different as we will need a way to store the articles that make up the blog. There are various types of databases, such as NoSQL or relational, among others, each of which has its pros and cons. For our blog, we are going to keep things simple and go with a relational database, such as MySQL or PostgreSQL. Feel free to use the database of your choice that best fits the needs of your application, but I am going to be using PostgreSQL for the purposes of this chapter.

Setting up the database

Crystal provides a database abstraction shard, `https://github.com/crystal-lang/crystal-db`, that defines the high-level API for database interactions. Each database implementation uses this as a base and implements how to get data from the underlying store. This provides a unified API and common features that all database implementations can leverage. In our case, we can make use of `https://github.com/will/crystal-pg` to handle interacting with our PG database.

Let's start by adding this dependency to your `shard.yml` dependencies section, which should now look like this:

```
dependencies:
  athena:
    github: athena-framework/framework
    version: ~> 0.16.0
  pg:
    github: will/crystal-pg
    version: ~> 0.26.0
```

Be sure to run `shards install` again, and require add `require "pg"` within `src/blog.cr`. This will install Crystal's database abstraction shard, along with the driver for Postgres. Crystal also has a few ORMs that could be used to easily interact with the database. However, for our purposes, I am going to just be using the default database abstractions to keep things simple. ORMs are essentially wrappers to what is provided by the driver, so an understanding of how they work under the hood can be good to have.

The base abstraction shard does provide a `DB::Serializable` module that
we can leverage to make things a bit easier on ourselves. This module works similarly to
`JSON::Serializable`, but for database queries, allowing us to instantiate an instance
of our type from a query we make. It is worth mentioning that this module does not
handle saving the instance to the database, only reading from it. So we will need to handle
that on our own, or maybe even implement some of our own abstractions.

Before we can get to getting the user registration set up, we need to get the database set up.
There are multiple ways to go about this, but the easiest I found is via `docker-compose`,
which will allow us to spin up a Postgres server that will be easy to manage and tear down
if needed. The `compose` file I am using looks like this:

```yaml
version: '3.8'
services:
  pg:
    image: postgres:14-alpine
    container_name: pg
    ports:
      - "5432:5432"
    environment:
      - POSTGRES_USER=blog_user
      - POSTGRES_PASSWORD=mYAw3s0meB!log
    volumes:
      - pg-data:/var/lib/postgresql/data
      - ./db:/migrations

volumes:
  pg-data:
```

While I am not going to get too in-depth with this, the gist of it is that we are defining
a pg container that will be using Postgres 14, exposed on the default port, using
environmental variables to set up the user and database, and finally creating a volume that
will allow the data to persist between when it starts and shuts down. We also are adding
a db/ folder as a volume. This is so that we have access to our migration files within the
container – more on this soon. This folder should be created before starting the server
for the first time, which could be done via `mkdir db` or whichever file manager you use.
Running `docker-compose up` will start the server. The `-d` option may be used if you
want to run it in the background.

Now that we have your database running, we need to configure the database settings, as well as creating the schema for our articles table. There are some shards out there for managing migrations, however, I am just going to store and run the SQL manually. If your project will have more than a few tables, using a migration tool could be super helpful, especially for projects you intend to keep around for a while. Let's create a new db/ folder to store our migration files, creating db/000_setup.sql with the following content:

```
CREATE SCHEMA IF NOT EXISTS "test" AUTHORIZATION "blog_user";
```

We do not technically need this just yet, however, it will come into play later on in *Chapter 14*, *Testing*. Next up, let's create db/001_users.sql with the following content:

```
CREATE TABLE IF NOT EXISTS "articles"
(
    "id"           BIGINT GENERATED ALWAYS AS IDENTITY NOT NULL
       PRIMARY KEY,
    "title"        TEXT                                NOT NULL,
    "body"         TEXT                                NOT NULL,
    "created_at"   TIMESTAMP                           NOT NULL,
    "updated_at"   TIMESTAMP                           NOT NULL,
    "deleted_at"   TIMESTAMP                           NULL
);
```

We are just storing some standard values along with timestamps and an auto-increment integer primary key.

Because our Postgres server is running within a Docker container, we need to use a docker command to run the migration files from within the container:

```
docker exec -it pg psql blog_user -d postgres -f /migrations/
000_setup.sql
docker exec -it pg psql blog_user -d postgres -f /migrations
/001_articles.sql
```

Persisting articles

Continuing where we left off from the last section, we were working on getting our articles persisted to the database.

The first thing we'll want to do is include the `DB::Serializable` module in our `Article` entity. As mentioned earlier, this module allows us to construct an instance of it, from `DB::ResultSet`, which represents the result of a query made against the database.

Because we have a few things that should happen before an article is actually persisted, let's go ahead and create some abstractions to handle this. Of course, if we were using an ORM, there would be built-in ways to do this, but it will be helpful to see how it could be done pretty easily and will also be a good segue into another Athena feature, DI.

Given that all we need is to run some logic before something is saved, we can just create a method called `#before_save` that we can call. You guessed it – before we save the object to the database. It would end up looking like this:

```
protected def before_save : Nil
  if @id.nil?
    @created_at = Time.utc
  end

  @updated_at = Time.utc
end
```

I made the method protected since it is more internal and not something we need to have as part of the public API. In the case of a new record, when there is not already an ID, we are setting the `created at` timestamp. The `updated_at` property is updated on every save given that is the purpose of that timestamp.

In some Crystal ORMs, as well as Ruby's `ActiveRecord`, it is common for there to be a `#save` method directly on the object that handles persisting it to the database. I am personally not a fan of this approach as I feel it violates the *single responsibility* SOLID principle given it handles both modeling what an article is in addition to persisting it to the database. Instead of taking this approach, we are going to create another type that will handle the persistence of `DB::Serializable` instances.

This type is going to be simple, but could definitely be much more complex as the more abstractions you add, the more you are essentially making your own ORM. These extra abstractions will not be required for our single entity/table blog but could be super beneficial for larger applications. However, at that point, it might be worth considering using an ORM. In the end, it comes down to your specific context, so do what makes the most sense.

The gist of this new type will be to expose a #persist method that accepts an instance of DB::Serializable. It will then call the #before_save method, if defined, and finally call a #save method where there will be an internal overload for our article entity. This way everybody is happy, and we stick to our SOLID principles. Let's create this type as src/services/entity_manager.cr. Be sure to add require "./services/*" to src/blog.cr as well. The implementation for it would look like this:

```
@[ADI::Register]
class Blog::Services::EntityManager
  @@connection : DB::Database = DB.open ENV["DATABASE_URL"]

  def persist(entity : DB::Serializable) : Nil
    entity.before_save if entity.responds_to? :before_save
    entity.after_save self.save entity
  end
  private def save(entity : Blog::Entities::Article) : Int64
    @@database.scalar(
      %(INSERT INTO "articles" ("title", "body", "created_at",
        "updated_at", "deleted_at") VALUES ($1, $2, $3, $4, $5)
          RETURNING "id";),
      entity.title,
      entity.body,
      entity.created_at,
      entity.updated_at,
      entity.deleted_at,
    ).as Int64
  end
end
```

In order to make our code easier to run on different machines, we are going to leverage an environmental variable for the connection URL. Let's call this DATABASE_URL. We can export this via the following:

```
export DATABASE_URL=postgres://blog_user:mYAw3s0meB\
!log@localhost:5432/postgres?currentSchema=public
```

Because the entity is not aware of the auto-generated ID from the database, we need a way to set that value. The `#save` method returns the ID such that we can apply it to the entity after saving via another internal method called `#after_save`. This method accepts the ID of the persisted entity and sets it on the instance. The implementation of that method is essentially just this:

```
protected def after_save(@id : Int64) : Nil
end
```

If we were dealing with more entities, we could of course make another module that includes `DB::Serializable` and add some of these extra helper methods, but given we only have one, that does not provide much benefit.

Lastly, and most importantly, we are making use of the `ADI::Register` annotation on the class itself. As mentioned in the first section, Athena makes heavy use of DI via a service container that is unique to each request, meaning the services within are unique to each request. This prevents the state within your services from leaking between requests, which could happen if you are using things such as class variables. However, that does not mean using a class variable is *always* a bad thing. It all depends on the context. For example, our entity manager is using one to keep a reference to `DB::Database`. In this case, it is fine since it is kept private within our class, and because it represents a pool of connections. Because of this, each request could get its own connection to the database if needed. We are also not storing any request-specific state within it, so it is kept pure.

The `ADI::Register` annotation tells the service container that this type should be treated as a service such that it could be injected into other services. Athena's DI features are incredibly powerful and I highly suggest reading through for a more in-depth list of its capabilities.

In our context, what this means in practice is that we can make Athena's DI logic inject an instance of this type wherever we may need to save an entity, such as a controller or another service. The primary benefit of this is that it makes the types that use it easier to test given we could inject a mock implementation within our unit tests to ensure we are not testing too much. It also helps keep code centralized and reusable.

Now that we have all the prerequisite work in place, we can finally set up **article persistence** with the first step being exposing our entity manager to `ArticleController`. To accomplish this, we can make the controller a service and define an initializer that creates an instance variable typed as `Blog::Services::EntityManager`, for example:

```
@[ADI::Register(public: true)]
class Blog::Controllers::ArticleController < ATH::Controller
```

```
def initialize(@entity_manager : Blog::Services::
  EntityManager);
  end


  # ...
end
```

For implementation reasons, the service has to be a public service, hence the `public: true` field within the annotation. A public service is allowed to be fetched directly by type or name from the container, instead of *only* being accessible via constructor DI. This may change in the future. Once we do this, we can reference our entity manager as we would any other instance variable.

At this point, we really only need to add one line to persist our articles. The `#create_article` method should now look like this:

```
def create_article(article : Blog::Entities::Article) :
  Blog::Entities::Article
  @entity_manager.persist article
  article
end
```

While the controller action looks simple, there is quite a bit going on under the hood:

1.   The request body converter will handle deserialization and running validations.

2.   The entity manager persists the deserialized entity.

3.   The entity can just be returned directly since it will have its ID set and be JSON serialized as expected.

Let's rerun our cURL request from earlier:

```
curl --request POST 'http://localhost:3000/article' \
--header 'Content-Type: application/json' \
--data-raw '{
    "title": "Title",
    "body": "Body"
}'
```

This will produce a response similar to this:

```
{
    "id": 1,
    "title": "Title",
    "body": "Body",
    "updated_at": "2022-04-09T04:47:09Z",
    "created_at": "2022-04-09T04:47:09Z"
}
```

Perfect! Now that we are correctly storing our articles. The next most obvious thing to handle is how to read the list of stored articles. Currently, though, the entity manager only handles persisting entities, not querying. Let's work on that next!

Fetching articles

While we could just add some methods to it to handle querying, it would be better to have a dedicated `Repository` type that is specific to querying that we could obtain via the entity manager. Let's create `src/entities/article_repository.cr` with the following content:

```
class Blog::Entities::Article::Repository
  def initialize(@database: DB::Database); end

  def find?(id : Int64) : Blog::Entities::Article?
    @database.query_one?(%(SELECT * FROM "articles" WHERE "id"
      = $1 AND "deleted_at" IS NULL;), id, as:
        Blog::Entities::Article)
  end

  def find_all : Array(Blog::Entities::Article)
    @database.query_all %(SELECT * FROM "articles" WHERE
      "deleted_at" IS NULL;), as: Blog::Entities::Article
  end
end
```

This is a pretty simple object that accepts `DB::Database` and acts as a place for all the article related queries to live. We need to expose this from the entity manager type, which we can do by adding the following method:

```
def repository(entity_class : Blog::Entities::Article.class) :
  Blog::Entities::Article::Repository
    @@article_repository ||= Blog::Entities::Article
      ::Repository.new
      @@database
  end
```

This approach will allow adding a `#repository` overload for each entity class if more are added in the future. Again, we could of course implement things in a fancier, more robust way, but given we will only have one entity, using overloads while caching the repository in a class variable is good enough. As the saying goes, *premature optimization is the root of all evil.*

Now that we have the ability to fetch all articles, as well as specific articles by ID, we can move onto creating the endpoints by adding the following methods to the article controller:

```
@[ARTA::Get("/article/{id}")]
def article(id : Int64) : Blog::Entities::Article
  article = @entity_manager.repository(Blog::Entities::Article)
    .find? id

  if article.nil?
    raise ATH::Exceptions::NotFound.new "An item with the
        provided ID could not be found."
  end
    article
end


@[ARTA::Get("/article")]
def articles : Array(Blog::Entities::Article)
  @entity_manager.repository(Blog::Entities::Article).find_all
end
```

The first endpoint calls its #find? method to return an article with the provided ID. If it does not exist, it returns a more helpful 404 error response. The next endpoint returns an array of all the stored articles.

Just like back when we started on the #create_article endpoint and learned about ATH::RequestBodyConverter, there is a better way to handle reading a specific article from the database. We can define our own param converter to consume the ID path parameter, fetch it from the database, and provide it to the action, all the while being generic enough to use for other entities we have. Create src/param_converters/database.cr with the following content, ensuring that this new directory is required within src/blog.cr as well:

```
@[ADI::Register]
class Blog::Converters::Database < ATH::ParamConverter
  def initialize(@entity_manager : Blog::Services
      ::EntityManager);
  end


  # :inherit:
  def apply(request : ATH::Request, configuration :
    Configuration(T)) : Nil forall T
    id = request.attributes.get "id", Int64

    unless model = @entity_manager.repository(T).find? id
      raise ATH::Exceptions::NotFound.new "An item with the
      provided ID could not be found."
    end

    request.attributes.set configuration.name, model, T
  end
end
```

Similar to the previous listener, we need to make the listener a service via the ADI::Register annotation. The actual logic involves retrieving the ID path parameter from the request's attributes, using that to look up the related entity, if any, and setting the entity within the request's attributes.

If the entity with the provided ID could not be found, we return a 404 error response.

The last key part to how this works relates to earlier in the chapter when we were looking into how Athena provides arguments to each controller action. One such way arguments are resolved is from the request's attributes, which can be thought of as a key/value store for arbitrary data related to the request, to which path and query parameters are added automatically.

In the context of our converter, the `configuration.name` method represents the name of the action parameter the converter relates to, based on the value provided in the annotation. We are using this to set the name of the attribute, `article` for example, to the resolved entity. Athena will then see that this controller action has a parameter called `article`, will check if there is an attribute with that name, and provide it to the action if it does exist. Using this converter, we can update the `#article` action to the following:

```
@[ARTA::Get("/article/{id}")]
@[ATHA::ParamConverter("article", converter:
  Blog::Converters::Database)]
def article(article : Blog::Entities::Article) :
  Blog::Entities::Article
  article
end
```

Ta-da! A seamless way to provide database entities directly as action arguments via their IDs. While we have quite a few article-related endpoints by now, we are still missing a way to update or delete an article. Let's focus on how to update an article first.

Updating an article

Updating database records may seem simple at first, but it actually can be quite complex due to the nature of the process. For example, to update an entity, you first need to get the current instance of it, then apply the changes to it. The changes are commonly represented as the request body to a PUT endpoint, with the ID of the entity included, unlike the POST endpoint. The problem lies in how to apply the changes from the new request body to the existing entity.

Athena's serializer has the concept of object constructors that control how the object being deserialized is first initialized. By default, they are instantiated normally via the `.new` method. It does offer the ability to define custom ones, which we could do in order to source the entity from the database, based on the ID property in the request body. We would then apply the rest of the request body onto the retrieved record. This ensures non-exposed database values are correctly handled as well as handling the hard part of applying the changes to the entity.

However, given this would get a bit in the weeds of how Athena's serializer works, and given our article only has two properties, we are not going to implement this. If you are curious what this would look like or want to try implementing it yourself, check out this cookbook recipe: `https://athenaframework.org/cookbook/object_constructors/#db`. It uses the Granite ORM, but switching it out in favor of our `EntityManager` should be pretty straightforward.

Instead of using an object constructor, we are just going to manually map the values from the request body and apply them to the entity fetched from the database. Before we can do this, we first need to update the entity manager to handle updates. The first step is to update #persist to check if the ID is set via the following:

```
def persist(entity : DB::Serializable) : Nil
  entity.before_save if entity.responds_to? :before_save

  if entity.id?.nil?
    entity.after_save self.save entity
  else
    self.update entity
  end
```

Where the #update method looks like this:

```
private def update(entity : Blog::Entities::Article) : Nil
  @@connection.exec(
    %(UPDATE "articles" SET "title" = $1, "body" = $2,
    "updated_at" = $3, "deleted_at" = $4 WHERE "id" = $5;),
    entity.title,
    entity.body,
    entity.updated_at,
    entity.deleted_at,
    entity.id
  )
end
```

From here, we can update our #update_article endpoint to look like this:

```
@[ARTA::Put("/article/{id}")]
@[ATHA::ParamConverter("article_entity", converter:
  Blog::Converters::Database)]
@[ATHA::ParamConverter("article", converter:
  ATH::RequestBodyConverter)]
def update_article(article_entity : Blog::Entities::Article,
    article : Blog::Entities::Article) : Blog::Entities::Article
  article_entity.title = article.title
  article_entity.body = article.body

  @entity_manager.persist article_entity
  article_entity
end
```

We are leveraging two param converters in this example. The first fetches the real article entity from the database, while the second constructs one based on the request body. We then apply the request body article to the article entity and pass it to #persist.

Let's say we make a request like this:

```
curl --request PUT 'http://localhost:3000/article/1' \
--header 'Content-Type: application/json' \
--data-raw '{
    "title": "New Title",
    "body": "New Body",
    "updated_at": "2022-04-09T05:13:30Z",
    "created_at": "2022-04-09T04:47:09Z"
}'
```

This would result in a response like this:

```
{
    "id": 1,     "title": "New Title",
    "body": "New Body",
    "updated_at": "2022-04-09T05:22:44Z",
    "created_at": "2022-04-09T04:47:09Z"
}
```

Perfect! The `title`, `body`, and `updated_at` timestamp were all updated as expected, while the `id` and `created_at` timestamps were unaltered from the database.

Last but not least, we need to be able to delete an article.

Deleting an article

We can handle deletes by once again updating our entity manager to have a `#remove` method, along with an `#on_remove` method on our entities that will handle setting the `deleted_at` property. We could then leverage the database param converter on a `DELETE` endpoint and simply provide `#remove` to the resolved entity.

Start off by adding this to the entity manager:

```
def remove(entity : DB::Serializable) : Nil
  entity.on_remove if entity.responds_to? :on_remove
  self.update entity
end
```

And this to our article entity:

```
protected def on_remove : Nil
  @deleted_at = Time.utc
end
```

Finally, the controller action would look like this:

```
@[ARTA::Delete("/article/{id}")]
@[ATHA::ParamConverter("article", converter:
  Blog::Converters::Database)]
def delete_article(article : Blog::Entities::Article) : Nil
  @entity_manager.remove article
end
```

We could then make a request such as `curl --request DELETE 'http://localhost:3000/article/1'` and see in the database its `deleted_at` column got set. Because the `#find?` method also filters out deleted items, trying to delete the same article again would result in a `404` error response.

In some cases, an API may need to support returning more than just JSON. Athena provides some ways to leverage content negotiation by handling multiple response formats via a singular return value from the controller action. Let's take a look.

Leveraging content negotiation

At this point, our blog is really coming together. We are able to create, fetch, update, and delete articles. We also have some pretty solid abstractions in place to aid future growth. As mentioned earlier in the chapter, having the controller actions directly return an object can help with handling multiple response formats. For example, say we wanted to augment our application by allowing it to return an article as HTML as well as JSON, depending on the `accept` header of the request.

In order to handle the generation of the HTML, we could make use of Crystal's built-in **Embedded Crystal (ECR)** feature, which is essentially like compile-time templating. However, it could help to have something a bit more flexible, much akin to PHP's Twig, Python's Jinja, or **Embedded Ruby (ERB)**. There is actually a Crystal port of Jinja, called Crinja that we can leverage. So first up, add the following as a dependency to your `shard.yml`, being sure to run `shards install` and require it within `src/blog.cr`:

```
crinja:
  github: straight-shoota/crinja
  version: ~> 0.8.0
```

Crinja has a `Crinja::Object` module that can be included to allow certain properties/methods from the type to be accessible within a template. It also has an `Auto` submodule that works much like `JSON::Serializable`. Because it is a module, it will also allow us to check if a specific object is renderable so that we can handle the error case of trying to render an object that is not able to be rendered.

The plan for how to set this up is as follows:

1. Set up content negotiation to allow the `GET /article/{id}` endpoint to be renderable as both JSON and HTML.

2. Include and configure `Crinja::Object::Auto` within our article entity.

3. Create an HTML template that will use the article data.

4. Define a custom renderer for HTML to wire everything together.

We also need a way to define which template the endpoint should use. We can leverage another incredibly powerful Athena feature, the ability to define/use custom annotations. This feature offers immense flexibility, as the possible uses are almost endless. You could define a `Paginated` annotation to handle pagination, a `Public` annotation to mark public endpoints, or in our case a `Template` annotation to map an endpoint to its Crinja template.

To create this custom annotation, we use the `configuration_annotation` macro as part of the `Athena::Config` component. This macro accepts the name of the annotation as the first argument, and then a variable amount of fields, which can also contain default values, very similar to the `record` macro. In our case, we only need to store the template's name, so the macro call would look like this:

```
ACF.configuration_annotation Blog::Annotations::Template, name
    : String
```

We'll get back to using this annotation shortly, but first, we need to address the other items on our to-do list. First up, configuring content negotiation. Add the following code to the `src/config.cr` file:

```
def ATH::Config::ContentNegotiation.configure :
  ATH::Config::ContentNegotiation?
  new(
    Rule.new(path: /^\/article\/\d+$/, priorities: ["json",
    "html"],
      methods: ["GET"], fallback_format: "json"),
    Rule.new(priorities: ["json"], fallback_format: "json")
  )
end
```

Similar to how we configured the CORS listener, we can do the same for the content negotiation feature. In this case, though, it is configured by providing a series of `Rule` instances that allow for fine-tuning the negotiation.

The `path` argument accepts a `Regex` that makes it so only endpoints that match the pattern will have that rule applied. Given we only want one endpoint to support both formats, we set up the regex to map to its path.

The `priorities` arguments control the formats that should be considered. In this case, we want to support JSON and HTML so we have those values set. The order of the values does matter. In a case in which the `accept` header allows for both formats, the first matching format in the array would be used, which in this case would be JSON.

Our second rule does not have a path so it is applied to all routes and only supports JSON. We are also setting `fallback_format` to JSON such that JSON would still be returned even if the *accept* header does not allow it. The fallback format could also be set to `nil` to try the next rule, or `false` to raise `ATH::Exceptions::NotAcceptable` if there is no servable format.

See `https://athenaframework.org/Framework/Config/ContentNegotiation/Rule/` for more information on how negotiation rules can be configured.

Now that we have that configured, we can move on to configuring our article entity to expose some of its data to Crinja. This is as simple as adding `include Crinja::Object::Auto` within the class, then adding the `@[Crinja::Attributes]` annotation to the entity class itself.

Next up we can create an HTML template to represent the article. Given this is for example purposes only, it is not going to look pretty, but it will do the job. Let's create `src/views/article.html.j2`, with the following content:

```
<h1>{{ data.title }}</h1>


<p>{{ data.body }}</p>


<i>Updated at: {{ data.updated_at }}</i>
```

We access the article values off at the data object that will represent the root data provided to the `render` call. This allows for the expansion of the exposed data outside of the article in the future.

Finally, we need to create an instance of `ATH::View::FormatHandlerInterface` that will handle the process of wiring everything up so that the controller action return value gets rendered via Crinja and returned to the client. Create `src/services/html_format_handler.cr` with the following content:

```
@[ADI::Register]
class HTMLFormatHandler
  include Athena::Framework::View::FormatHandlerInterface

  private CRINJA = Crinja.new loader: Crinja::Loader::
    FileSystem
    Loader.new "#{__DIR__}/../views"

  def call(view_handler : ATH::View::ViewHandlerInterface, view
  : ATH::ViewBase, request : ATH::Request, format : String) :
    ATH::Response
```

```
    ann_configs = request.action.annotation_configurations

    unless template_ann = ann_configs[Blog::Annotations::
      Template]?
      raise "Unable to determine the template for the
        '#{request.attributes.get "_route"}' route."
    end

    unless (data = view.data).is_a? Crinja::Object
      raise ATH::Exceptions::NotAcceptable.new "Cannot convert
    value of type '#{view.data.class}' to '#{format}'."
    end

    content = CRINJA.get_template(template_ann.name).
      render({data: view.data})

    ATH::Response.new content, headers: HTTP::Headers{"content-
      type" => "text/html"}
  end

  def format : String
    "html"
  end
end
```

Other than doing some stuff we should be familiar with by now, such as registering it as a service and including the interface module, we are also defining a #format method that returns the format that this type handles. We also created a singleton instance of Crinja that will load the templates from the src/views folder. Crinja reads the templates on each call to #get_template, so there is no need to restart the server when you only made changes to a template. However, as it stands at the moment, it would require the path to exist and be valid in both development and production environments. Consider using an environmental variable to provide the path.

Lastly, we defined a #call method that has access to various information that can be used in part to render the response. In our case, we only need the view and request parameters, the latter of which is used to get all of the annotation configurations defined on its related route. This is where the annotation we created earlier comes into play as we can check if there is an instance of it applied to the controller action related to the current request. See https://athenaframework.org/Framework/View/ for more information on what is exposed via these parameters.

Next up, we handle some error contexts such as if the endpoint does not have the template annotation, or the value returned is not renderable via Crinja. I purposefully am raising generic exceptions so that a 500 error response is returned given we do not want to leak internal information outside of the API.

Finally, we use Crinja to fetch the template based on the name in the annotation and render it, using the value returned from the controller action as the value of the data object. We then use the rendered content as the response body to ATH::Response, setting the response content-type to text/html.

To enable this behavior, we simply need to apply the @ [Blog::Annotations::Template("article.html.j2")] annotation to our #article method within ArticleController. We can test everything out by making another request:

```
curl --request GET 'http://localhost:3000/article/1' --header
'accept: text/html'
```

The response in this context should be our HTML template. If you were to set the header to application/json or remove it altogether, the response should be JSON.

Summary

And there you have it, a blog implementation that leverages some of the cooler Athena features that in turn made the implementation easy and highly flexible. We used param converters to handle both deserializing the request body, and also looking up and providing a value from the database. We created a custom annotation and format handler to support multiple format responses via content negotiation. And most importantly, we scratched the surface of the DI component by showing how it makes reusing objects easy as well as how the *container per request* concept can be used to prevent the bleeding of state between requests.

As you can imagine, Athena leverages quite a few metaprogramming concepts in order to implement its features. In the next chapter, we are going to be exploring a core metaprogramming feature, macros.

Further reading

- `https://athenaframework.org/EventDispatcher/`
- `https://athenaframework.org/Console/`
- `https://athenaframework.org/Routing/`

Part 4: Metaprogramming

This part is intended to cover the more advanced metaprogramming features and techniques, with a focus on annotations. This information is generally not well documented. Without further ado, let's dive into how to make use of these more advanced features.

This part contains the following chapters:

- *Chapter 10, Working with Macros*
- *Chapter 11, Introducing Annotations*
- *Chapter 12, Leveraging Compile-Time Type Introspection*
- *Chapter 13, Advanced Macro Usages*

10
Working
with Macros

In this chapter, we are going to explore the world of metaprogramming. Metaprogramming can be a great way to DRY up your code by consolidating boilerplate code into reusable chunks, or by processing data at compile time to generate additional code. First, we are going to take a look at the core piece of this feature: **macros**.

We will cover the following topics in this chapter:

- Defining macros
- Understanding the macro API
- Exploring macro hooks

By the end of this chapter, you will be able to understand when and how macros can be applied to reduce the amount of boilerplate code in an application.

Technical requirements

For this chapter, you will need a working installation of Crystal.

You can refer to *Chapter 1, An Introduction to Crystal*, for instructions on getting Crystal set up.

All of the code examples in this chapter can be found in the `Chapter 10` folder of this book's GitHub repository: `https://github.com/PacktPublishing/Crystal-Programming/tree/main/Chapter10`.

Defining macros

In Crystal, a macro has two meanings. Generally, it refers to any code that runs or expands at compile time. However, more specifically, it can refer to a type of method that accepts AST nodes at compile time, whose body is pasted into the program at the point the macro is used. An example of the latter is the `property` macro, which you saw in previous chapters, which is an easy way to define both a getter and a setter method for a given instance variable:

```
class Example
  property age : Int32

  def initialize(@age : Int32); end
end
```

The preceding code is equivalent to the following:

```
class Example
  @age : Int32

  def initialize(@age : Int32); end

  def age : Int32
    @age
  end

  def age=(@age : Int32)
  end
end
```

As we mentioned earlier, macros accept AST nodes at compile time and output Crystal code that is added to the program as if it was manually typed. Because of this, `property age : Int32` is not part of the final program, only what it expands to – the instance variable declaration, the getter method, and the setter method. Similarly, because macros operate on AST nodes at compile time, the arguments/values that are used within a macro must also be available at compile time. This includes the following:

- Environment variables
- Constants
- Hardcoded values
- Hardcoded values generated via another macro

Because the arguments must be known at compile time, macros are *not* a replacement for normal methods, even if the outcome seems to be the same in both cases. Take this small program, for example:

```
macro print_value(value)
  {{pp value}}
  pp {{value}}
end


name = "George"


print_value name
```

Running this program would produce the following output:

```
name
"George"
```

The main thing to notice is the output of `value` when it was within the macro context. Because macros accept AST nodes, the macro does *not* have access to the current value of a runtime variable such as `name`. Instead, the type of `value` within the macro context is a `Var`, which represents a local variable or block argument. This can be confirmed by adding a line to the macro that consists of `{{pp value.class_name}}`, which would end up printing `"Var"`. We will learn more about AST nodes later in this chapter.

It is easy to abuse macros because of the power they provide. However, as the saying goes: *with great power comes great responsibility*. The rule of thumb is that if you can accomplish what you want with a normal method, use a normal method and use macros as infrequently as possible. This is not to say macros should be avoided at all costs, but more that they should be used strategically as opposed to as the solution to every problem you come across.

A macro can be defined using the `macro` keyword:

```
macro def_method(name)
  def {{name.id}}
    puts "Hi"
  end
end


def_method foo


foo
```

In this example, we defined a macro called `def_method` that accepts one argument. Overall, macros are very similar to normal methods in terms of how they are defined, with the main differences being as follows:

- Macro arguments cannot have type restrictions
- Macros cannot have return type restrictions
- Macro arguments do not exist at runtime, so they may only be referenced within the macro syntax

Macros behave similarly to class methods in regards to how they are scoped. Macros can be defined within a type and invoked outside of it by using the class method syntax. Similarly, macro invocations will look for the definition within the type's ancestor chain, such as parent types or included modules. Private macros can also be defined, which would only make it visible within the same file if it's declared at the top level, or only within the specific type it was declared.

Macro syntax consists of two forms: `{{ ... }}` and `{% ... %}`. The former is used when you want to output some value into the program. The latter is used as part of the control flow of the macro, such as loops, conditional logic, variable assignment, and so on.

In the previous example, we used the double curly brace syntax to paste the `name` argument's value into the program as the method's name, which in this case is `foo`. We then called the method, which resulted in the program printing `Hi`.

Macros can also expand to multiple things and have more complex logic for determining what gets generated. For example, let's define a method that accepts a variable number of arguments and create a method to access each value, optionally only for odd numbers:

```
macro def_methods(*numbers, only_odd = false)
  {% for num, idx in numbers %}
    {% if !only_odd || (num % 2) != 0 %}
      # Returns the number at index {{idx}}.
      def {{"number_#{idx}".id}}
        {{num}}
      end
    {% end %}
  {% end %}
  {{debug}}
end


def_methods 1, 3, 6, only_odd: true


pp number_0
pp number_1
```

There is more going on in this example than what we can see! Let's break it down. First, we defined a macro called `def_methods` that accepts a variable number of arguments with an optional Boolean flag defaulted to `false`. The macro expects you to provide it a series of numbers, using which it will create methods to access the number, using the index of each value to create a unique method name. The optional flag will force the macro to only create methods for odd numbers, even if even numbers were also passed to the macro.

The purpose of using the `splat` and `named` arguments is to show that macros are similar to methods, which could be written the same way. However, the difference is more obvious when you get into the body of the macro. Normally, the `#each` method is used to iterate a collection. In the case of a macro, you must use the `for item, index in collection` syntax, which can also be used to iterate a fixed number of times or over the key/values of a `Hash`/`NamedTuple` via `for i in (0..10)` and `for key, value in hash_or_named_tuple`, respectively.

The main reason #each cannot be used is that the loop needs access to the actual program to be able to paste in the generated code. It is possible to use #each within a macro, but it must be used within the macro syntax, and cannot be used to generate code. This is best demonstrated with an example:

```
{% begin %}
  {% hash = {"foo" => "bar", "biz" => "baz"} %}

  {% for key, value in hash %}
    puts "#{{{key}}}=#{{{value}}}"
  {% end %}
{% end %}

{% begin %}
  {% arr = [1, 2, 3] %}
  {% hash = {} of Nil => Nil %}

  {% arr.each { |v| hash[v] = v * 2 } %}

    puts({{hash}})
{% end %}
```

In this example, we iterated over the keys and values of a hash, generating a puts method call that prints each pair. We also used ArrayLiteral#each to iterate over each value and set a computed value in a hash literal, which we then print. In most cases, the for in syntax can be used in place of #each, but #each cannot be used in place of for in. Put more simply, because the #each method uses a block, there is not a way for it to output generated code. As such, it can only be used to iterate, not generate, code.

The next thing our def_methods macro does is use an if statement to determine whether it should generate a method or not for the current number. if/unless statements in macro land work identically to their runtime counterparts, albeit within the macro syntax.

Next, notice that this method has a comment on it that includes {{idx}}. Macro expressions are evaluated in both comments and normal code. This allows comments to be generated based on the expanded value of the macro expressions. However, this feature also makes it impossible to comment out macro code as it would still be evaluated as normal.

Finally, we have the logic that creates the method. In this case, we interpolated the index from the loop into a string representing the name of the method. Notice that we used the `#id` method on the string. The `#id` method returns the value as `MacroId`, which essentially normalizes the value as the same identifier, no matter what type the input is. For example, calling `#id` on `"foo"`, `:foo`, and `foo` results in the same value of `foo` being returned. This is helpful as it allows the macro to be called with whatever identifier the user prefers, while still producing the same underlying code.

At the very end of the macro definition, you may have noticed the `{{debug}}` line. This is a special macro method that can be invaluable when debugging macro code. When used, it will output the macro code that will be generated on the line that it was called on. In our example, we would see the following output on the console before the expected values are printed:

```
# Returns the number at index 0.
def number_0
1
end


# Returns the number at index 1.
def number_1
3
end
```

As a macro becomes more and more complex, this can be incredibly useful in ensuring it is generating what it should be.

It is also possible for a macro to generate other macros. However, special care needs to be taken when doing so to ensure the inner macro's expressions are escaped correctly. For example, the following macro is similar to the previous example, but instead of defining the methods directly, it creates another macro and immediately invokes it, resulting in the related methods being created:

```
macro def_macros(*numbers)
  {% for num, idx in numbers %}
    macro def_num_{{idx}}_methods(n)
      def num_\{{n}}
        \{{n}}
    end
```

```
        def num_\{{n}}_index
            {{idx}}
        end
    end


    def_num_{{idx}}_methods({{num}})
    {% end %}
end


def_macros 2, 1


pp num_1_index # => 1
pp num_2_index # => 0
```

In the end, the macros expand and define the four methods. The key thing to notice in this example is the usage of \{{. The backslash escapes the macro syntax expression so that it is not evaluated by the outer macro, which means it is only expanded by the inner macro. Macro variables from the outer macro can still be referenced within the inner macro by using the variable within the inner macro *without* escaping the expression.

The need to escape each macro syntax expression within the inner macro can be pretty tedious and error-prone. Fortunately, the verbatim call can be used to simplify this. The inner macro shown in the previous example could also be written as follows:

```
macro def_num_{{idx}}_methods(n)
    {% verbatim do %}
    def num_{{n}}
        {{n}}
    end

    def num_{{n}}_index
        {{idx}}
    end
    {% end %}
end
```

However, if you were to run this, you would see that it does not compile. The one downside of verbatim is that it does not support any variable interpolation. In other words, this means that the code within the verbatim block cannot use variables defined outside of it, such as idx.

To be able to access this variable, we need to define another escaped macro variable outside of the verbatim block within the inner macro that is set to the expanded value of the outer macro's idx variable. Put more simply, we need to add \{% idx = {{idx}} %} above the {% verbatim do %} line. This ultimately ends up expanding {% idx = 1 %} within the inner macro, in the case of the second value.

As macros expand to Crystal code, it is possible for the code that's generated by the macro to create a conflict with the code defined around the macro expansion. The most common issue would be overriding local variables. The solution to this is to use fresh variables as a means to generate unique variables.

Fresh variables

If a macro uses a local variable, it is assumed that that local variable is already defined. This feature allows a macro to make use of predefined variables within the context where the macro expands, which can help reduce duplication. However, it also makes it easy to accidentally override a local variable by one defined in the macro, as shown in this example:

```
macro update_x
    x = 1
end


x = 0
update_x
puts x
```

The update_x macro expands to the x = 1 expression, which overrides the original x variable, resulting in this program printing a value of 1. To allow the macro to define variables that will not conflict, **fresh variables** must be used, like so:

```
macro dont_update_x
    %x = 1
    puts %x
end

x = 0
```

```
dont_update_x
puts x
```

Unlike the earlier example, this will print a value of 1, followed by a value of 0, thus showing that the expanded macro did not modify the local x variable. Fresh variables are defined by prefixing a % symbol to a variable name. Fresh variables may also be created concerning another compile-time macro value. This can be especially useful in loops where a new fresh variable using the same name should be defined for each iteration of the loop, like so:

```
macro fresh_vars_sample(*names)
  {% for name, index in names %}
    %name{index} = {{index}}
  {% end %}
  {{debug}}
end


fresh_vars_sample a, b, c
```

The previous program will iterate over each of the arguments that were passed to the macro and will define a fresh variable for each item, using the index of the item as the variable's value. Based on the debug output, this macro expands to the following:

```
__temp_24 = 0
__temp_25 = 1
__temp_26 = 2
```

One variable is defined for each iteration of the loop. The Crystal compiler keeps track of all the fresh variables and assigns each a number to ensure they do not conflict with each other.

Non-macro definition macros

All of the macro code we have written/looked at so far has been in the context of a macro definition. While this is one of the most common places to see macro code, macros can also be used outside of a macro definition. This can be useful for conditionally defining code based on some external value, such as an environment's var, compile-time flag, or a constant's value. This can be seen in the following example:

```
{% if flag? :release %}
  puts "Release mode!"
```

```
{% else %}
  puts "Non-release mode!"
{% end %}
```

The `flag?` method is a special macro method that allows us to check for either user-provided or built-in compile-time flags. One of the main use cases for this method is to define some code that's specific to a particular OS and/or architecture. The Crystal compiler includes some built-in flags that can be used for this, such as `{% if flag?(:linux) && flag?(:x86_64) %}`, which would only execute if the system compiling the program is using a 64-bit Linux OS.

Custom flags may be defined using the `--define` or `-D` options. For example, if you wanted to check for `flag? :foo`, the flag could be defined by executing `crystal run -Dfoo main.cr`. Compile-time flags are either present or not; they cannot include a value. However, environmental variables could be a good substitute if more flexibility is required.

Environment variables can be read at compile time via the `env` macro method. A good use case for this is the ability to embed build time information into the binary, such as the build epoch, the build time, and so on. This example will set the value of a constant during compile time to either the value of the `BUILD_SHA_HASH` environment variable or an empty string if it was not set (all of this takes place at compile time):

```
COMMIT_SHA = {{ env("BUILD_SHA_HASH") || "" }}


pp COMMIT_SHA
```

Running this code would normally print an empty string, while setting the related `env` variable would print that value. Having this value being set via the `env` variable as opposed to generated within the macro itself via a system call is much more portable as it is not dependent on Git, and is also much easier to integrate with external build systems such as Make.

One limitation of macros is that the generated code from the macro must also be valid Crystal code on its own, as shown here:

```
def {{"foo".id}}
  "foo"
end
```

This preceding code is not a valid program because the method is incomplete and not fully defined within the macro. This method can be included within the macro by wrapping everything within {% begin %}/{% end %} tags, which would look like this:

```
{% begin %}
  def {{"foo".id}}
    "foo"
  end
{% end %}
```

At this point, you should have a strong introductory understanding of what macros are, how to define them, and what use cases they are designed to address, allowing you to keep your code DRY. Next, we are going to look at the macro API so that we can create more complex macros.

Understanding the macro API

The examples in the previous section utilized various variables of different types within the macro context, such as the numbers we iterate over, the strings we use to create identifiers, and the Booleans we compare to conditionally generate code. It would be easy to assume that this maps directly to the standard `Number`, `String`, and `Bool` types. However, that is not the case. As we mentioned in the *Defining macros* section of this chapter, macros operate on AST nodes and, as such, have their own set of types that are similar to their related normal Crystal types, but with a subset of the API. For example, the types we have worked with so far include `NumberLiteral`, `StringLiteral`, and `BoolLiteral`.

All macro types live under the `Crystal::Macros` namespace within the API documentation, which is located at `https://crystal-lang.org/api/Crystal/Macros.html`. The most common/useful types include the following:

- `Def`: Describes a method definition
- `TypeNode`: Describes a type (class, struct, module, lib)
- `MetaVar`: Describes an instance variable
- `Arg`: Describes a method argument
- `Annotation`: Represents an annotation that's applied to a type, method, or instance variable (more on this in the next chapter)

Crystal provides a convenient way to obtain an instance of the first two types in the form of the @def and @type macro variables. As their names imply, using @def within a method will return a Def instance representing that method. Similarly, using @type will return a TypeNode instance for the related type. The other types can be accessed via the methods based on one of those two types. For example, running the following program would print "The hello method within Foo":

```
class Foo
  def hello
    {{"The #{@def.name} method within #{@type.name}"}}
  end
end


pp Foo.new.hello
```

Another more advanced way of obtaining a TypeNode is via the parse_type macro method. This method accepts a StringLiteral, which could be dynamically constructed, and returns one of a handful of macro types depending on what the string represented. See the method documentation within https://crystal-lang.org/api/Crystal/Macros.html for more information

As we mentioned earlier, the macro API allows us to invoke a fixed subset of the normal API methods on the literal types. In other words, it allows us to call ArrayLiteral#select but not ArrayLiteral# each_repeated_permutation, or StringLiteral#gsub but not StringLiteral#scan.

In addition to these primitive types, the previously mentioned macro types expose their own set of methods so that we can fetch information about the related type, such as the following:

- The return type, its visibility, or the arguments of a method
- The type/default value of a method argument
- What union/generic arguments a type has, if any

There are, of course, too many to mention here, so I suggest checking out the API documentation for the full list. In the meantime, let's put some of these methods to use:

```
class Foo
  def hello(one : Int32, two, there, four : Bool, five :
    String?)
```

```
  {% begin %}
    {{"#{@def.name} has #{@def.args.size}
      arguments"}}
    {% typed_arguments = @def.args.select(&.restriction) %}
    {{"with #{typed_arguments.size} typed
      arguments"}}
    {{"and is a #{@def.visibility.id} method"}}
  {% end %}
end
end


Foo.new.hello 1, 2, 3, false, nil
```

This program will output the following:

```
"hello has 5 arguments"
"with 3 typed arguments"
"and is a public method"
```

The first line is printing the name of the method and how many arguments it has via `ArrayLiteral#size` because `Def#args` returns `ArrayLiteral(Arg)`. We are then making use of the `ArrayLiteral#select` method to get an array containing only arguments that have a type restriction. `Arg#restriction` returns `TypeNode` based on the restriction's type, or `Nop`, which is a false value that's used to represent an empty node. Finally, we use `Def#visibility` to find out the level of visibility of the method. It returns `SymbolLiteral`, so we are invoking `#id` on it to get a generic representation of it.

There is another special macro variable, `@top_level`, that returns `TypeNode`, which represents the top-level namespace. If we don't use this, the only other way to access it is to invoke `@type` within the top-level namespace, making it impossible to reference it within another type. Let's look at how this variable could be used:

```
A_CONSTANT = 0

module Foo; end

{% if @top_level.has_constant?("A_CONSTANT") && @top_level
  .has_constant?("Foo") %}
  puts "this is printed"
```

```
{% else %}
  puts "this is not printed"
{% end %}
```

In this example, we made use of `TypeNode#has_constant?`, which returns `BoolLiteral` if the related `TypeNode` has the provided constant, supplied either as `StringLiteral`, `SymbolLiteral`, or `MacroId` (the type you get from calling `#id` on another type). This method works for both actual constants as well as types.

Understanding the macro API is critical to being able to write macros that make use of information derived from a type and/or method. I would highly suggest reading through the API documentation for some of the macro types we talked about in this section to fully understand what methods are available.

Before we move on to the next section, let's apply what we have learned so far to recreate the standard library's `property` macro.

Recreating the property macro

Commonly, the `property` macro accepts a `TypeDeclaration` instance that represents the name, type, and default value, if any, of an instance variable. The macro uses this definition to generate an instance variable, as well as a getter and setter for it.

The `property` macro also handles a few additional use cases, but for now, let's focus on the most common one. Our implementation of this macro would look like this:

```
macro def_getter_setter(decl)
  @{{decl}}

  def {{decl.var}} : {{decl.type}}
    @{{decl.var}}
  end

  def {{decl.var}}=(@{{decl.var}} : {{decl.type}})
  end
end
```

We can define the instance variable by using `@{{decl}}` because it will expand to the proper format automatically. We could have also used `@{{decl.var}} : {{decl.type}}`, but the other way was shorter and handles default values better. The longer form would need to explicitly check for and set the default value, if any, while the shorter form handles that for us. However, the fact that you can reconstruct a node manually using the methods it exposes is not a coincidence. AST nodes are abstract representations of something within a program, such as the declaration of a type, or a method, or the expression of an `if` statement, so it only makes sense that you can construct what the node represents using the node itself.

The rest of our `def_getter_setter` macro builds out the getter and setter methods for the defined instance variable. From here, we can go ahead and use it:

```
class Foo
  def_getter_setter name : String?
  def_getter_setter number : Int32 = 123
  property float : Float64 = 3.14
end


obj = Foo.new


pp obj.name
obj.name = "Bob"
pp obj.name


pp obj.number
pp obj.float
```

Running this program would result in the following output:

```
nil
"Bob"
123
3.14
```

And there you have it! A successful reimplementation of the most common form of the `property` macro! Here, it is easy to see how macros can be used to reduce the amount of boilerplate and repetition within your application.

The last macro concept we are going to discuss in this chapter is macro hooks, which allow us to tap into various Crystal events.

Exploring macro hooks

Macro hooks are special macro definitions that are invoked by the Crystal compiler in some situations at compile time. These include the following:

- `inherited` is invoked when a subclass is defined, where `@type` is the inheriting type.

- `included` is invoked when a module is included, where `@type` is the including type.

- `extended` is invoked when a module is extended, where `@type` is the extending type.

- `method_missing` is invoked when a method is not found and is passed a single `Call` argument.

- `method_added` is invoked when a new method is defined in the current scope and is passed a single `Def` argument.

- `finished` is invoked after the semantic analysis phase, so all the types and their methods are known.

The first three and `finished` definitions are the most common/useful ones, so we are going to focus on those here. The first three hooks all work essentially the same – they just execute in different contexts. For example, the following program demonstrates how they work by defining various hooks and printing a unique message when that hook is executed:

```
abstract class Parent
  macro inherited
    puts "#{{{@type.name}}} inherited Parent"
  end
end

module MyModule
  macro included
    puts "#{{{@type.name}}} included MyModule"
  end

  macro extended
    puts "#{{{@type.name}}} extended MyModule"
  end
```

```
end

class Child < Parent
  include MyModule
  extend MyModule
end
```

The preceding code would print the following output:

Child inherited Parent
Child included MyModule
Child extended MyModule

These hooks can be quite helpful when you want to add methods/variables/constants to another type in cases where normal inheritance/module semantics would not work. An example of this is where you want to add both instance and class methods to a type when a module is included. Because of how module inclusion/extension works, there is currently no way to add both types of methods to a type from a single module.

A workaround is to nest another ClassMethods module within the primary one. However, this would require the user to manually include the primary module and extend the nested module, which is not the greatest user experience. A better option would be to define a macro included hook in the primary module that extends the ClassMethods module. This way, the macro will expand within the included class, automatically extending the class methods module. This would look something like this:

```
module MyModule
  module ClassMethods
    def foo
      "foo"
    end
  end

  macro included
    extend MyModule::ClassMethods
  end

  def bar
    "bar"
  end
end
```

```
end

class Foo
  include MyModule
end

pp Foo.foo
pp Foo.new.bar
```

This way, the user only needs to include the module to get both types of methods, resulting in an overall better user experience.

`macro finished` is primarily used when you want to execute some macro code *only* after Crystal is aware of all of the types. In some cases, not having your macro code in a finished hook could result in incorrect results. Stay tuned! We will cover this in more detail in *Chapter 15, Documenting Code.*

Summary

Metaprogramming is one area where Crystal excels. It provides us with a pretty powerful system that can be used for code generation and reducing boilerplate/repetition, while still being fairly simple compared to other languages. However, this power should be used sparingly when appropriate.

In this chapter, we learned how and when to use macros to reduce boilerplate, how to tap into various Crystal events via macro hooks, and were introduced to the macro API to support creating more advanced macros.

In the next chapter, we are going to look at annotations and how they can be used in conjunction with macros to store data that can be read at compile time.

11
Introducing Annotations

As mentioned in the previous chapter, macros can be a powerful tool for generating code in order to reduce duplication and keep your application DRY. However, one of the limitations of macros, especially those outsides of a macro definition, is that it is challenging to access data to use within the macro since it must be accessible at compile time, like an environmental variable or constant.

Neither of these are great options most of the time. In order to better solve this, we need to explore the next Crystal metaprogramming concept: **annotations**.

We will cover the following topics in this chapter:

- What are annotations?
- Storing data within annotations
- Reading annotations

By the end of this chapter, you should have a solid understanding of what annotations are and how to use them.

Technical requirements

The requirement for this chapter is as follows:

- A working installation of Crystal

You can refer to *Chapter 1*, *An Introduction to Crystal*, for instructions on getting Crystal set up.

All of the code examples used in this chapter can be found in the Chapter 11 folder on GitHub: https://github.com/PacktPublishing/Crystal-Programming/tree/main/Chapter11.

What are annotations?

Simply put, an **annotation** is a way to attach metadata to certain features in the code that can subsequently be accessed at compile time within a macro. Crystal comes bundled with some built-in annotations that you may have already worked with, such as @[JSON::Field] or the @[Link] annotation, which was covered in *Chapter 7*, *C Interoperability*. While both of these annotations are included by default, they do differ in regard to their behavior. For example, the JSON::Field annotation exists in Crystal's standard library and is implemented/used in a way that you could replicate in your own code with your own annotation. The Link annotation, on the other hand, has a special relationship with the Crystal compiler and some of its behavior cannot be reproduced in user code.

Custom annotations can be defined via the annotation keyword:

```
annotation MyAnnotation; end
```

That is all there is to it. The annotation could then be applied to various items, including the following:

- Instance and class methods
- Instance variables
- Classes, structs, enums, and modules

An annotation can be applied to various things by putting the name of the annotation within the square brackets of the @[] syntax, as in the following example:

```
@[MyAnnotation]
def foo
  "foo"
```

```
end

@[MyAnnotation]
class Klass
end

@[MyAnnotation]
module MyModule
end
```

Multiple annotations may also be applied to the same item:

```
annotation Ann1; end
annotation Ann2; end

@[Ann1]
@[Ann2]
@[Ann2]
def foo
end
```

In this specific context, it does not really make sense to use more than one annotation as there is not a way to tell them apart; however, it will make more sense when you add data to the annotation, which is the topic of the next section.

Okay, so annotations are something that can be applied to various things in code to store metadata about it. *But what are they actually good for?* The main benefit they provide is that they are implementation-agnostic. In other words, this means you can just annotate something and a related library could read the data from it without needing a dedicated macro definition in order to create the instance variable, method, or type.

An example of this would be, say you have an ORM model that you want to be *validatable*. For example, if one of the libraries you have installed uses a custom macro such as `column id : Int64`, it may make the other libraries non-functional because the annotation may not be correctly applied to the instance variable or method. However, if all of the libraries make use of annotations, then they are all working with standard Crystal instance variables, so there is no possibility for libraries to conflict and it makes things look more natural.

Additionally, annotations are more futureproof and flexible compared to macro definitions for this specific use case. Next, let's talk about how to store data within an annotation.

Storing data within annotations

Similar to a method, an annotation supports both positional and named arguments:

```
annotation MyAnnotation
end
```

```
@[MyAnnotation(name: "value", id: 123)]
def foo; end
```

```
@[MyAnnotation("foo", 123, false)]
def bar; end
```

In this example, we defined two empty methods, where each method has an annotation applied to it. The first one is solely using named arguments, while the second is using solely positional arguments. A better example of applying multiple annotations of the same type can be demonstrated when each annotation has data included within it. Here is an example:

```
annotation MyAnnotation; end
```

```
@[MyAnnotation(1, enabled: false)]
@[MyAnnotation(2)]
def foo
end
```

As the values on each annotation can be different, the related library could create multiple methods or variables, for example, based on each annotation and the data within it. However, this data isn't any good if you cannot access it! Let's take a look at how to do that next.

Reading annotations

In Crystal, you normally invoke a method on an object in order to access some data stored within. Annotations are no different. The Annotation type exposes three methods that can be used to access the data defined on the annotation in different ways. However, before you can access the data on the annotation, you need to get a reference to an Annotation instance. This can be accomplished by passing the Annotation type to the #annotation method defined on the types that support annotations, including TypeNode, Def, and MetaVar. For example, we can use this method to print the annotation applied to a specific class or method, if present:

```
annotation MyAnnotation; end
@[MyAnnotation]
class MyClass
  def foo
    {{pp @type.annotation MyAnnotation}}
    {{pp @def.annotation MyAnnotation}}
  end
end


MyClass.new.foo
```

The #annotation method will return NilLiteral if no annotation of the provided type is applied. Now that we have access to the applied annotation, we are ready to start reading data from it!

The first, most straightforward way is via the #[] method, which may look familiar as it is also used as part of the Array and Hash types, among others. This method has two forms, with the first taking NumberLiteral and returning the positional value at the provided index. The other form accepts StringLiteral, SymbolLiteral, or MacroId and returns the value with the provided key. Both of these methods will return NilLiteral if no value exists at the provided index, or with the provided key.

The other two methods, #args and #named_args, do not return a specific value, but instead return a collection of all of the positional or named arguments within the annotation as TupleLiteral and NamedTupleLiteral, respectively.

First up, let's see how we could work with data stored in a class, using the data from the annotation to construct some output:

```
annotation MyClass; end
Annotation MyAnnotation; end
@[MyClass(true, id: "foo_class")]
class Foo
  {% begin %}
    {% ann = @type.annotation MyClass %}
    {% pp "#{@type} has positional arguments of:
      #{ann.args}" %}
    {% pp "and named arguments of #{ann.named_args}" %}
    {% pp %(and is #{ann[0] ? "active".id : "not
      active".id}) %}
    {% status = if my_ann = @type.annotation MyAnnotation
                  "DOES"
                else
                  "DOES NOT"
                end %}
    {% pp "#{@type} #{status.id} have MyAnnotation applied." %}
  {% end %}
end
```

Running this program would output the following:

```
"Foo has positional arguments of: {true}"
"and named arguments of {id: \"foo_class\"}"
"and is active."
"Foo DOES NOT have MyAnnotation applied."
```

We can also do a similar thing with an annotation applied to a method:

```
annotation MyMethod; end

@[MyMethod(4, 1, 2, id: "foo")]
def my_method
  {% begin %}
    {% ann = @def.annotation MyMethod %}
```

```
      {% puts "\n" %}
      {% pp "Method #{@def.name} has an id of #{ann[:id]}" %}
      {% pp "and has #{ann.args.size} positional arguments" %}
      {% total = ann.args.reduce(0) { |acc, v| acc + v } %}
      {% pp "that sum to #{total}" %}
   {% end %}
 end


 my_method
```

Running this program would output the following:

```
"Method my_method has an id of \"foo\""
"and has 3 positional arguments"
"that sum to 7"
```

In both of these examples, we made use of all three methods, as well as some of the collection types themselves. We also saw how to handle an optional annotation by following similar `nil` handling logic as you would in your non-macro Crystal code. If our class did have the annotation applied, we could access any additional data from it via the `my_ann` variable, much as we did with the `ann` variable on the previous lines. This pattern can be incredibly useful to allow the macro logic to be influenced by the presence or absence of the annotation. This can lead to more readable code that otherwise would require a single annotation with many different fields.

Related to the earlier example of multiple annotations on a single item, the `#annotation` method returns the *last* annotation applied to a given item. If you want to access *all* of the applied annotations, you should use the `#annotations` method instead. This method works almost identically to the other method but returns `ArrayLiteral(Annotation)` instead of `Annotation?`. For example, we could use this method to iterate over multiple annotations in order to print the index of the annotation along with the value that it is storing:

```
annotation MyAnnotation; end


@[MyAnnotation("foo")]
@[MyAnnotation(123)]
@[MyAnnotation(123)]
def annotation_read
   {% for ann, idx in @def.annotations(MyAnnotation) %}
```

```
    {% pp "Annotation #{idx} = #{ann[0].id}" %}
  {% end %}
end


annotation_read
```

Running this would print the following:

```
"Annotation 0 = foo"
"Annotation 1 = 123"
"Annotation 2 = 123"
```

That is all there is to it. Annotations themselves are a pretty simple feature but can be quite powerful when paired with some other Crystal metaprogramming features.

Summary

In this chapter, we looked at how to define and use annotations to augment various Crystal features with additional metadata, including how to store both named and positional arguments, how to read single and multiple annotations, and what advantages/ use cases annotations fulfill over macros.

Annotations are a vital metaprogramming feature that we will definitely make use of in the coming chapters. Up until now, all of the macro code we have written when accessing type or method data has been in the context of that type or method.

In the next chapter, we are going to explore the compile-time type introspection feature of Crystal, which will introduce new ways to access the same information.

12
Leveraging Compile-Time Type Introspection

In the previous chapters, we have mainly been using macros within types and methods themselves in order to access compile-time information or read annotations. However, this greatly reduces the effectiveness of macros to be able to dynamically react as new types are added or annotated. The next Crystal metaprogramming concept that we are going to take a look at is that of **compile-time type introspection**, which will cover the following topics:

- Iterating type variables
- Iterating types
- Iterating methods

By the end of this chapter, you should be able to create macros that generate code using instance variables, methods, and/or type information along with data read off of annotations.

Technical requirements

The requirement for this chapter is as follows:

- A working installation of Crystal

You can refer to *Chapter 1*, *An Introduction to Crystal*, for instructions on getting Crystal set up.

All the code examples used in this chapter can be found in the `Chapter 12` folder on GitHub: `https://github.com/PacktPublishing/Crystal-Programming/tree/main/Chapter12`.

Iterating type variables

One of the most common use cases for type introspection is that of iterating over a type's instance variables. The simplest example of this would be adding a `#to_h` method to an object that returns `Hash` using the type's instance variables for the key/values. This would look like this:

```crystal
class Foo
  getter id : Int32 = 1
  getter name : String = "Jim"
  getter? active : Bool = true

  def to_h
    {
      "id"     => @id,
      "name"   => @name,
      "active" => @active,
    }
  end
end

pp Foo.new.to_h
```

Which, when executed, would print the following:

```crystal
{"id" => 1, "name" => "Jim", "active" => true}
```

However, this is less than ideal because you need to remember to update this method *every time* an instance variable is added or removed. It also does not handle the case where this class is extended, and more instance variables are added.

We could improve it by using a macro to iterate over the instance variables of the type in order to build out the hash. The new #to_h method would look like this:

```
def to_h
  {% begin %}
    {
      {% for ivar in @type.instance_vars %}
        {{ivar.stringify}} => @{{ivar}},
      {% end %}
    }
  {% end %}
end
```

If you remember from *Chapter 10, Working with Macros*, we need to wrap this logic within begin/end in order to make everything a valid Crystal syntax. We then use the #instance_vars method on the TypeNode instance retrieved via the special @type macro variable. This method returns Array(MetaVar), which includes information about each instance variable, such as its name, type, and default value.

Finally, we iterate over each instance variable using a for loop, using a string representation of the instance variable's name as the key, and, of course, its value as the value of the hash. Running this version of the program results in the same output as before, but with two major benefits:

- It automatically handles newly added/removed instance variables.
- It would include instance variables defined on child types since the macro expands for each concrete subclass because it uses the @type macro variable.

Similar to iterating instance variables, class variables may also be accessed via the TypeNode#class_vars method. However, there is one major gotcha when wanting to iterate over a type's instance/class variables.

> **WARNING**
> Instance variables can only be accessed in the context of a method. Trying to do so outside of a method will always result in an empty array, even if used within a macro finished hook.

This is basically a limitation of the Crystal compiler at the moment, which *may* be implemented in some form in the future. But, until then, it is best to keep this in mind to avoid wasting time debugging something that just isn't going to work. Check out `https://github.com/crystal-lang/crystal/issues/7504` for more information on this limitation.

Another use case for iterating instance variables is to opt-in instance variables to some external logic that could be included by a module. For example, say we have an `Incrementable` module that defines a single `#increment` method that, as the name applies, will increment certain opted-in variables. The implementation of this method could use `@type.instance_vars` along with `ArrayLiteral#select` to determine which variables should be incremented.

First up, let's look at the code for the `Incrementable` module:

```
module Incrementable
  annotation Increment; end

  def increment
    {% for ivar in @type.instance_vars.select &.annotation
          Increment %}
      @{{ivar}} += 1
    {% end %}
  end
end
```

We first define our module, along with an annotation within it. We then define the method that filters the type's instance variables to only the ones that have the annotation applied. For each of those variables, we increment it by one. Next, let's take a look at the type that will include this module:

```
class MyClass
  include Incrementable

  getter zero : Int32 = 0

  @[Incrementable::Increment]
  getter one : Int32 = 1
```

```
    getter two : Int32 = 2

    @[Incrementable::Increment]
    getter three : Int32 = 3
  end
```

This is a pretty simple class that just includes our module, defines some instance variables via the `getter` macro, and applies the annotation defined within the module to a couple of variables. We can test our code by creating and running the following small program:

```
obj = MyClass.new

pp obj

obj.increment

pp obj
```

In this program, we are creating a new instance of our class we defined in the last example, printing the state of that object, calling out the `increment` method, and then printing the state of the object again. The first line of output shows that each instance variable's value matches the name of the variable. However, the second line of output shows that variables `one` and `three` have indeed been incremented by one.

Granted, this example is pretty trivial, but the applications can be much more complex and powerful, which we will touch on a bit more in the next chapter. Until then, let's move on from iterating instance/class variables to how to iterate types.

Iterating types

Much of what we talked about and demonstrated in the last section can also be applied to types themselves. The one major benefit of iterating over types is that they are not constrained by the same limitation as instance variables are. In other words, you *don't* need to be in the context of a method in order to iterate over types. Because of this, the possibilities are almost endless!

You could iterate types within the context of another class to generate code, iterate on the top level to generate additional types, or even within a method to build out a sort of pipeline using annotations to define the order.

In each of these contexts, any data that is available at compile time could be used to alter how the code gets generated, such as environmental variables, constants, annotations, or data extracted from the type itself. All in all, it is a very powerful feature that has a lot of useful applications. But before we can start to explore some of those use cases, we first need to learn how types can be iterated. There are four primary ways in which types can be iterated:

1. Over all or direct subclasses of a parent type
2. Over types that include a specific module
3. Over types that apply specific annotation(s)*
4. Some combination of the previous three ways

The first two are pretty self-explanatory. The third method has an *asterisk* as there is a catch that we will discuss a bit later in the chapter. The fourth deserves some further explanation. It basically means that you can use a combination of the first three to filter down further to the types you want. An example of this could be iterating over all types that inherit from a specific base class *and* that have a specific annotation applied that has a field with a specific value.

The most common way of iterating over types is via the subclasses of a parent type. This could either be *all* subclasses of that type, or only the direct subclasses. Let's take a look at how you would go about doing it.

Iterating a type's subclasses

Before we get into more complex examples, let's focus on a simpler use case of iterating over subclasses of a type using the following inheritance tree:

```
abstract class Vehicle; end
abstract class Car < Vehicle; end

class SUV < Vehicle; end

class Sedan < Car; end
class Van < Car; end
```

The first thing we need is `TypeNode` of the parent type whose subclasses we want to iterate over. In our case, it will be `Vehicle`, but it does not necessarily have to be the topmost type. We could have just as easily picked `Car` if that was better suited to our needs.

If you remember back to the first chapter in this part, we were able to obtain `TypeNode` using the special `@type` macro variable. However, this would only work if we wanted to iterate over the types in the context of the `Vehicle` type. If you want to iterate outside of that type, you will need to use the full name of the parent type.

Once we have `TypeNode`, there are two methods we could use depending on exactly what we want to do. `TypeNode#subclasses` can be used to get the direct subclasses of that type. `TypeNode#all_subclasses` can be used to get all the subclasses of that type, including subclasses of the subclasses, and so on. For example, add the following two lines to a file, along with the inheritance tree shown previously:

```
{{pp Vehicle.subclasses}}
{{pp Vehicle.all_subclasses}}
```

Compiling the program will result in two lines being printed to the console, the first being `[Car, SUV]` and the second `[Car, Sedan, Van, SUV]`. The second line is longer because it is also including subclasses of the `Car` type, which is not included in the first line because `Van` and `Sedan` are not direct children of the `Vehicle` type.

Also notice that the array contains both concrete and abstract types. It is worth pointing this out because if you wanted to iterate over the types and instantiate them, it would fail because the abstract `Car` type would be included. In order for this example to work, we need to filter the list of types down to those that are non-abstract. Both methods in the earlier example return `ArrayLiteral(TypeNode)`. Because of this, we can leverage the `ArrayLiteral#reject` method to remove abstract types. The code for this would look like this:

```
{% for type in Vehicle.all_subclasses.reject &.abstract? %}
   pp {{type}}.new
{% end %}
```

Running this would ultimately print a new instance of the `Sedan`, `Van`, and `SUV` types. We can take this idea of filtering a step further to include more complex logic, such as using annotation data in determining whether a type should be included.

For example, say we wanted to get a subset of types that have an annotation, excluding those with a specific annotation field. For this example, we will be using the following types:

```
annotation MyAnnotation; end
```

```
abstract class Parent; end
```

```
@[MyAnnotation(id: 456)]
class Child < Parent; end

@[MyAnnotation]
class Foo; end

@[MyAnnotation(id: 123)]
class Bar; end

class Baz; end
```

We have five classes, including one abstract. We also defined an annotation and applied it to some of the types. Additionally, some of those annotations also include an `id` field that is set to some number. Using these classes, let's iterate over only the ones that have an annotation and either no `id` field or an ID that is an even number.

Notice, however, unlike the previous examples, that there is no direct parent type that all types inherit from, nor is there a specific module that is included in each. *So how are we going to filter down to the type we want?* This is where the asterisk from the beginning of the chapter comes into play. There is not a direct way to simply get all types with a specific annotation yet. However, we can use the same pattern of iterating over all subclasses of a type in order to replicate this behavior.

Iterating types with a specific annotation

In Crystal, `Object` is the topmost type of all types. Because *all* types implicitly inherit from this type, we can use it as the base parent type to filter down to the types we want.

However, since this approach needs to iterate over *all* types, it is much less efficient than a more focused approach. In the future, there may be a better way to go about it, but for now, depending on the exact use case/API you want to support, this is a decent workaround.

For example, this approach is required if the types you want to iterate over do not already share some sort of common user-defined type and/or included module. However, because this type is also the parent type to types in the standard library, you will need to have some way to filter it down, such as via an annotation.

The code to actually do the filtering looks similar to previous examples, just with a bit more complex filtering logic. Ultimately, it would look like the following:

```
{% for type in Object.all_subclasses.select { |t| (ann =
   t.annotation(MyAnnotation)) && (ann[:id] == nil || ann[:id]
     % 2 == 0) } %}
  {{pp type}}
{% end %}
```

We are using `ArrayLiteral#select` in this case because we only want the types for which this block returns `true`. The logic mirrors the requirements we mentioned earlier. It selects types that have our annotation, and either do not have an `id` field or an `id` field with an even number. Building this example would correctly print the expected types: `Child` and `Foo`.

Iterating types that include a specific module

The third way we can iterate types is by querying for those types that include a specific module. This can be achieved via the `TypeNode#includers` method, where `TypeNode` represents the module, for example:

```
module SomeInterface; end

class Bar
  include SomeInterface
end

class Foo; end

class Baz
  include SomeInterface
end

class Biz < Baz; end

{{pp SomeInterface.includers}}
```

Building this program would output the following:

```
[Bar, Baz]
```

The one thing to note when using the #includers method is that it *only* includes types that directly include this module, not any types that then inherit from it. However, it would be possible to then call #all_subclasses on each type returned via #includers if that fits your use case. Of course, any of the previously mentioned filtering logic also applies here since #includers returns ArrayLiteral(TypeNode).

In all of these examples, we have started with a base parent type and worked our way down through all of that type's subclasses. It is also possible to do the opposite; start at a child type and iterate through its ancestors. For example, let's look at the ancestors of the Biz class by adding the following code to our program and running it:

```
{{pp Biz.ancestors}}
```

This should output the following:

```
[Baz, SomeInterface, Reference, Object]
```

Notice we get the direct parent type, the module that its superclass includes, and some of the implicit superclasses of the type, including the aforementioned Object type. Once again, the #ancestors method returns ArrayLiteral(TypeNode), so it could be filtered as we have in previous examples.

The next metaprogramming feature we are going to look at is how to iterate over the methods of a type.

Iterating methods

Iterating methods have a lot in common with iterating types, just with a different macro type. The first thing we need in order to iterate over methods is TypeNode, representing the type whose methods we are interested in. From there, we can call the #methods method, which returns ArrayLiteral(Def) of all the methods defined on that type. For example, let's print an array of all the method names within a class:

```
abstract class Foo
   def foo; end
end
```

```
module Bar
  def bar; end
end

class Baz < Foo
  include Bar

  def baz; end

  def foo(value : Int32); end

  def foo(value : String); end

  def bar(x); end
end

baz = Baz.new
baz.bar 1
baz.bar false

{{pp Baz.methods.map &.name}}
```

Running this would output the following:

```
[baz, foo, foo, bar]
```

Notice that similar to the #includers method, only methods explicitly defined within the type are printed. Also notice that the #foo method is included once for each of its overloads. However, even though #bar is invoked with two unique types, it is only included once.

The filtering logic we talked about in the last section also applies to iterating methods. Checking for annotations can be an easy way to *mark* methods that some other construct should act upon. If you think back to the first section's Incrementable module, you could easily do something similar, but substituting instance variables with methods. Methods also have added flexibility since they do not need to be iterated in the context of a method.

If you remember the iterating instance variables section earlier in the chapter, there was a dedicated `TypeNode#class_vars` method to access class variables. In the case of class methods, there is no equivalent method. It is possible to iterate over them, however. The majority of the time, `TypeNode` is going to represent the instance type of a type, which is why it is used to iterate over the instance variables or instance methods of that type. However, there is a method that can be used to get another `TypeNode` that represents the **metaclass** of that type, from which we could access its class methods. There is also a method that will return the instance type if `TypeNode` represents the class type.

These methods are `TypeNode#class` and `TypeNode#instance`. For example, if you had `TypeNode` representing a `MyClass` type, the former method would return a new `TypeNode` representing `MyClass.class`, whereas the latter method would turn `MyClass.class` into `MyClass`. Once we have a `TypeNode` class type, it is then as simple as calling `#methods` on it; for example:

```
class Foo
  def self.foo; end
  def self.bar; end
end


{{pp Foo.class.methods.map &.name}}
```

Running this would output the following:

```
[allocate, foo, bar]
```

You may be wondering where the `allocate` method came from. This method is added automatically by Crystal for use within the constructor in order to allocate the memory required to instantiate it. Given you most likely do not want to include this method in your logic, be sure to have some way to filter it out.

As types themselves can be iterated, you could combine that concept with iterating methods. In other words, it is possible to iterate over types and then iterate over each of those type's methods. This can be incredibly powerful as a means of autogenerating code such that the end user only needs to apply some annotations or inherit/include some other type.

Summary

And there you have it; how to introspect instance/class variables, types, and methods at compile time! This metaprogramming technique can be used to create powerful code generation logic that can make applications easy to extend and use, all the while making the application more robust by reducing the chance of typos or user error.

Next up, in the final chapter of this part, we are going to look at some examples of how all of the metaprogramming concepts learned so far can be combined into more advanced patterns/features.

Further reading

As mentioned earlier, there are a lot more methods on `TypeNode` that are out of scope. However, I highly suggest checking out the documentation at `https://crystal-lang.org/api/Crystal/Macros/TypeNode.html` to learn more about what additional data could be extracted.

13
Advanced Macro Usages

In the last few chapters, we have looked at various metaprogramming concepts, such as macros, annotations, and how they can be used together to allow for introspecting types, methods, and instance variables at compile time. However, for the most part, we used them independently. These concepts can also be combined in order to allow for the creation of even more powerful patterns! In this chapter, we are going to explore a few of these, including:

- Using annotations to influence runtime logic
- Exposing annotation/type data at runtime
- Determining a constant's value at compile time
- Creating custom compile-time errors

By the end of this chapter, you should have a deeper understanding of metaprogramming in Crystal. You should also have some ideas of the non-directly apparent use cases for metaprogramming that will allow you to create unique solutions to problems in your application.

Technical requirements

Before we dive into the chapter, you'll need the following installed on your system:

- A working installation of Crystal

You can refer to *Chapter 1, An Introduction to Crystal*, for instructions on getting Crystal set up.

All of the code examples used in this chapter can be found in the `Chapter 13` folder on GitHub: `https://github.com/PacktPublishing/Crystal-Programming/tree/main/Chapter13`.

Using annotations to influence runtime logic

As we learned in *Chapter 11, Introducing Annotations*, annotations are a great way to add additional metadata to various Crystal features such as types, instance variables, and methods. However, one of their major limitations is that the data held within them is only available at compile time.

In some cases, you may want to implement a feature using *annotations* to customize something, but the logic that needs that data cannot be generated with macros alone and needs to execute at runtime. For example, say we wanted to be able to print instances of objects in various formats. This logic could use annotations to mark which instance variables to expose, as well as configure *how* they get formatted. A high-level example of this would look like this:

```
annotation Print; end


class MyClass
  include Printable

  @[Print]
  property name : String = "Jim"

  @[Print(format: "%F")]
  property created_at : Time = Time.utc
```

```
  @[Print(scale: 1)]
  property weight : Float32 = 56.789
end


MyClass.new.print
```

Where the output of this could be the following:

```
---
name: Jim
created_at: 2021-11-16
weight: 56.8
---
```

In order to implement this, the printing logic needs to have access to both the annotation data and the value of the instance variable that should be printed. In our case, the Printable module takes care of this by defining a method that handles iterating over and printing each applicable instance variable. This would ultimately look like this:

```
module Printable
  def print(printer)
    printer.start
    {% for ivar in @type.instance_vars.select(&.annotation
      Print) %}
      printer.ivar({{ivar.name.stringify}}, @{{ivar.name.id}},
        {{ivar.annotation(Print).named_args.double_splat}})
    {% end %}
    printer.finish
  end

  def print(io : IO = STDOUT)
    print IOPrinter.new(io)
  end
end
```

The majority of the logic happens in the #print (printer) method. This method will print the starting pattern, which, in this case, is the three dashes. It then uses a macro for loop to iterate over the instance variables of the including type. The instance variables are filtered such that only those with the Print annotation are included. Then, for each of those variables, the #ivar method on the printer is called with the name and value of the instance variable as well as any named arguments defined on the annotation. Finally, it prints the ending pattern, which is also three dashes.

To support supplying values from the annotation, we are also leveraging the NamedTupleLiteral#double_splat method along with Annotation#named_args. This combination will provide any key/value pairs defined on the annotation as named arguments to the method call.

The #print (io) method serves as the main entry point to print an instance. It allows the provision of a custom I/O to which the data should be printed, but, by default, is STDOUT. The I/O is used to create another type that actually does the printing:

```
struct IOPrinter
  def initialize(@io : IO); end

  def start
    @io.puts "---"
  end

  def finish
    @io.puts "---"
    @io.puts
  end

  def ivar(name : String, value : String)
    @io << name << ": " << value
    @io.puts
  end

  def ivar(name : String, value : Float32, *, scale :
    Int32 = 3)
    @io << name << ": "
    value.format(@io, decimal_places: scale)
    @io.puts
```

```
    end

    def ivar(name : String, value : Time, *, format : String
      = "%Y-%m-%d %H:%M:%S %:z")
      @io << name << ": "
      value.to_s(@io, format)
      @io.puts
    end
  end
```

This type defines the start and end methods as well as an overload for each of the supported instance variable types, each with specific values and defaults related to that type. By using a separate type with overloads, we are able to catch mistakes earlier by them being compile-time errors, such as if you were to use the annotation on an unsupported type, or did not supply a value on the annotation for a required argument. This example goes to show how flexible and powerful Crystal's annotations can be when combined with other concepts such as composition and overloads. However, there are cases where you might want to separate the logic from the type itself, such as in order to keep things loosely coupled.

In the next section, we will take a look at how we can take what we have learned so far a step further by allowing annotation/type data to be used at runtime such that they could be used as and where needed.

Exposing compile-time data at runtime

As we left off in the previous section, exposing annotation data outside of the type itself can be a good way to keep things less coupled. This concept focuses on defining a struct that represents the parameters of the related annotation, along with other metadata related to the item the annotation was applied to.

If the struct representing the annotation's data has required parameters that are expected to be provided via the annotation, the program would not compile if those values were not provided. It also handles the case where the parameters have a default value. Additionally, if there is an unexpected field on the annotation, or an argument was not of the correct type, it would not compile either. This makes adding/removing properties from the struct far easier as they do not need to *all* be explicitly set within a `StringLiteral`.

There is currently a Crystal RFC that proposes making this pattern more of a built-in feature by making the annotation and the struct one and the same. See `https://github.com/crystal-lang/crystal/issues/9802` for more information.

There are a few ways to go about how to actually expose the structs:

- Define a method that returns an array of them.
- Define a method that returns a hash that exposes them by the instance variable's name.
- Define a method that accepts the name of the instance variable and returns it.

Each of these approaches has its pros and cons, but they all have something in common. There needs to be some entry point on the instance/type itself that exposes the data. The main reason for this is that instance variables can only be iterated in the context of a method.

Additionally, there are two main ways to handle the structs themselves. One option is to make the method an instance method and include the value of each instance variable within the struct. This approach has a few downsides, such as making it harder to memorize and does not handle updates very well. For example, you call the method and get a struct for a given instance variable, but then the value of that instance variable changes before the actual logic is executed. The value in the struct could only represent the value at the time the method was called.

Another approach is to make the method a lazily initialized memorized class method. This approach is ideal because:

1. It only creates the hash/array for types that are used instead of every type/instance.
2. It caches the structs so that they only need to be created once.
3. It makes more sense since the majority of the data is going to be specific to a given type, and not an instance of that type.

For the purposes of this example, we are going to create a module that defines the lazily initialized class method that will return a hash of that type's properties. But before we do that, let's spend a moment thinking about what data we want to store within our struct. Most commonly, the struct will represent an instance variable along with data from an annotation applied to it. In this case, our struct is going to have the following fields:

1. `name` – The name of the property
2. `type` – The type of property
3. `class` – The class the property is a part of

4. `priority` – An optional numeric value from the annotation

5. `id` – A required numeric value from the annotation

What data you need is, of course, highly dependent on the exact use case, but generally, name, type, and class are good to have in all cases. The type could either be that of the instance variable, or the return type of a method, for example.

We can make use of the `record` macro to make it super easy to create our struct. In the end, this would look like this:

```
abstract struct MetadataBase; end
record PropertyMetadata(ClassType, PropertyType, PropertyIdx)
  < MetadataBase,
  name : String,
  id : Int32,
  priority : Int32 = 0 do
  def class_name : ClassType.class
    ClassType
  end

  def type : PropertyType.class
    PropertyType
  end
end
```

We are making use of generics in order to provide the type of class and instance variable. We also have another generic variable that we will get into shortly. We exposed these generics as methods since the generic types will already be scoped to each instance, and as such there is no need to also store them as instance variables.

Each record will have a name and we also added our two extra properties to it. Since the `priority` value is optional, we made it have a default value of `0` while the ID is required so it does not have a default value.

Next up, we need to create the module that will build and expose the hash of property metadata. We can leverage some macro concepts we learned a few chapters ago, such as macro hooks and verbatim. This module would ultimately end up looking like this:

```
annotation Metadata; end

module Metadatable
```

```
macro included
  class_property metadata : Hash(String, MetadataBase) do
    {% verbatim do %}
      {% begin %}
        {
          {% for ivar, idx in @type.instance_vars.select &.
            annotation Metadata %}
            {{ivar.name.stringify}} => (PropertyMetadata(
              {{@type}}, {{ivar.type.resolve}},{{idx}}
            ).new({{ivar.name.stringify}},
              {{ivar.annotation(Metadata).named_args
              .double_splat}}
            )),
          {% end %}
        } of String => MetadataBase
      {% end %}
    {% end %}
  end
end
end
```

We are also making use of the block version of the `class_getter` macro to handle defining the lazy getter for us. The included hook is used to ensure the getter is defined within the class the module is included in. The verbatim and begin macro features are also used to ensure the child macro code executes within the context of the including type, not the module itself.

The actual macro logic is pretty simple, doing a lot of what we did in the previous section. In this example, however, we are also passing some generic values when instantiating our `PropertyMetadata` instance.

At this point, our logic is ready to try out. Create a class that includes the module and some properties that use the annotation, for example:

```
class MyClass
  include Metadatable

  @[Metadata(id: 1)]
  property name : String = "Jim"

  @[Metadata(id: 2, priority: 7)]
  property created_at : Time = Time.utc
  property weight : Float32 = 56.789
end


pp MyClass.metadata["created_at"]
```

If you were to run this program, you would see that it outputs a `PropertyMetadata` instance with both the values from the annotation and the instance variable itself set correctly. However there is still one thing we need to handle; how can we access the value of the related metadata instance? This is precisely what we are going to explore next.

Accessing the value

A little-known fact about generics is that you can also pass a number as the value of a generic argument. This is primarily to support the `StaticArray` type, which uses the syntax of `StaticArray(Int32, 3)` to denote a static array of three `Int32` values.

As mentioned earlier, our `PropertyMetadata` type has a third generic variable that we have been setting to the index of the related instance variable. The main use case for this is so that we can then use this to extract the value that the metadata instance represents in conjunction with another trick.

In case you were wondering, no, there is not a way to magically obtain the value out of thin air just because we have the index of the instance variable and `TypeNode` of the type it belongs to. We will need an actual instance of `MyClass` to extract from. To account for this, we have to add some additional methods to `PropertyMetadata`:

```
def value(obj : ClassType)
  {% begin %}
    obj.@{{ClassType.instance_vars[PropertyIdx].name.id}}
  {% end %}
```

```
  end

  def value(obj) : NoReturn
    raise "BUG: Invoked default value method."
  end
```

The other trick that makes this implementation possible is the ability to access instance variables of a type directly, even if they do not have a getter via the `obj.@ivar_name` syntax. I will preface this by saying you should not use this often, if ever, outside of very specific use cases such as this. It is an anti-pattern and should be avoided whenever possible. 99% of the time, you should instead define a getter method to expose an instance variable's value instead.

With that said, the implementation uses the index of the instance variable in order to access the name of it to use it to construct the earlier syntax. Because all of this happens at compile time, the actual method that gets added, for the `name` instance variable, for example, would be:

```
def value(obj : ClassType)
  obj.@name
end
```

We also defined another overload that raises an exception if you pass an object instance that is not of the same type as represented by the metadata instance. This is mainly to make the compiler happy when there is more than one `Metadatable` type. In practice, it should never happen as the end user would not be interacting with these metadata instances directly since it would be an internal implementation detail.

We can go ahead and try it out by adding the following to our program and running it:

```
my_class = MyClass.new

pp MyClass.metadata["name"].value my_class
```

You should see the value of the name property be printed in your terminal, which, in this case, would be `"Jim"`. There is one downside to this implementation. The type of value returned from the `#value` method will consist of a union of all properties that have the annotation with a given type. For example, `typeof(name_value)` would return `(String | Time)`, which results in an overall less efficient memory representation.

This pattern works great for allowing the implementation of powerful internal APIs, but should be used sparingly, nor used within a hot path of an application, or even publicly exposed for that matter.

If you remember back to *Chapter 9*, *Creating a Web Application with Athena*, where you were applying validation constraint annotations, Athena's Validator component is implemented using this pattern, albeit with quite a bit more complexity.

Granted, this is most likely not a pattern that you will need very often, if ever, but it is good to know if the need ever arises. It also is a good example of how powerful macros can be when you think slightly outside of the box. As an added bonus, we can once again take this pattern a step further.

Modeling an entire class

In the previous section, we looked at how we can use a struct to represent a specific item, such as an instance variable or method along with data from an annotation applied to it. Another pattern involves creating a dedicated type to contain this data instead of using an array or hash directly. This pattern can be useful for decoupling the metadata about a type from the type itself, as well as allowing the addition of more methods/properties without needing to pollute the actual type.

For this to work, you need to be able to iterate over the properties and build out the hash or array within another type's constructor. Even though there is a limitation on reading instance variables off of a type, it does not say that it *has* to be a method within the type itself. Given a constructor is just a method that returns `self`, that will not be an issue. Even so, we still need a reference to `TypeNode` of the type we are interested in.

Because macros have access to generic information, also when within the context of a method, we can have this `ClassMetadata` type accept a generic type argument in order to pass a reference to `TypeNode`. Additionally, we could continue to pass the generic type around to other types/methods that need it.

For example, using the same `PropertyMetadata` type as in the last section:

```
annotation Metadata; end
annotation ClassConfig; end


class ClassMetadata(T)
  def initialize
    {{@type}}


    {% begin %}
```

```
      @property_metadata = {
        {% for ivar, idx in T.instance_vars.select &.
          annotation Metadata %}
          {{ivar.name.stringify}} => (
            PropertyMetadata({{@type}}, {{ivar.type.resolve}},
              {{idx}}).new({{ivar.name.stringify}},
                {{ivar.annotation(Metadata).named_args
                  .double_splat}})
            ),
          {% end %}
        } of String => MetadataBase


      @name = {{ (ann = T.annotation(ClassConfig)) ?
        ann[:name] : T.name.stringify}}
    {% end %}
  end


  getter property_metadata : Hash(String, MetadataBase)
  getter name : String
end
```

Where the Metadatable module now looks like this:

```
module Metadatable
  macro included
    class_getter metadata : ClassMetadata(self) {
      ClassMetadata(self).new }
  end
end
```

Most of the logic is the same as in the previous example, except that instead of directly returning a hash, the .metadata method now returns an instance of ClassMetadata that exposes the hash. In this example, we also introduced another annotation to demonstrate how to expose data when an annotation could be applied to the class itself, such as customizing the name by using @[ClassConfig(name: "MySpecialName")].

In the next section, we are going to take a look at how you can use macros and constants together to *register* things that can be used/iterated over at a later point in time.

Determining a constant's value at compile time

Constants in Crystal are constant but not frozen. In other words, this means if you define a constant as an array, you would not be able to change its value to String, but you could push/pop values to/from the array. This, coupled with macros being able to access the constant's value, lead to a fairly common practice of using macros to mutate constants at compile time so that the values could later be used/iterated over in a finished hook.

With the introduction of annotations, this pattern is no longer as useful as it once was. However, it can still be helpful when you want to allow the user to be able to influence some aspect of your macro logic and there is no place to apply an annotation. One of the main benefits of this approach is that it can be called anywhere within the source code and still be applied, unlike annotations, which need to be applied to a related item.

For example, say we wanted to have a way to register types at compile time to allow them to be resolved by their string name at runtime. In order to implement this feature, we will define a constant as an empty array, and a macro that will push types to the array constant at compile time. We will then update the macro logic to check this array and skip instance variables with types that are included in the array. The first part of the implementation would look like this:

```
MODELS = [] of ModelBase.class

macro register_model(type)
  {% MODELS << type.resolve %}
end

abstract class ModelBase
end

class Cat < ModelBase
end

class Dog < ModelBase
end
```

Here we define the mutable constant that will contain the registered types, the types themselves, and the macro that will register them. We are also calling #resolve on the type passed to the macro because the type of the macro argument would be Path. The #resolve method resolves the path into TypeNode, which is what instance variable types are represented as. The #resolve method only needs to be used when the type is passed by name, such as an argument to a macro, while the @type macro variable will always be TypeNode.

Now that we have the registration side of things defined, we can move onto the runtime side. This part is simply a method that generates a case statement using the values defined within the MODELS constants, for example:

```
def model_by_name(name)
  {% begin %}
    case name
    {% for model in MODELS %}
      when {{model.name.stringify}} then {{model}}
    {% end %}
    else
      raise "model unknown"
    end
  {% end %}
end
```

From here we can go ahead and add the following code:

```
pp {{ MODELS }}
pp model_by_name "Cat"


register_model Cat
register_model Dog


pp {{ MODELS }}
pp model_by_name "Cat"
```

After running it, you will see the following printed to your terminal:

```
[]
Cat
[Cat, Dog]
Cat
```

We can see that the first array is empty because no types have been registered, even though the `"Cat"` string can be successfully resolved even when the related type is registered after it. The reason for this is that registration happens at compile time, while resolution happens at runtime. In other words, the model registration happens before the program ever starts to execute, no matter where in the source code the types are registered.

After registering the two types, we can then see that the MODELS array contains them. Finally, it shows once again that it was able to be resolved when called either before or after the registration of the related type. As mentioned earlier in this chapter, macros do not have the same sort of typing as normal Crystal code. Because of this, it is not possible to add type restrictions to macros. This means the user is free to pass whatever they want to the `.register_model` macro, which could result in not-so-obvious errors. For example, say they accidentally passed `"Time"` instead of `Time`, this would result in the following error: `undefined macro method 'StringLiteral#resolve'`. In the next section, we are going to explore a way to make the source of the error a bit more obvious.

Creating custom compile-time errors

Compile-time errors are one of the benefits of a compiled language. You are made aware of problems immediately versus needing to wait until that code is executed to find out there was a bug. However, because Crystal does not know the context around a specific error, it will always output the same error message for the same type of error. The last feature we are going to discuss in this chapter resolves around emitting your own custom compile-time errors.

Custom compile-time errors can be a great way to add additional information to the error message that makes the end user's life much easier by making it clearer what needs to be done to fix the problem. Going back to the example at the end of the last section, let's update our `.exclude_type` macro to provide a better error message if an unexpected type is passed.

In the past few chapters, we have made use of various top-level macro methods, such as #env, #flag, and #debug. Another top-level method is #raise, which will raise a compile-time error and allow the provision of a custom message. We can use this, with some conditional logic, to raise if the value passed to our macro is not Path. Our updated macro would look like this:

```
macro exclude_type(type)
  {% raise %(Expected argument to 'exclude_type' to be
    'Path', got '#{type.class_name.id}'.) unless type.is_a?
```

```
        Path %}
    {% EXCLUDED_TYPES << type.resolve %}
  end
```

Now, if we were to call the macro with `"Time"`, we would get an error:

```
In mutable_constants.cr:43:1


43 | exclude_type "Time"
     ^-----------
Error: Expected argument to 'exclude_type' to be 'Path',
   got 'StringLiteral'.
```

In addition to displaying our custom message, it also highlights the macro call that produced the error and shows the line number. However, there is one thing we can do to potentially improve this error even more.

All of the macro types we have worked with extend from a base `ASTNode` macro type that provides the base methods that are common to all nodes, which is where the `#id` method that we used a few times comes from. This type also defines its own `#raise` method, which works the same as the top-level one, but will highlight the specific node it was called on.

We can refactor our logic to use this by using `type.raise` instead of just `raise`. Unfortunately, in this case, the resulting error highlighting is the same. There are some outstanding bugs in Crystal related to this, so hopefully it improves over time. Regardless, it is still a good practice to follow as it both makes it more clear to the reader what the invalid value is, but also sets the code up to be future proof.

Restricting generic types

Generics in Crystal provide a good way of reducing duplication by allowing a type to be parameterized to support using it with multiple concrete types. A good example of this would be the `Array(T)`, or `Hash(K, V)` types. Crystal generics, however, do not currently provide a native way to restrict what types a generic type could be created with. Take the following code, for example:

```
abstract class Animal
end

class Cat < Animal
```

```
end

class Dog < Animal
end

class Food(T)
end

Food(Cat).new
Food(Dog).new
Food(Int32).new
```

In this example, there is a generic food type that should only accept a subclass of Animal. However, it is perfectly okay, by default, to be able to instantiate a Food instance using a non-Animal type, like Int32. We can use a custom compile-time error within the constructor of Food to ensure that T is a child of Animal. This would end up looking like this:

```
class Food(T)
  def self.new
    {% raise "Non animal '#{T}' cannot be fed." unless T <=
      Animal %}
  end
end
```

With this new code, trying to do Food(Int32).new would raise a compile-time error.

Being able to define your own custom compile time errors can go a long way in reducing the amount of time required to debug an issue. Otherwise, vague errors could be augmented with additional context/links, and overall made more user friendly.

Summary

Hurray! We have reached the end of the metaprogramming part of the book, covered a lot of content along the way, and showed off just how powerful Crystal macros can be. I am hopeful that you can apply your deeper understanding of macros and these patterns to solve challenging problems you may come across as part of your future projects.

In the next part, we are going to explore various Crystal supporting tools, such as how to test, document, and deploy your code, as well as how to automate that process!

Part 5: Supporting Tools

Crystal comes bundled with various supporting features and tooling to help with everything needed to create robust and usable applications, once the application itself has been written. This includes a testing framework to ensure the application continues to function as expected, and a documentation system to make it easier for others to learn how to use the application, and is supported by the nature of the language itself, which makes it easy to deploy. Let's get started!

This part contains the following chapters:

14
Testing

If you remember back in *Chapter 4, Exploring Crystal via Writing a Command-Line Interface*, a `spec/` folder was created when scaffolding the project. This folder contained all of the **tests** related to the application, but what are tests and why should I write them? Tests, in short, are an automated way to ensure your code is still working as intended. They can be immensely helpful as your application grows since the time and effort required to manually test everything for every change simply becomes infeasible. In this chapter, we will cover the following topics:

- Why test?
- Unit testing
- Integration testing

By the end of this chapter, you should understand the benefits of testing and how to write general unit tests and integration tests within the context of the Athena Framework.

Technical requirements

You will require the following for this chapter:

- A working installation of Crystal

You can refer to *Chapter 1, An Introduction to Crystal,* for instructions on getting Crystal set up.

All of the code examples used in this chapter can be found in the `Chapter 14` folder on GitHub at the following link:

`https://github.com/PacktPublishing/Crystal-Programming/tree/main/Chapter14`

Why test?

Within both of the two larger projects we worked through so far, and all of the other examples, we have been manually running them after changes were made to ensure they produced the expected output, such as returning the correct response, producing the desired transformation, or simply printing the correct value to the terminal.

This process is fine when there are only a handful of methods/flows. However, as the application grows, it can become infeasible to test each method or flow on its own after every change. Granted—you could revert to only testing things directly related to what you changed, but this could lead to missed bugs within other logic that makes use of it. **Testing** is a process of writing additional code that makes assertions in an automated fashion to ensure the code executes as expected.

Testing can also be a good way to ensure no that a change does not result in unintentionally breaking public **application programming interface** (**API**) of your application since the tests would be testing the public API and, by extension, the private API.

Some people—or companies—may be hesitant about spending additional time and money on something that brings essentially no value to the customer/user of the application. However, the little amount of time it would take to write some tests can end up saving countless hours in the long run by preventing bugs from making it into production.

There are various types of testing, each of which has its own goal. Some of these include the following:

- **Unit testing**: Testing a specific function/method in isolation
- **Integration testing**: Testing the integration of various types together, mocking external communications (database, external APIs, and so on)
- **Functional testing**: Similar to integration testing, but with less mocking and more specific assertions, such as a specific value returned from the database versus just asserting a query was made
- **End-to-end (E2E) testing**: Similar to functional testing, but usually including the **user interface** (**UI**) and absolute minimal mocking
- **Security testing**: Validating that there are no known security flaws within the code

Each of these types of testing has its pros, cons, and goals. However, we are going to be primarily focusing on the unit and integration/functional side of things, starting with unit testing.

Unit testing

Unit testing refers to when you want to test a specific method, whether it be on the top level or as part of an object, in isolation. Testing it in isolation is an important part of this type of testing. Doing this ensures that you are *only* testing the logic you want and not the logic of its dependencies.

Crystal comes bundled with the `Spec` module, which provides the tools required to test your code. For example, say you have the following method that returns the sum of two values as part of `add.cr`:

```
def add(value1, value2)
  value1 + value2
end
```

The related tests for this could look like this:

```
require "spec"
require "./add"

describe "#add" do
  it "adds with positive values" do
    add(1, 2).should eq 3
  end

  it "adds with negative values" do
    add(-1, -2).should eq -3
  end

  it "adds with mixed signed values" do
    add(-1, 2).should eq 1
  end
end
```

We first require the Spec module, and then use the #describe method to create a grouping of related tests—in this case, all the ones related to the #add method. We then use the #it method to define specific test cases in which we assert it returns the correct value. We have a few of these defined for example purposes. Ideally, you would have a test case for each flow that the code could go through, being sure to add new ones as bugs are fixed.

If you were testing this method as part of a shard, you would want to create a file within the spec/ folder, with a name that ends in _spec—such as spec/add_spec.cr. Normally, the tests follow the same organizational style as the source code, such as using the same subfolders and such. You would then be able to run crystal spec, which would run all the specs defined in the folder. Otherwise, you could also run this file as you would any other Crystal program if it is a one-off test. It is also suggested to use the --order=random option with crystal spec. This will run all the test cases in a random order, which can help identify cases where one spec requires a previous one to run first, which is not something you want.

The spec/spec_helper.cr file, which was generated by the crystal init command, is used as an entry point to a project's tests. This file usually requires spec, the source code of the project, as well as any other spec-specific files, such as fixtures or mocks. Global test helpers may also be defined here. Each test should require this file to have access to the Spec module and these other helpers.

In the previous example, we were only making use of the eq assertion, or that two values are equal. However, the Spec module provides many other assertions, as shown in the following example:

```
require "spec"

it do
  true.should be_true
  nil.should be_nil
  10.should be >= 5
  "foo bar baz".should contain "bar"
  10.should_not eq 5

  expect_raises Exception, "Err" do
    raise Exception.new "Err"
  end
end
```

Check out `https://crystal-lang.org/api/Spec/Expectations.html` for a full list. This example also demonstrates that an outer `#describe` block is not required. However, it is generally recommended to include one as it helps with the organization of your tests. An `#it` block *is* required, however, as failures will not be reported correctly without it.

As the amount of code in an application grows, so will the number of tests. This can make debugging specific test cases harder. In this case, the `focus: true` argument can be added to a `#describe` or `#it` block. This will only execute that one spec, as in the following example:

```
it "does something", focus: true do
    1.should eq 1
end
```

Just be sure to remove it before committing!

The `Spec` module also provides some additional methods that can be used to more precisely control the execution of your test cases. Some of these are listed here:

- `#pending`: This method is used to define a test case for something that is not fully implemented yet but will be in the future—for example, `pending "check cat" { cat.alive? }`. The block of the method is never executed but can be used to describe what the test should do.

- `#pending!`: The `#pending!` method is similar to the previous method but can be used to dynamically skip a test case. This can be useful for ensuring system-level dependencies/requirements are satisfied before running the test case.

- `#fail`: Lastly, this method can be used to manually fail a test case. This can be used in conjunction with custom conditional logic to create more complex assertions that the built-in ones cannot handle.

Tagging tests

Tags are a way to organize specs into groups, such that a subset of them could be executed. Similar to focusing a spec, tags are applied to either `#describe` or `#it` blocks via the `tags` argument, as follows:

```
require "spec"

describe "tags" do
  it "tag a", tags: "a" do
```

```
      end

    it "tag b", tags: "b" do
    end
  end
```

From here, you could use the `--tag` option via `crystal spec` to control which ones get executed, as outlined here:

- `--tag 'a' --tag 'b'` will include specs tagged with a *OR* b.

- `--tag '~a' --tag '~b'` will include specs not tagged with a *AND* not tagged with b.

- `--tag 'a' --tag '~b'` will include specs tagged with a, but not tagged with b.

The final command could end up looking like this: `crystal spec --tag 'a'`. Next up, we're going to take a look at how to handle inner object dependencies by creating mocks.

Mocking

The previous example with the `#add` method did not have any external dependencies, but remember in *Chapter 4, Exploring Crystal via Writing a Command-Line Interface,* how we made the `NotificationEmitter` type a constructor argument versus using it directly within the `#process` method? The `NotificationEmitter` type is a dependency of the `Processor` type.

The reason we made it a constructor argument is so that it follows our *SOLID design principles* (where **SOLID** stands for **single-responsibility principle, open-closed principle, Liskov substitution principle, interface segregation principle**, and **dependency inversion principle**), in turn making the type easier to test by allowing a mock implementation to be used in place of that argument. The mock allows you to assert it is called correctly and set it up to return values such that the test cases are the same each time.

Let's take a look at a simplified example here:

```
module TransformerInterface
  abstract def transform(value : String) : String
end


struct ShoutTransformer
```

```
  include TransformerInterface

  def transform(value : String) : String
    value.upcase
  end
end

class Processor
  def initialize(@transformer : TransformerInterface =
    ShoutTransformer.new); end

  def process(value : String) : String
    @transformer.transform value
  end
end


puts Processor.new.process "foo"
```

Here, we have a `TransformerInterface` type that defines the required
method each transformer must implement. We have a single implementation of it,
`ShoutTransformer`, that upcases—or converts—the value to uppercase letters.
We then have a `Processor` type that uses a `TransformerInterface` type as part of
its #process method, defaulting to the shout transformer. Running this program would
result in `FOO` being printed to your terminal.

Because we want to test our `Processor` type in isolation, we are going to create a mock
transformer implementation to use within our test. This ensures that we are not testing
more than is required. Have a look at the following example:

```
class MockTransformer
  include TransformerInterface

  getter transform_arg_value : String? = nil

  def transform(value : String) : String
    @transform_arg_value = value
  end
end
```

This implements the same API as the others but doesn't actually transform the value and just exposes it via an instance variable. We could then leverage this in a test as follows, being sure to also require `Processor` and `MockTransformer` if they are not defined within the same file:

```
require "spec"

describe Processor do
  describe "#process" do
    it "processes" do
      transformer = MockTransformer.new
      Processor.new(transformer).process "bar"
      transformer.transform_arg_value.should eq "bar"
    end
  end
end
```

Because the mock transformer stores the value, we can use it to ensure it was called with the expected value. This would catch the cases of it not being called or being called with an unexpected value, both of which would be bugs. The mock implementation also does not need to be private. It could be exposed as part of the project itself such that the end user could use it in their tests too.

Hooks

A core tenet of testing is that each test case is independent of the others, such as not relying on the state from a previous test. However, multiple tests may require the same state to test what they are focusing on. Crystal provides a handful of methods as part of the `Spec` module that can be used to define callbacks at certain points in the test life cycle.

These methods can be helpful in centralizing the setup/teardown of the required state for the tests. For example, say you wanted to ensure a global environmental variable was set before running any test, and a few test cases have another variable but not any of the other tests. To do this, you could leverage the `.before_suite`, `#before_each`, and `#after_each` methods. You can see an example of this in the following code snippet:

```
require "spec"

Spec.before_suite do
  ENV["GLOBAL_VAR"] = "foo"
```

```
end

describe "My tests" do
  it "parent1" do
    puts "parent test 1: #{ENV["GLOBAL_VAR"]?}
      - #{ENV["SUB_VAR"]?}"
  end

  describe "sub tests" do
    before_each do
      ENV["SUB_VAR"] = "bar"
    end

    after_each do
      ENV.delete "SUB_VAR"
    end

    it "child1" do
      puts "child test: #{ENV["GLOBAL_VAR"]?}
        - #{ENV["SUB_VAR"]?}"
    end
  end

  it "parent2" do
    puts "parent test 2: #{ENV["GLOBAL_VAR"]?}
      - #{ENV["SUB_VAR"]?}"
  end
end
```

This example does just what we want. The `.before_suite` method runs once before any test runs, while the `#before_each` and `#after_each` methods would run before/after each test case in the current context, such as a specific `#describe` block. Running it would result in it printing the following:

```
parent test 1: foo -
child test: foo - bar
parent test 2: foo -
```

A key thing to point out is that some of these methods exist both as instance methods and class methods. The class method versions will affect *all* test cases no matter where they are defined, while the instance method versions will be scoped to the current context.

Another type of hook is `around_*` methods. You can think of them as a combination of before/after methods, but allowing precise control over when, or if, a test or test group is executed. For example, we could simplify the inner `#describe` block of the earlier example by replacing the before/after hook with the following:

```
around_each do |example|
  ENV["SUB_VAR"] = "bar"
  example.run
  ENV.delete "SUB_VAR"
end
```

Unlike the other blocks, this method yields a `Spec::Example` type, which exposes information about the related test case, such as its description, tags, and whether it's focused. Also, unlike the other blocks, the test case must be manually executed via the `#run` method. Alternatively, it could not be executed at all, using the information from the example, or other external data to determine that.

While unit tests can be a good way to ensure specific parts of an application, they are not good at testing the interaction between those parts. For that, we will need to start making use of integration/functional tests.

Integration testing

The overall process of writing integration tests is very similar to unit testing. The same expectations are used, the same syntax can be used, and the general guidelines/organizational structure also remains the same. The main difference comes down to *what* is being tested. For example, in the previous section, we created a mock so that we could limit the scope of our test. However, in an integration test, you want to use mocks sparingly such that you fully test the real integration of your types within the application.

Mocks can still be useful in cases where there is external communication involved, such as with third-party API clients whereby you do not make real requests to their servers every time the tests are run. The database layer *could* also be mocked but using a real test database can be very helpful, given it is a core part of an application.

A common form of integration testing is within the context of a web framework. You make a request to one of your endpoints and assert that you get the expected response, either by checking the response body or just asserting that you get the expected status code. Let's use our blog application from *Chapter 9, Creating a Web Application with Athena*, and write some integration tests for it.

But before we get into writing our integration tests, we should spend some time taking a look at Athena's `Spec` component as it will be used to create integration tests, but can also be used for unit testing if so desired.

Athena's `Spec` component provides commonly useful testing methods as well as an alternate **domain-specific language** (**DSL**) for writing tests. Unlike other testing shards, the `Spec` component boils down to standard `Spec` module features, as opposed to rewriting how tests are written and run.

The primary goal of the `Spec` component is to promote reusability and extendibility by using a more **object-oriented programming** (**OOP**) approach. For example, say we have a `Calculator` type that has `#add` and `#subtract` methods that look like this:

```
struct Calculator
  def add(value1 : Number, value2 : Number) : Number
    value1 + value2
  end

  def substract(value1 : Number, value2 : Number) : Number
    value1 - value2
  end
end
```

An example test file using the `Spec` component for our `Calculator` type would look like this:

```
struct CalculatorSpec < ASPEC::TestCase
  @target : Calculator

  def initialize : Nil
    @target = Calculator.new
  end

  def test_add
    @target.add(1, 2).should eq 3
```

```
    end

    test "subtract" do
        @target.subtract(10, 5).should eq 5
    end
end
```

Each method starting with `test_` boils down to an `#it` method from the `Spec` module. The `test` macro can also be used to simplify the creation of these methods. Because the tests are defined within a struct, you can use inheritance and/or composition to allow the reuse of logic for groups of related tests. It also allows projects to expose abstract types that make creating tests for certain types easier. This is exactly the approach the Athena Framework took in regard to its `ATH::Spec::APITestCase` type. See `https://athenaframework.org/Framework/Spec/APITestCase/` and `https://athenaframework.org/Spec/TestCase/#Athena::Spec::TestCase` for more information.

Getting back to our blog's integration tests, let's start by testing the article controller by creating a new file to contain them: `spec/controllers/article_controller_spec.cr`. Then, add the following content to it:

```
require "../spec_helper"

struct ArticleControllerTest < ATH::Spec::APITestCase
end
```

We can also delete the default `spec/blog_spec.cr` file.

`APITestCase` provides a `#request` method that can be used to send requests to our API, but also provides helper methods for common **HyperText Transfer Protocol (HTTP)** verbs such as `#get` and `#post`. It is also implemented in such a way that no actual `HTTP::Server` type is needed. This allows you to test the application's logic in a faster, more reliable manner. However, as mentioned at the beginning of this chapter, E2E testing is also important in order to test the full interaction of the system.

Let's start by testing the endpoint to get a specific article by **identifier (ID)** by adding the following method within `ArticleControllerTest`:

```
def test_get_article : Nil
    response = self.get "/article/10"
    pp response.status, response.body
end
```

Before we can try out this test case, we first need to make `spec/spec_helper.cr` aware of the abstract test case type, as well as configure it to run our `Athena::Spec` component-based tests. Update `spec/spec_helper.cr` so that it looks like this:

```
require "spec"
require "../src/blog"


require "athena/spec"


ASPEC.run_all
```

In addition to requiring the `Spec` module and our blog's source code, we are also requiring the spec helpers provided by the `Framework` component. Lastly, we need to call `ASPEC.run_all` to ensure these types of tests actually run. However, since Athena's `Spec` component is optional, we do need to add it as a development dependency by adding the following code to your `shard.yml` file, followed by `shards install`:

```
development_dependencies:
  athena-spec:
    github: athena-framework/spec
    version: ~> 0.2.3
```

Running `crystal spec` highlights an issue with our test setup. The response to the request is entirely based on the state of your development database. For example, if you do not have a database created/running, you get a `500` HTTP response. If you happen to have an article with ID `10`, you will get a `200` response as it worked as expected.

Mixing your development database data with your test data is not a good idea as it makes things harder to manage and leads to less robust tests. To alleviate this, we are going to leverage the `test` schema created back in *Chapter 9*, *Creating a Web Application with Athena*. The set-up **Structured Query Language** (**SQL**) file set the owner to the same user as our development database so that we can reuse the same user. Because we also set things up to leverage an environmental variable, we do not need to change any code to support this. Simply export `DATABASE_URL=postgres://blog_user:mYAw3s0meB\!log@ localhost:5432/postgres?currentSchema=test`, and things should just work. Another thing we will need to do is handle creating tables as well as creating/removing fixture data. We are going to cheat a bit and leverage the raw Crystal DB API for this since it is a bit outside the scope of our `EntityManager` type.

As mentioned earlier in the chapter, we can leverage some of Crystal's `Spec` module callbacks to handle this. Let's get started by adding the following code to your `spec/spec_helper.cr` file:

```
DATABASE = DB.open ENV["DATABASE_URL"]

Spec.before_suite do
  DATABASE.exec File.read "#{__DIR__}/../db/000_setup.sql"
  DATABASE.exec "ALTER DATABASE \"postgres\" SET
    SEARCH_PATH TO \"test\";"
  DATABASE.exec File.read "#{__DIR__}/../db/001_articles.sql"
end

Spec.after_suite do
  DATABASE.exec "ALTER DATABASE \"postgres\" SET SEARCH_PATH TO
    \"public\";"
  DATABASE.close
end

Spec._each do

end
```

Here, we are creating a constant to represent a connection pool to our database. We are then defining a callback that runs once before any test executes. Within this callback, we are running our database migration files to ensure the schema and tables are in place before running the tests. We also execute a query to ensure that our tables/queries will be executed against our `test` schema. Finally, we have another callback that runs after all the tests have been executed to clean up a bit by resetting the search path back to the `public` schema and closing the connection pool.

Now that we have tables to store our data, we need to handle cleaning up, and we have already scaffolded out where we are going to do that. Update the `Spec.before_each` block so that it looks like this:

```
Spec.before_each do
  DATABASE.exec "TRUNCATE TABLE \"articles\" RESTART IDENTITY;"
end
```

Here, we are cleaning up any articles that may have been created as part of each integration test. By doing this here, we are able to ensure our tests will not interfere with one another.

At this point, if we were to run the specs again, we would now be met with a 404 error response since we did not do anything related to saving any article fixtures. Let's do that next.

To keep things focused and simple, we are just going to execute raw SQL inserts for the purposes of this chapter. Feel free to define some abstractions and helper methods, and leverage a third-party fixture library—or what have you—if you want.

Because we are automatically cleaning up our table after each test case, we can freely insert whichever data our specific test case requires. In our case, we need to insert an article with an ID of 10. We also should make some assertions against the response to ensure it is what we expect. Update our GET article test so that it looks like this:

```
def test_get_article : Nil
  DATABASE.exec <<-SQL
    INSERT INTO "articles" (id, title, body, created_at,
      updated_at) OVERRIDING SYSTEM VALUE
    VALUES (10, 'TITLE', 'BODY', timezone('utc', now()),
      timezone('utc', now())));
  SQL

  response = self.get "/article/10"

  response.status.should eq HTTP::Status::OK

  article = JSON.parse response.body
  article["title"].as_s.should eq "TITLE"
  article["body"].as_s.should eq "BODY"
end
```

Because of having GENERATED ALWAYS AS IDENTITY on the **primary key** (**PK**) in our tables, we need to include OVERRIDING SYSTEM VALUE within our INSERT statements to allow us to specify the ID we want.

In our GET article test, we are asserting that the request was successful and that it returns the expected data. We can also test the **HyperText Markup Language** (**HTML**) flow by setting an `accept` header as part of the request. Let's define another test case for that, as follows:

```
def test_get_article_html : Nil
  DATABASE.exec <<-SQL
    INSERT INTO "articles" (id, title, body, created_at,
      updated_at) OVERRIDING SYSTEM VALUE
    VALUES (10, 'TITLE', 'BODY', timezone('utc', now()),
      timezone('utc', now())));
  SQL

  response = self.get "/article/10", headers: HTTP::Headers
    {"accept" => "text/html"}

  response.status.should eq HTTP::Status::OK
  response.body.should contain "<p>BODY</p>"
end
```

We could also easily test the creation of an article, like this:

```
def test_post_article : Nil
  response = self.post "/article", body: %({"title":"TITLE",
    "body":"BODY"})

  article = JSON.parse response.body
  article["title"].as_s.should eq "TITLE"
  article["body"].as_s.should eq "BODY"
  article["created_at"].as_s?.should_not be_nil
  article["id"].raw.should be_a Int64
end
```

No matter which way you go about it, in the end, our article-controller integration tests turned out to be pretty simple and powerful. They provide a means to test the full flow of a request, including your listeners, param converters, and format handlers. It also allows the testing of any custom serialization or validation logic as part of the request/response payload.

Summary

Tests are one of those things that may seem like a waste of time to write but ultimately pay off in the long run in terms of time regained by preventing bugs from making it into production. The earlier you get test coverage on a type, the better.

In this chapter, we learned how to use the `Spec` module to write unit tests and the `Athena::Spec` component to write integration tests. Since these are the two most common types of tests, understanding how to write good tests—as well as learning the benefits of *why* writing tests is such a good idea—can be incredibly helpful in ensuring the overall reliability of an application.

In the next chapter, we are going to take a look at another thing that's just as important as tests—how to document your code/project.

15
Documenting Code

No matter how well implemented a **shard** is, if the user does not know how to use it, then they will not be able to make full use of it or will give up entirely. Having well-documented code can be just as important as having well-written or well-tested code. As suggested by `https://documentation.divio.com`, proper documentation for a software product should cover four separate areas:

- Tutorials
- How-to guides
- Explanations
- References

Each of these areas lets you consume the documentation, depending on what you want to do – for example, wanting to solve a specific problem versus figuring out the parameters to a specific method. While the first three are best handled via code, Crystal comes with some easy-to-use code documentation features that can make creating reference documentation pretty painless.

In this chapter, we are going to cover the following topics:

- Documenting Crystal code
- Documentation directives
- Generating the documentation

After completing this chapter, you should have an understanding of the tools and features you can use to document your code. This will ultimately allow the users of the shard to get up and running quickly, and easily learn how to use it.

Technical requirements

For this chapter, you will need a working installation of Crystal.

Please refer to *Chapter 1, An Introduction to Crystal*, for instructions on getting Crystal set up.

All the code examples for this chapter can be found in the `Chapter 15` folder in this book's GitHub repository: `https://github.com/PacktPublishing/Crystal-Programming/tree/main/Chapter15`.

Documenting Crystal code

Code comments that are added to types, methods, macros, and constants are counted as documentation comments. The compiler lets us extract the documentation to create an HTML website to present it. We will get into this later in this chapter.

For a comment to act as documentation, it must be applied directly above the item, without any empty lines. Empty lines are allowed but must also be prefixed with a # symbol so that the comment chain is not broken. Let's look at a simple example:

```
# This comment is not associated with MyClass.

# A summary of what MyClass does.
class MyClass; end
```

In this example, there are two comments: one is associated with `MyClass`, while the other is not. The first paragraph should be used as the summary, defining the purpose and functionality of the item. The **first paragraph** comprises all the text, up to a period or an empty comment line, as shown here:

```
# This is the summary
# this is still the summary
#
# This is not the summary.
def foo; end
```

```
# This is the summary.
# This is no longer the summary.
def bar; end
```

Here, the #foo method has a multiline summary that is ended by the empty new line. On the other hand, the #bar method uses a period to denote the end of the summary and the beginning of the body. Crystal generates HTML and JSON documentation based on the doc comments. More on how to actually generate the documentation later in the chapter, but for now let's just take a look at how it will look:

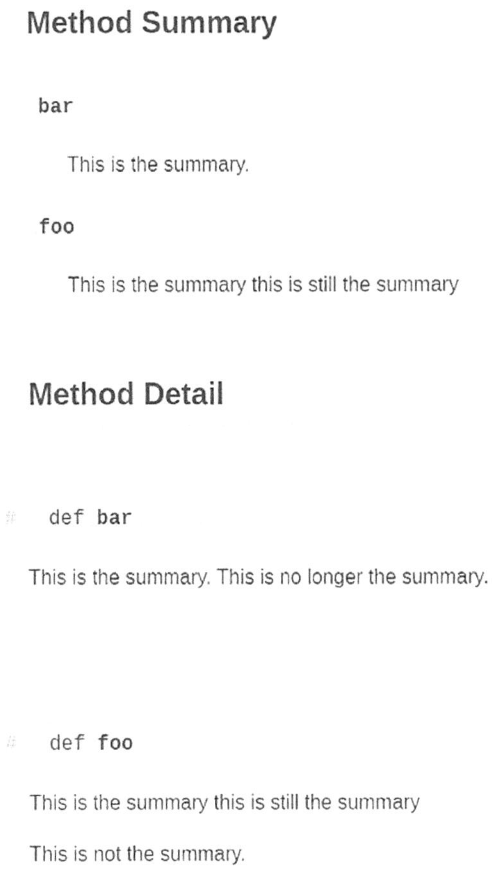

Method Summary

bar

This is the summary.

foo

This is the summary this is still the summary

Method Detail

def bar

This is the summary. This is no longer the summary.

def foo

This is the summary this is still the summary

This is not the summary.

Figure 15.1 – Generated method documentation

While having well-written summaries and descriptions can be invaluable, they are not isolated. Commonly, a method can accept/return instances of another type, or a type can be closely related to another. In such cases, being able to link them together can make navigating the documentation much easier.

Linking an API feature

An API feature can be linked to another by enclosing the feature in single backticks. Let's look at an example:

```
# Creates and returns a default instance of 'MyClass'.
def create : MyClass; end
```

These items are then automatically resolved and converted into links when the documentation is generated. Features within the same namespace can be linked with relative names:

- We can use `#foo` to reference an instance method
- We can use `.new` to reference a class method
- We can use `MyClass` to reference another type or constant

Features that are defined in other namespaces must use their fully-qualified paths; that is, `MyOtherClass#foo`, `MyOtherClass.new`, and `MyOtherClass::CONST`, respectively. Specific overloads can also be linked by using the full signature, such as `#increment` or `#increment(by)`.

If a method has a return type or if a parameter has a type restriction, Crystal will automatically link these to the related type if those types are defined within the same project. Types defined in Crystal's standard library or external shards are not linked by default.

If you want to add supplemental documentation to a method parameter, it is recommended that you italicize the name of the parameter, like so:

```
# Returns of sum of *value1* and *value2*.
def add(value1 : Int32, value : Int32); end
```

Documentation comments support most markdown features, such as code fences, ordered/unordered lists, headings, quotes, and more. Let's take a look at those next!

Formatting

One of the most common markdown features you will use when documenting code is **code fences**. These can be used to provide syntax highlighting for chunks of code that show how to use a method or type, as follows:

```
# ## Example
#
```

```
#  ''' 
#  value = 2 + 2 => 4
#  value #  : Int32
#  '''
module MyModule; end
```

The preceding code creates a subheading with a code fence. By default, the language of the fence is Crystal, but this can be overridden by explicitly tagging the language you wish to use, such as ```yaml. It is also a common practice to use `# => value` to denote the value of something within the code block. `# : Type` can also be used to show the type of a specific value.

Another reason to use the `# => value` syntax is to allow future tools to be used, which could run the example code and ensure that the output matches the expected output, ultimately leading to more reliable and robust documentation.

In some cases, you may wish to emphasize a particular sentence to denote that something needs to be fixed or warn the reader about something. Several **admonition keywords** can be used for this purpose, like so:

```
# Runs the application.
#
# DEPRECATED: Use '#execute' instead.
def run; end
```

The preceding example would generate documentation that looks like this:

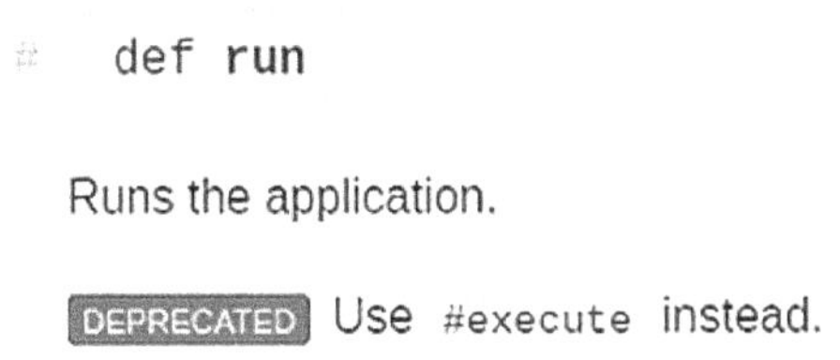

```
      def run
```

Runs the application.

DEPRECATED Use `#execute` instead.

Figure 15.2 – Example admonition usage

The admonition keyword must be the first word on the line and must be in uppercase. The colon is optional but is suggested for readability.

> **Tip**
>
> See `https://crystal-lang.org/reference/syntax_and_ semantics/documenting_code.html#admonitions` for the full list of admonition keywords.

In the previous example, we used the `DEPRECATED` admonition to denote a deprecated method. However, this only affects the generated documentation and will not help users identify deprecated methods/types unless they were to look at the documentation.

In cases where you want to fully deprecate a type or method, it is suggested to use *deprecated annotation* (`https://crystal-lang.org/api/Deprecated.html`). This annotation will add the `DEPRECATED` admonition for you, as well as provide compiler warnings to make it more obvious what is deprecated to the end user.

In addition to the various admonitions, Crystal also includes several directives that can be used in documentation comments and influence how the documentation gets generated. Let's take a look at those next.

Documentation directives

Crystal also provides several directives that inform the documentation generator how it should treat documentation for a specific feature. These include the following:

- `:ditto:`
- `:nodoc:`
- `:inherit:`

Let's take a closer look at what they do.

Ditto

The `:ditto:` directive can be used to copy the documentation from the previous definition, like so:

```
# Returns the number of items within this collection.
def size; end

# :ditto:
def length; end

# :ditto:
```

```
#
# Some information specific to this method.
def count; end
```

When the documentation is generated, `#length` would have the same sentence as `#size`. `#count` would also have this sentence, in addition to another sentence that's specific to that method. This can help reduce duplication for a series of related methods.

Nodoc

Documentation is only generated for the public API. This means that private and protected features are hidden by default. However, in some cases, a type or method cannot be private, but it still should not be considered as part of the public API. The `:nodoc:` directive can be used to hide public features from the documentation, like so:

```
# :nodoc:
#
# This is an internal method.
def internal_method; end
```

This directive *must* be on the first line. The following lines may still be used for internal documentation.

Inherit

Inheritance changes the way documentation is handled in some contexts. For example, if a method in the parent type has a documentation comment, it is automatically copied to the child method, assuming that the child method has the same signature and no documentation comment. The following is an example of this:

```
abstract class Vehicle
  # Returns the name of 'self'.
  abstract def name
end

class Car < Vehicle
  def name
    "car"
  end
end
```

Here, the documentation of `Car#name` would be as follows:

```
#   def name

Description copied from class Vehicle

Returns the name of self .
```

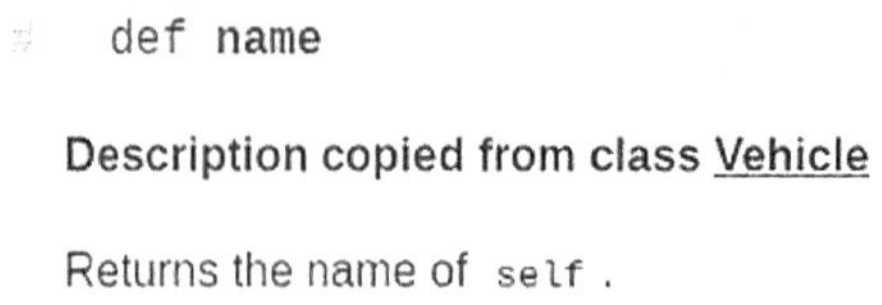

Figure 16.3 – Default documentation inheritance behavior

This feature makes it clear where the documentation is coming from, but in some cases, you may want to omit the `Description copied from ...` text. This can be accomplished by applying the `:inherit:` directive to the child method, like so:

```
class Truck < Vehicle
  # Some documentation specific to *name*'s usage within
  # 'Truck'.
  #
  # :inherit:
  def name : String
    "truck"
  end
end
```

In this case, because the `:inherit:` directive was used, the documentation of `Truck#name` would be as follows:

```
#   def name : String

Some documentation specific to name's usage within Truck .

Returns the name of self .
```

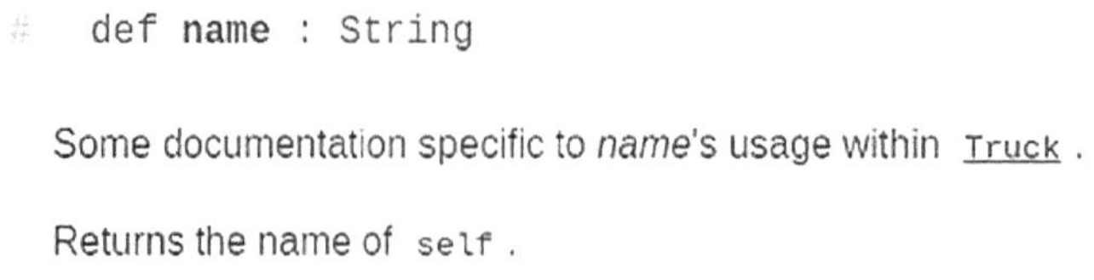

Figure 15.4 – Documentation inheritance behavior with :inherit:

> **Important Note**
> Inheriting documentation only works on instance and non-constructor methods.

This feature can be incredibly helpful in reducing duplication when there are a lot of child types or implementations of an interface.

While all the documentation we have been writing is important, it will not do much good if the user needs to look at the code itself to see it. To make it useful and available to users, it needs to be generated. Let's learn how to do that.

Generating the documentation

Similar to the `crystal spec` command we learned about in *Chapter 14*, *Testing*, there is also a `crystal docs` command. The most common scenario for generating code is within the context of a shard. In this case, all you need to do to generate the documentation is run `crystal docs`. This will process all the code within `src/` and output the generated website within a `docs/` directory in the root of the project. From here, you can open `docs/index.html` in your browser to view what was generated. Future invocations of `crystal docs` will overwrite the previous files.

We can also pass an explicit list of files to this command; for example, `crystal docs one.cr two.cr three.cr`. This will generate documentation for code within, or required by, all these files. You can use this to include external code within the generated documentation. For example, say you have a project that depends on two other shards within the same namespace. You could pass the main entry point file for each project to `crystal docs`, which would result in the generated website containing the documentation for all three projects. This would look something like `crystal docs lib/project1/src/main.cr lib/project2/src/main.cr src/main.cr`. The order may need to be adjusted so that it matches how `project1` and `project2` are required within `src/main.cr`.

Manually providing the files to use is required when you're not using the command within the context of a shard since neither the `src/` folder nor the `shard.yml` file will exist. The `shard.yml` file is used to generate the documentation to determine the name of the project and its version. Both of these can be customized via the `--project-name` and `--project-version` options. The former is required if it's not within the context of a shard, while the latter will default to the current branch name, suffixed by `-dev`. If you are not within the context of a GitHub repository, then it must also be provided explicitly.

In addition to generating HTML, this command also generates an `index.json` file that represents the documentation in a machine-readable format. This can be used to extend/customize how the documentation is displayed; for example, `https://mkdocstrings.github.io/crystal/index.html`. Now that we have generated the documentation, let's spend some time talking about what to do with it so that others can view it. We are also going to touch on how to handle versioning the documentation as your application progresses.

Hosting the documentation

Requiring each user to generate the documentation for your project is less than ideal and stops them from perusing it, ultimately leading to less adoption. A better solution would be to host a pre-generated version of the documentation so that users can easily find and view it.

The generated documentation is fully static HTML, CSS, and JavaScript, which allows it to be hosted as you would any website, such as via Apache, Nginx, and so on. However, these options require a server, which most people probably do not have access to, to solely host HTML documentation. A common alternative solution is to leverage `https://pages.github.com/`. A guide for how to do this can be found within the Crystal reference material: `https://crystal-lang.org/reference/guides/hosting/github.html#hosting-your-docs-on-github-pages`.

Documentation versioning

The documentation that's generated for a specific version should never need to be touched again. Because of this, in some cases, it can be beneficial to publish the documentation for multiple versions of your application. This is especially helpful when you support multiple versions of your application instead of just the latest.

The doc generator does come with a relatively simple built in version selector, however how to use it is not documented. The gist of it is that when generating the documentation, a URL pointing to a JSON file representing the available versions can be provided to power the version selector dropdown.

For example, the JSON versions file for the standard library can be found at `https://crystal-lang.org/api/versions.json`. The file contents is a simple JSON object with a single versions array, where each object within the array contains the name of the version and the path that version's generated documentation can be found at.

Using the same URL as Crystal's versions file, the command to generate the documentation would be `crystal docs --json-config-url=/api/versions.json`.

While this does handle the UI side of things, generating the config file and planting the generated documentation at each path is not something it handles for you. Depending on your requirements, this built in way may be sufficient. But using a third-party solution, or something you build yourself are also options if you require additional features.

Summary

And there you have it! Everything you need to know about how to best document your code. The typed nature of Crystal helps remove some of the burdens of writing documentation as it will handle the basics. Using a flavor of markdown for code comments also helps by keeping the documentation close to the code, reducing the likelihood that it becomes outdated.

Now that we know how to write a well-designed, tested, and documented application, it is time to move on to the final step: deploying it! In the next chapter, we are going to learn how shards should be versioned, how to create a production binary, and how to distribute it using Docker.

16
Deploying Code

One of the major benefits of Crystal is that its binaries can be statically linked. This means that all of the runtime dependencies of the program are included within the binary itself. If the binary was dynamically linked instead, the user would be required to have those dependencies installed to use the program. Similarly, since it compiles to a single binary, distributing it is much simpler since the source code does not need to be included.

In this chapter, we are going to cover the following topics:

- Versioning your shard
- Creating production binaries
- Distributing your binary

By the end of this chapter, you will have a portable, performant binary that can be distributed to the end users of your application.

Technical requirements

The requirement for this chapter is as follows:

- A working installation of Crystal

Please refer to *Chapter 1*, *An Introduction to Crystal*, for instructions on getting Crystal set up.

All the code examples for this chapter can be found in the `Chapter 16` folder in this book's GitHub repository: `https://github.com/PacktPublishing/Crystal-Programming/tree/main/Chapter16`.

Versioning your shard

The first thing you need to do before you can deploy a project is create a new release. As you learned in *Chapter 8*, *Using External Libraries*, it is strongly suggested that all Crystal shards, especially libraries, follow semantic versioning (`https://semver.org`) to make dependencies more maintainable by allowing reproducible installs and an expectation of stability.

Because of this, any non-backward compatible change in the public API must result in a new major version of the shard. An example of this could be renaming a method, removing a method, altering the name of a method parameter, and so on. However, code can be deprecated as part of a minor release with the indication that it will be altered/removed in the next major version.

Crystal provides the `https://crystal-lang.org/api/Deprecated.html` annotation, which can be used to produce deprecation warnings when applied to methods or types. In some cases, a program may need to support multiple major versions of a shard at one time. This can be solved by checking the version of the shard at compile time, along with some conditional logic to generate the correct code based on the current version.

The `VERSION` constant is accessible at compile time and is a good source for the current shard's version. The following is an example:

```
module MyShard
  VERSION = "1.5.17"
end


{% if compare_versions(MyShard::VERSION, "2.0.0") >= 0 %}
  puts "greater than or equal to 2.0.0"
{% else %}
```

```
  puts "less than 2.0.0"
{% end %}
```

Additional branches can be added if multiple version ranges are required.

A **release** is nothing more than a Git tag on a specific commit. How to create a release depends on what host you are using. See the following links for instructions on how to do so for your specific host:

- `https://docs.github.com/en/repositories/releasing-projects-on-github/managing-releases-in-a-repository#creating-a-release`

- `https://docs.gitlab.com/ee/user/project/releases/#create-a-release`

> **Important Note**
> The `release` tag *must* start with a `v` – for example, `v1.4.7`, not `1.4.7`.

Before creating the release, you should make sure you update any references to the version within source files, such as within `shard.yml` or any `VERSION` constants.

If the project is a library, that's all there is to it. Other applications would then be able to use the new version by either running `shards install` or `shards update`, depending on if it is a new or existing dependency. If the project is an application, then there are a few more steps you must complete to allow users to download pre-built binaries to use it.

Creating production binaries

While foreshadowed in *Chapter 6, Concurrency*, we have mainly been building binaries with the `crystal build file.cr` command and its run equivalent. These commands are fine during development but they do not produce a fully optimized binary for a production workload/environment that would be suitable for distribution.

To build a release binary, we need to pass the `--release` flag. This will tell the LLVM backend that it should apply all the optimizations it can to the code. Another option that we can pass is `--no-debug`. This will tell the Crystal compiler to not include any debug symbols, resulting in a smaller binary. Further symbols can be removed via the `strip` command. See `https://man7.org/linux/man-pages/man1/strip.1.html` for more information.

After building with these two options, you would end up with a smaller, more performant binary that would be suitable for benchmarking or use within a production environment. However, it would not be portable, which means that it would still require that the user has all of the Crystal runtimes and application-specific system dependencies installed. To create a more portable binary, we would need to statically link it.

Static linking is as simple as adding the `--static` option, but with a catch. The catch is that not all dependencies play well with static linking, with `libc` being the main offender, given that Crystal depends on it. Instead, `musl-libc` can be used, which has better static linking support. While not the only way, the recommended way to build a static binary is to use **Alpine Linux**. Official Crystal Docker images based on Alpine are provided that can be used to simplify this process.

This does require the native dependencies for the app to have static versions available within the base image. The `--static` flag does not 100% guarantee that the resulting binary will be fully statically linked either. In some cases, statically linking may be less ideal than dynamically linking.

For example, if a critical bug is discovered and fixed in a dependency, the binary would need to be recompiled/released using the new version of that package. If it was dynamically linked, the user could just upgrade the package and it would start to use the new version.

Static linking also increases the size of the binary since it needs to include the code for all its dependencies. In the end, it would be worth thinking about which approach you should take, depending on the requirements of the program you are distributing.

An example command to do this would look like this:

```
docker run --rm -it -v $PWD:/workspace -w /workspace
crystallang/crystal:latest-alpine crystal build app.cr --
static --release --no-debug
```

This runs a container using the latest Crystal Alpine image, mounts the current directory into it, builds a static production binary, and then exits and removes the container.

We can ensure the resulting binary is statically linked by using the `ldd` command, which is available on Linux. The macOS users can use `otool -L`. Passing this command with the name of our binary will return any shared objects it is using, or statically linked if it does not have any. This command could be used to check new binaries to prevent any surprises later on when you go to run it in a different environment.

Now that we have a portable, production-ready binary ready to go, we need a way to distribute it so that users can easily install and use it. However, if your application is made for internal use and does not need to be distributed to end users, all you need to do at this point is deploy the binary and run it. There is a multitude of ways to go about this, depending on your use case, but at a high level, all it boils down to is copying/moving the binary to where it should live and running it.

Distributing your binary

The simplest form of distribution would be to add the binary we built in the previous section to the assets of the release. This would allow anyone to download and run it, assuming a binary existed for their OS/architecture combination. The binary we created in the previous section would work on any computer using the same underlying OS and architecture that it was compiled on – in this case, **x86_64 Linux**. Other CPU architectures/OSs, such as macOS and Windows, would need dedicated binaries.

Via Docker

Another common way to distribute your binary is by including it within a Docker image that could then be used directly. The portable nature of Crystal makes creating these images easy. We can also leverage multi-stage builds to build the binary in an image that contains all the required dependencies, but then extract it into a more minimal image for distribution. The resulting **Dockerfile** for this process could look like this:

```
FROM crystallang/crystal:latest-alpine as builder

WORKDIR /app

COPY ./shard.yml ./shard.lock ./
RUN shards install --production

COPY . ./
RUN shards build --static --no-debug --release --production

FROM alpine:latest
WORKDIR /
```

```
COPY --from=builder /app/bin/greeter .

ENTRYPOINT ["/greeter"]
```

First, we must use the base Crystal Alpine image as a base, with a `builder` alias (more on this soon). Then, we must set our `WORKDIR`, which represents what the directory's future commands will be based on. Next, we must copy the `shard.yml` and `shard.lock` files to install any non-development-dependent shards. We do these as separate steps so that they are treated as different layers in the image. This helps with performance since it will only rerun those steps if something changes in one of those files, such as adding/editing a dependency.

Finally, as the final command in this stage of the build, we build a static release binary, which will ultimately be created in `/app/bin` as that is the default output location. Now that this step is complete, we can move on to the second stage of the build.

The start of the second stage of the build starts with using the latest version of Alpine as a base. Because the binary is static, we could use a scratch as the base. However, I like using Alpine as it is already quite minimal size-wise, but also provides you with a package manager in case you still need some subset of dependencies, which in most cases you will.

Here, we must set our `WORKDIR` again and copy the binary inside it. The `COPY` command has a `--from` option, which allows you to specify which stage of the build it should use as the source. In this case, we can reference the `builder` alias we defined in the first stage. Finally, we must set the entry point of the image to our binary so that any arguments that are passed to the image will be forwarded to the binary itself within the container.

Now that we have defined our Dockerfile, we need to build an image using it. We can do this by running `docker build -t greeter .`. This will build an image tagged as `greeter`, which we could then run via `docker run --rm greeter --shout George`. Because we defined the entry point of the image to the binary, this would be identical to running `./greeter --shout George` with a local copy of the binary. The `--rm` option will remove the container after it exits, which is helpful for one-off invocations so that they do not pile up.

It is also possible to extract the binary from a container. But before we can do this, we need to get a container ID. You can view existing containers via the `docker ps -a` command. If you run our image without the `--rm` flag, you would see an exited container from that invocation. If you do not currently have an existing container, one can be created via the `docker create greeter` command, which returns a container ID that we can use in the next step.

Docker also provides a `cp` command, which can be used to extract a file from a container. For example, to extract the `greeter` binary to the current folder, the command would be `docker cp abc123:/greeter ./`, where you should replace `abc123` with the container ID that the file should be extracted from.

Even if your project is for internal use, Docker can still be a good tool in orchestrating deployments as each version of the project lives in its own image. This allows various tools, such as Kubernetes, to handle scaling and deployments with ease once they've been set up.

Via package manager(s)

Another way to distribute your binary is by adding it to your package manager(s) of choice. While walking through how to do this is a bit outside of the scope of this book, it is worth mentioning as it can make the **user experience** (**UX**) much better since the user can install/update your project, just like how they do the rest of their packages. A few common package managers that could be used include the following:

- Snap
- macOS's Homebrew
- Arch Linux's AUR

Ultimately, this is an optional step. Providing a pre-built binary and instructions to build from the source is most likely going to be enough to start with.

Summary

Due to the single binary, and portability, of Crystal binaries, deploying an application is essentially as simple as copying a binary somewhere and running it. There is no need to include the source code or to exclude non-production files in your build process as all of that is taken care of for you when the correct options are used.

However, while the process is relatively straightforward, when combined with running tests and generating documentation, there are quite a few steps involved that, after a while, can get tedious to do manually every time a new version is ready to be released. In the next and final chapter, we are going to take a look at how to automate some of these processes.

Further reading

There is a lot more content related to deploying projects than we can cover in this one chapter. Check out the following links for more information on the topics we covered:

- `https://crystal-lang.org/reference/guides/static_linking.html`

- `https://docs.docker.com/develop/develop-images/baseimages`

- `https://crystal-lang.org/2019/06/19/snapcraft-summit-montreal.html`

17
Automation

Congratulations on making it this far! We have covered a lot, but alas have reached the last chapter. In the previous few chapters, we have looked into how to take a project from working to fully usable and easy to maintain by writing tests, documenting how it works, and distributing it to end users. However, it can be easy to forget to do one or more of those steps, which would defeat the whole purpose. In this chapter, we are going to explore how to automate those processes, as well as a few new ones, so that you do not need to think of them at all! By doing this, we are going to cover the following topics:

- Formatting code
- Linting code
- Continuous integration with GitHub Actions

Technical requirements

The requirements for this chapter are as follows:

- A working installation of Crystal
- A dedicated GitHub repository

You can refer to *Chapter 1*, *An Introduction to Crystal*, for instructions on getting Crystal set up as well as `https://docs.github.com/en/get-started/quickstart/create-a-repo` for setting up your repository.

All of the code examples used in this chapter can be found in the `Chapter 17` folder on GitHub: `https://github.com/PacktPublishing/Crystal-Programming/tree/main/Chapter17`.

Formatting code

Some of the most heated arguments in programming can be over the smallest things, such as whether you should use tabs or spaces for indentation, or how many of each. Crystal tries to prevent these scenarios from ever happening in the first place by providing a standardized, enforceable code style that should be used in every project.

These are some of the examples of what the formatter does:

- Removes extra whitespace at the end of the lines.

- Unescape characters that do not need to be escaped, such as `F\oo` and `Foo`.

- Adds/removes indentation as needed, including replacing `;` with newlines in some cases.

While not everyone may agree with everything the formatter does, that is kind of the point of it. It is intended to provide a standard and *not* be customizable with the goal that it takes the choice out of the equation. However, this does not mean there are not any areas that can be improved or cases of incorrect formatting.

This code style is provided by a Crystal command, much like the `spec`, `run`, or `build` commands we have used in past chapters. The simplest way to use the formatter is to run `crystal tool format` within your code base. This will go through every source file and format it according to Crystal's standard. Some IDEs even have support for the formatter and will run it automatically when you save. See *Appendix A, Tooling Setup*, for more details on how to set that up.

However, there are cases where you may *not* want to automatically reformat the code, but just determine whether it is valid. In this case, you can pass the `--check` option, which will make the command return a non-zero exit code if any changes would have been made to the code. This can be helpful as part of automation scripts/workflows that use exit codes to determine whether the command was successful.

In addition to ensuring your code is formatted correctly, it can also be a good idea to *lint* it as well. Linting would identify any code smells or idiomatic issues that should be resolved. Let's take a look at that next!

Linting code

Static analysis is the act of analyzing the source code of a program in order to identify code issues without needing to actually execute the program. This process is primarily used to detect security, stylistic, or non-idiomatic code issues.

These static analysis tools are nothing new to programming languages. However, the typed nature of Crystal handles most of what an external static analysis tool would handle, without needing anything other than the compiler itself. While the compiler would catch type-related errors, it would not catch more idiomatic issues, such as code smells or using non-optimal methods.

In Crystal, the go-to static analysis tool is `https://github.com/crystal-ameba/ameba`. This tool is usually installed as a development dependency by adding this to your `shard.yml` file and then running `shards install`:

```
development_dependencies:
  ameba:
    github: crystal-ameba/ameba
version: ~> 1.0
```

When installed, Ameba will build and output itself into the `bin/` folder of your project that could then be run via `./bin/ameba`. When executed, Ameba will go through each of your Crystal files, checking for any issues. Let's create a test file to demonstrate how it works:

1. Create a new directory and a new `shard.yml` file within it. The easiest way to do that is to run `shards init`, which will create the file for you.

2. Next, add Ameba as a development dependency and run `shards install`.

3. Finally, create another file within this folder with the following content:

```
[1, 2, 3].each_with_index do |idx, v|
  pp v
end


def foo
  return "foo"
end
```

4. We can then run Ameba and see something like the following output:

```
Inspecting 2 files


F.


test.cr:1:31
[W] Lint/UnusedArgument: Unused argument 'idx'. If
it's necessary, use '_' as an argument name to
indicate that it won't be used.
> [1, 2, 3].each_with_index do |idx, v|
                               ^

test.cr:6:3
[C] Style/RedundantReturn: Redundant 'return' detected
> return "foo"
  ^----------^


Finished in 2.88 milliseconds
2 inspected, 2 failure
```

Ameba checked our test file, and while the code itself is valid, it found some errors. These errors are not the type of things that would prevent the code from executing, but more so related to the overall maintainability and readability of it. The output of Ameba displays each failure, including what the error is, what file/line/column the error is located at, and what category of error it is.

Similar to checking the format, Ameba will also return a non-zero exit code if there is at least one error detected. On the other hand, Ameba is meant to be more configurable than the formatter. For example, you are able to tweak the default limits, disable/enable specific rules, or suppress errors within the code itself.

Now that we know how to ensure our code is well formatted and free of code quality issues, we can now move on to automating all of these processes.

Continuous integration with GitHub Actions

Continuous integration involves automating workflows that live in a centralized location to ensure various things about the code being written. What exactly it does is up to you, but the most common use case is to build, test, and lint the code as changes are made. This process provides an automated way to ensure only valid code is being merged into your project's repository.

There are numerous providers that can be used for this; however, given GitHub is the most likely place your project will be hosted, and because it already has some good tooling for Crystal, we are going to be using **GitHub Actions** for our continuous integration needs.

Before we get into setting up our workflows, we should first think about everything that we want them to do. Based on what we did in the last few chapters, I came up with this list:

1. Ensure the code is formatted correctly.
2. Ensure coding standards against the code via Ameba.
3. Ensure our tests pass.
4. Deploy documentation when a new version is released.

Regarding *step 3*, there are a few additional enhancements that we could do to improve it, such as running on different platforms, or also testing against Crystal's nightly build, the latter of which can be a great way to be alerted regarding upcoming breaking changes or regressions that may need fixed/reported, which ultimately leads to much more stable code as you are not scrambling to fix an issue the day of a new Crystal release.

Running against multiple platforms can also be a good way to find issues before they make it into production. However, depending on what your application is doing, it may not be needed. For example, if you are writing a web application that is only ever going to run on a **Linux** server, there is little point in also testing it against **macOS**. On the other hand, if you are creating a CLI-based project that will be distributed across various platforms, then testing against each supported one is a good idea.

Related to how there are many different providers that we could use, there are also numerous ways to set up each workflow that ultimately does the same thing. The workflows covered during this chapter are what I have found best fit my needs/desires. Feel free to customize them as needed to best fit your needs.

Formatting, coding standards, and tests

To start, let's first scaffold out our workflow file. There is a specific directory structure that GitHub expects, so be sure to follow along. You can either scaffold out a new shard to test this with or add it to an existing project:

1. Create a `.github` folder within the root of your project, on the same level as `shard.yml`, for example.

2. From within that folder, create another folder called `workflows`.

3. Finally, create a file called `ci.yml`. The file could be called whatever you want, but given it will contain all of our continuous integration jobs, `ci` felt like a good choice.

   You can then add the following content to the `ci.yml` file:

   ```
   name: CI

   on:
     pull_request:
       branches:
         - 'master'
     schedule:
       - cron: '37 0 * * *' # Nightly at 00:37


   jobs:
   ```

   Each workflow file should define its name, and what triggers it to run. In this example, I named the workflow `CI` and set it up to run whenever a pull request is made into the `master` branch. It will also run daily at 37 minutes past midnight. In GitHub Actions, a **workflow** represents a collection of related jobs, where a **job** is a set of steps that will execute to accomplish some goal. As you can see, we stubbed out the `jobs` map, which is where all of our jobs will be defined.

For demonstration purposes, we are going to run our tests against both the latest and nightly releases of Crystal, as well as run them on both Linux and macOS. As mentioned earlier, feel free to adjust the platforms as you see fit. GitHub Actions supports a concept called **matrices**, which allow us to define a single job that will create additional jobs for each combination. We will get to this shortly. First, let's focus on the two more straightforward jobs – formatting and coding standards.

Go ahead and update our `ci.yml` file's `jobs` map to look like this:

```
jobs:
  check_format:
    runs-on: ubuntu-latest
    steps:
      - uses: actions/checkout@v2
      - name: Install Crystal
        uses: crystal-lang/install-crystal@v1
      - name: Check Format
        run: crystal tool format --check
  coding_standards:
    runs-on: ubuntu-latest
    steps:
      - uses: actions/checkout@v2
      - name: Install Crystal
        uses: crystal-lang/install-crystal@v1
      - name: Install Dependencies
        run: shards install
      - name: Ameba
        run: ./bin/ameba
```

At a high level, these jobs are pretty similar. We set them up to both run on the latest **Ubuntu** version, using the latest **Crystal Alpine Docker image**. The steps for each are slightly different of course, but they both start off by checking out your project's code.

The formatting check can just run `crystal tool format --check`. If it is not formatted correctly, it will return a non-zero exit code, as we learned a little while ago, which will fail the job. The coding standards job starts out the same, but will also run `shards install` in order to install Ameba. Finally, it runs Ameba, which will also return a non-zero exit code in the event of failure. Next, let's move on to the job that will run our tests.

Add the following code to the `jobs` map:

```
  test:
    strategy:
      fail-fast: false
      matrix:
```

```
        os:
            - ubuntu-latest
            - macos-latest
        crystal:
            - latest
            - nightly
    runs-on: ${{ matrix.os }}
    steps:
        - uses: actions/checkout@v2
        - name: Install Crystal
          uses: crystal-lang/install-crystal@v1
          with:
            crystal: ${{ matrix.crystal }}
        - name: Install Dependencies
          run: shards install
        - name: Specs
          run: crystal spec --order=random --error-on-
            warnings
```

This job is a bit more complex than the last two. Let's break it down!

This job introduces the `strategy` mapping, which includes data describing *how* the job should be executed. The two primary features we are using include `fail-fast` and `matrix`. The former makes it so that if one of the jobs created via the matrix were to fail, it does not fail all of them. We want this to be `false` so that, for example, a failure on Crystal nightly on a specific platform does not fail all the other jobs.

As alluded to earlier, the matrix mapping, as the name implies, allows the definition of a matrix that will create a job for each combination of the matrix values. In the end, our matrix will define four jobs:

- Crystal latest on Ubuntu

- Crystal nightly on Ubuntu

- Crystal latest on macOS

- Crystal nightly on macOS

Additional parts of the job's configuration are templated in order to use the values from the matrix, such as to set what the job runs on and what version of Crystal to install. We are also making use of `https://github.com/crystal-lang/install-crystal` to install Crystal, which works cross-platform.

We are then running `shards install` to install any dependencies. If your project does not have any dependencies, feel free to remove this step. Finally, we are running the specs in a random order as well as erroring when any warnings from any dependencies, including Crystal itself, are encountered. The main reason for this is to bring future deprecations from the Crystal nightly job to light so that they can be addressed.

From here, you could look into adding some branch protection rules, for example, `https://docs.github.com/en/repositories/configuring-branches-and-merges-in-your-repository/defining-the-mergeability-of-pull-requests/about-protected-branches#require-status-checks-before-merging`, to require certain checks to pass before a pull request can be merged.

Now that we are enforcing formatting, coding standards, and tests, we can move on to deploying our documentation.

Deploying documentation

There are many different ways we could go about handling our **documentation deployments**, both in terms of what features we want to support, where they will be hosted, and how the documentation needs to be built. For example, you may want to support displaying the documentation for each version of your application, or you may want to self-host it, or you may need to include documentation from other shards.

For the example we are going to walk through, I will be hosting the documentation via `https://pages.github.com`, with only the latest version, with no external dependencies. As such, you will need to be sure to set up **GitHub Pages** for your repository.

> **Tip**
> See `https://docs.github.com/en/pages/quickstart` for more information on how to get that set up.

Now that that is out of the way, we can get on to setting up the workflow! Because deploying documentation is something that only needs to happen when a new release is published, we are going to make a dedicated workflow for it. Start off by creating a `deployment.yml` file within the `workflows` folder. You can add the following content to this file:

```yaml
name: Deployment

on:
  release:
    types:
      - created

jobs:
  deploy_docs:
    runs-on: ubuntu-latest
    steps:
      - uses: actions/checkout@v2
      - name: Install Crystal
        uses: crystal-lang/install-crystal@v1
      - name: Build
        run: crystal docs
      - name: Deploy
        uses: JamesIves/github-pages-deploy-action@4.1.5
        with:
          branch: gh-pages
          folder: docs
          single-commit: true
```

Starting off the same as we did before, we give a name to this workflow and define when it should run. Given your documentation is public, you would not want it to update with possibly breaking changes every time something is merged in. Instead, we set this workflow up to run when a new release is created, so that the documentation is always consistent with the latest stable release of the project.

Step wise, we are checking out the code, installing Crystal, building the documentation via running `crystal docs`, and finally uploading the documentation to GitHub Pages.

We are making use of an external action to handle deploying the documentation. There are quite a few other actions that support this, or you could also do it manually, but I found that this one works quite well and is easy to set up. You can check out `https://github.com/JamesIves/github-pages-deploy-action` for more information regarding this action.

We are providing a few configuration options to the action. The first two are required and represent what branch in our repository the documentation should be *uploaded* to, and the second represents the source of the documentation to upload. You can choose whatever you want as the branch name. I just named it `gh-pages` to keep it clear what it is used for.

Also, since `crystal docs` outputs to the `docs/` folder, I specified that as the source folder. I am also setting the `single-commit` option to `true`. This essentially resets the history of our branch so that there is only ever a single commit on that branch. This is fine in our case because the documentation can easily be regenerated if needed, so there is no need to keep that history around.

At this point, all of our workflows are defined. The **CI workflow** will ensure code coming into the project is valid and working as intended, and the **Deployment workflow** will deploy our documentation to GitHub Pages when a new release is created. Once this happens, you can navigate to the **Pages URL** for your repository to see the results.

You could also add additional things to the Deployment workflow, such as building/publishing release binaries automatically.

Summary

And there you have it! Continuous integration can be a great way to more easily manage contributions as you have an automated way that can enforce your standards and make it easier to debug/be notified of any issues that do arise. It can also help automate the deployment process. It is also customizable and flexible enough to handle virtually any use case.

Once again, congratulations on finishing the book! There has been a lot of content within various areas of Crystal that hopefully provided some helpful information that can be put to use on your future projects or, better yet, serve as a reference for some of the more advanced topics.

Appendix A
Tooling Setup

The Crystal compiler is responsible for analyzing Crystal code and producing debug and release-grade executables. The usual flow of writing code and then using the compiler to build and run your application can be entirely done using the command-line interface, but it quickly gets tedious.

This appendix will teach you how to configure and use Crystal from **Visual Studio Code** with standard IDE features, such as syntax highlighting, code completion, hovering over symbols for more information, exploring the classes and methods defined in a file, building the project, and running it. If you use other code editors, the instructions should be similar.

Installing the Crystal compiler

The first step is to make sure the Crystal compiler is correctly installed. Try running the `crystal --version` command from your terminal. You can skip to the next section if it successfully shows the compiler version and target architecture.

Go to `https://crystal-lang.org/install` and check the exact instructions for your operating system. On **macOS**, Crystal is available from **Homebrew**. On most Linux distributions, Crystal is available from a repository. Crystal is also available for BSD systems.

Installing the compiler on Windows

On **Windows**, the Crystal compiler is still experimental (as of **Crystal 1.4.0**). So, you must enable the **Windows Subsystem for Linux** (**WSL**) and use a Linux distribution inside Windows.

If you haven't used WSL yet, enabling it is simple. You will need to be running either **Windows 10** or **Windows 11**. Open Windows PowerShell, select **Run as Administrator**, and run the `wsl --install` command.

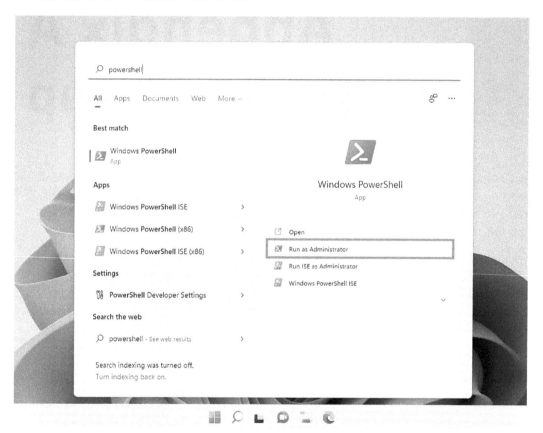

Figure 18.1 – Running PowerShell as an administrator

By default, it will use **WSL2** with **Ubuntu**, as shown in the following screenshot. It's a good default if you haven't used Linux before:

Figure 18.2 – Enabling WSL

After these steps are done, proceed with installing Crystal inside WSL using the Ubuntu instructions from the official site, as previously mentioned.

Installing Visual Studio Code

If you don't have Visual Studio Code, you can install it from the official site at `https://code.visualstudio.com/`. It's a popular, free, and powerful code editor.

If you use Windows and WSL, then install the **Remote - WSL** extension. It will allow Visual Studio Code to connect to WSL.

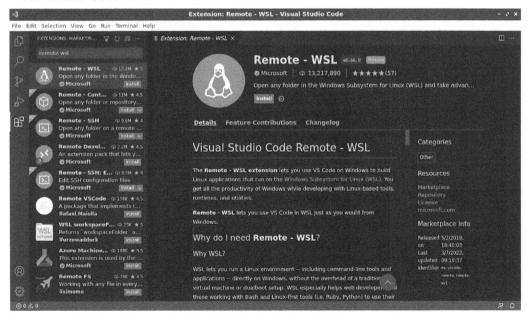

Figure 18.3 – Installing the Remote - WSL extension

After installing this extension, you will see a small green icon in the bottom-left corner of your screen. Use it to open a WSL window.

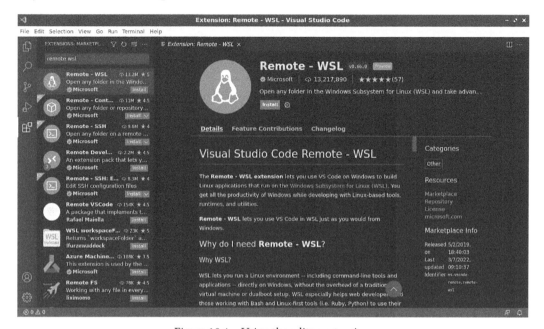

Figure 18.4 – Using the editor extension

Search for and install the **Crystal Language** extension from the Crystal language tools.

Figure 18.5 – Installing the Crystal Language extension

It will provide you with syntax highlighting, code formatting, and a project outline.

Figure 18.6 – Enabling the Crystalline language server

To unlock the full potential of the extension, it also needs a language server. We recommend using **Crystalline** for that. It will enable code completion, error reporting, go to definition, and symbol information on hover.

You can find the installation instructions at `https://github.com/elbywan/crystalline#pre-built-binaries`. The link shows the command to download and install it on macOS and Linux. If you use Windows, follow the Linux instructions inside WSL.

To enable some extra features, go to the Visual Studio Code settings (**File | Preferences | Settings**) and search for `Crystal`. You can turn on more or fewer features, but be aware that analyzing Crystal code isn't lightweight, and it can be slow for larger projects depending on your computer:

1. The first options enable code completion, hovering, and the go to definition feature; enable those.

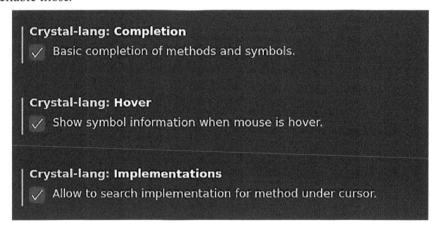

Figure 18.7 – Optional extension features

2. Next, you can choose what kind of problems are reported. This is helpful to allow you to spot errors before trying to run the code. The syntax option is the default and checks for the most common errors. You can also use build to check for all compile-time errors (more expensive) or none to disable the feature altogether.

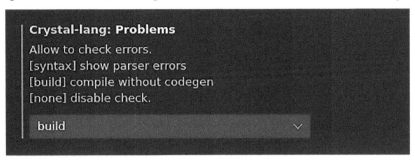

Figure 18.8 – Problem detection level

3. Finally, you can optionally configure the language server. It will enable a more complete analysis of code completion and symbol information based on the inferred type of the variables. Here, add the path of the Crystalline executable you installed earlier. Be aware that the language server is experimental, and it might not provide accurate information on all cases.

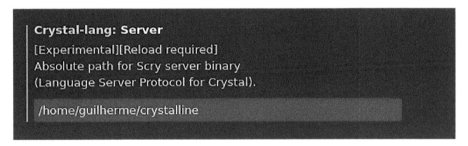

Figure 18.9 – Setting up the language server

Appendix B
The Future of Crystal

Crystal has recently graduated as stable and production-ready with the release of version **1.0.0** in March 2021. As of April 2022, the latest version is 1.4.1, which has many refinements. Still, there is much work ahead, and many areas of the language will see improvement in further releases. All development and design discussions happen in the open in the official GitHub repository, and there is plenty of opportunity for contribution from outsiders.

Today, Crystal is already used by several companies in production. You can find a public list of some of those on Crystal's Wiki here: `https://github.com/crystal-lang/crystal/wiki/Used-in-production`. Adoption is expected to rise even further now that there is a proper policy of *no breaking changes* being introduced. Source code built now will compile fine with no changes on all future *1.x* versions.

Windows

Crystal supports **Linux**, **macOS**, and **FreeBSD**, but it cannot run natively on **Windows** today. All other platforms are Unix-like and are reasonably similar. On the other hand, Windows is an entirely different thing and requires considerable effort to be correctly supported. This is one of the most requested features, and work has been underway to provide proper Windows support. Running Crystal inside **Windows Subsystem for Linux (WSL)** is supported, but this is mostly intended for developers.

Crystal 1.0.0 was released with very early support to get simple programs compiled to Windows, but this doesn't mean you can already use it for everything: concurrent I/O features (files, sockets, console, and so on), for example, are still missing. Fortunately, implementations for each of those primitives are being contributed by the community and should be available on one of the following *1.x* versions.

You can check the current progress on GitHub issue **#5430**. If this issue is already closed when you happen to be reading this book, then Windows is a supported target on the current release. Yay!

WebAssembly

WebAssembly is a new standard for a compilation target that is quickly growing in popularity, and not just on the web. It offers portability to run anywhere with near-native speed: web browsers, cloud servers, embedded devices, plugins, blockchains, and more. Also, it allows different languages to interoperate in a convenient format, and it is secure and verifiable before execution.

There is ongoing work to add targeting support to the compiler and the standard library, making it easy to write a Crystal program that can run anywhere and accepts WebAssembly. The Crystal 1.4.0 release shipped with the initial experimental implementation, with most of the standard library already working.

Please refer to issue **#12002** for an up-to-date progress status.

Multithreading

Concurrent programming is a significant theme when exploring Crystal. You can create lightweight threads (known as **fibers**) with the spawn method. By default, Crystal distributes work across a single CPU core using an asynchronous event loop. This is a simple and very efficient approach that relieves the programmer from dealing with thread synchronization and data races. When doing an I/O operation, only the current fiber is blocked; all others can run in the meantime. In most cases, scalability can be achieved by running multiple Crystal instances to take advantage of multiple cores. Concurrency will be discussed in greater detail in *Chapter 8, Using External Libraries*.

Nonetheless, there are cases when true multithreading becomes a need. For example, when working with CPU-intensive processing, having concurrent fibers isn't enough. Being able to run multiple fibers at once with parallelism is a must. For this, Crystal has an experimental flag, -Dpreview_mt, that enables your program to use all cores. Each core will have its own event loop to run fibers and I/O operations.

This mode is experimental, and not every feature works well with it yet. Special care must be taken with data synchronization. The recommended and safe approach is to use channels for all communication between fibers and avoid sharing global state. Still, it works and can be used for testing. A couple of the possible evolutions it might have before it is deemed as ready for production are as follows:

- **Work stealing**: When one CPU core becomes idle because it has no fiber to run (maybe they are all waiting on some I/O operation), it must be able to *steal* a resumable fiber from another core and continue with it. This prevents a CPU core from becoming idle when there is work to be done.

- **Preemptive scheduling**: This ensures that a single fiber can't use too much CPU time before another fiber can run. This is done by pausing long-running fibers and doing a context switch forcefully.

Structured concurrency

Concurrency is the act of having many computations that are going on at the same time. Different languages deal with this concept differently. For example, Erlang has actors, JavaScript has promises, .NET has tasks, and Go has goroutines. Each of these provides a different abstraction on how to understand and handle the ongoing jobs and communicate data between them.

Crystal provides some low-level concurrency primitives with fibers, channels, and the `select` statement. They are quite powerful and allow a program to handle concurrency as it sees fit. But the standard library still lacks a higher-level tool for structured concurrency, where the lifetime and data flow of each job is clearly stated and predictable. Having this will make concurrent programming less error-prone and easier to reason about. More about this can be found by reading up on issue **#6468**.

Incremental compilation and better tooling

Crystal uses a type inference system that applies to the whole program at once to analyze and identify every expression type on the program. This is different from the usual type inference of other languages because it works across method boundaries, and argument types don't need to be explicitly typed. It has a cost, however. Analyzing the entire program for types requires, well, the entire program, all at once. Any change to any line in any file causes the whole analysis to be repeated from the start.

Compiling and analyzing Crystal programs is a little slower than in other languages, but this is the tradeoff for the excellent performance and awesome syntax, semantics, and expressiveness.

There are extensions for many code editors and IDEs supporting Crystal, but they are mainly based on the compiler itself, and thus they don't offer incremental analysis of the program and the developer often has to wait a few seconds before getting feedback such as type information on hover or semantic errors. This will most likely be developed as a custom language server.

Using integrated debuggers does work, but they don't yet provide full Crystal support for inspecting any kind of variable at runtime or evaluating expressions.

Work has been done in the past to improve compile time, such as caching intermediary results or some semantic changes in the language itself. But rethinking the type checker to work incrementally will take a lot of effort and time. It is clear that the major selling point of Crystal is its expressiveness and the fact that it's a joy to use; any change made will have to preserve this. Still, the feedback loop is a pain point currently, and improvements will come over time to address this. If you want to learn more about this challenge, look at issue **#10568**. There are also many other issues about different aspects of the tooling support.

How to get in touch with the community

The topics listed previously and many more are subjects of daily discussion by the community, a place for understanding use cases, arguing about different implementation approaches, and organizing efforts to cooperate. Anyone is welcome to join.

The primary channel is the forum at `https://forum.crystal-lang.org/`. Any kind of discussion can happen there, from hypothetical features to seeking help and code reviews, from looking for Crystal jobs to sharing projects you've created.

If you are looking for other ways to interact, please take a look at `https://crystal-lang.org/community`; it aggregates links from many different platforms.

Finally, there is the GitHub repository, where collaboration about the language's development happens, at `https://github.com/crystal-lang/crystal`. It is the place to go if you want to contribute to the standard library or the compiler itself with code, documentation improvements, or issues.

Anywhere you go, you will find a passionate community there to help, share experiences, and work together.

Index

Symbols

A

B

X

Other Books You May Enjoy

If you enjoyed this book, you may be interested in these other books by Packt:

Polished Ruby Programming

Jeremy Evans

ISBN: 9781801072724

- Use Ruby's core classes and design custom classes effectively
- Explore the principles behind variable usage and method argument choice
- Implement advanced error handling approaches such as exponential backoff
- Design extensible libraries and plugin systems in Ruby
- Use metaprogramming and DSLs to avoid code redundancy
- Implement different approaches to testing and understand their trade-offs
- Discover design patterns, refactoring, and optimization with Ruby
- Explore database design principles and advanced web app security

Modern CMake for C++

Rafał Świdziński

ISBN: 9781801070058

- Understand best practices for building C++ code

- Gain practical knowledge of the CMake language by focusing on the most useful aspects

- Use cutting-edge tooling to guarantee code quality with the help of tests and static and dynamic analysis

- Discover how to manage, discover, download, and link dependencies with Cmake

- Build solutions that can be reused and maintained in the long term

- Understand how to optimize build artifacts and the build process itself

Build Your Own Programming Language

Clinton L. Jeffery

ISBN: 9781800204805

- Perform requirements analysis for the new language and design language syntax and semantics
- Write lexical and context-free grammar rules for common expressions and control structures
- Develop a scanner that reads source code and generate a parser that checks syntax
- Build key data structures in a compiler and use your compiler to build a syntax-coloring code editor
- Implement a bytecode interpreter and run bytecode generated by your compiler
- Write tree traversals that insert information into the syntax tree
  Implement garbage collection in your language

Packt is searching for authors like you

If you're interested in becoming an author for Packt, please visit `authors.packtpub.com` and apply today. We have worked with thousands of developers and tech professionals, just like you, to help them share their insight with the global tech community. You can make a general application, apply for a specific hot topic that we are recruiting an author for, or submit your own idea.

Share Your Thoughts

Now you've finished *Crystal Programming*, we'd love to hear your thoughts! Scan the QR code below to go straight to the Amazon review page for this book and share your feedback or leave a review on the site that you purchased it from.

https://packt.link/r/1801818673

Your review is important to us and the tech community and will help us make sure we're delivering excellent quality content.

www.ingramcontent.com/pod-product-compliance
Ingram Content Group UK Ltd.
Pitfield, Milton Keynes, MK11 3LW, UK
UKHW052114140225
455135UK00007B/47